The EMERGING DIACONATE

Servant Leaders in a Servant Church

WILLIAM T. DITEWIG

Paulist Press
New York/Mahwah, NJ

ADVANCE PRAISE FOR *THE EMERGING DIACONATE*

"A great guide to where the diaconate has been and, more importantly, to where it is going. *The Emerging Diaconate* blends historical scholarship and liturgical reflection, leadership theory and theological analysis, quantitative data and personal story, to paint a richly textured portrait of today's deacon. Pointing to the "servant-ecclesiology" of the Second Vatican Council, Deacon Ditewig situates the diaconate within the context of the mission of the whole church, an approach that not only illuminates this important order, but also provides a model for understanding the many ministries at work in the church today."

—Edward P. Hahnenberg, PhD
Author of *Ministries: A Relational Approach* and
A Concise Guide to the Documents of Vatican II

"Even forty years after the restoration of the permanent diaconate, the theology and experience of the diaconate are still emerging. That is no surprise since the larger ministerial life of the church is in a period of epochal transition with priests serving multiple communities assisted by professional pastoral staffs and with the advent of lay ecclesial ministry. Deacon Ditewig effectively shows us where deacons fit in this ministerial landscape. This engaging account of the diaconate ranges from statistical descriptions of the scope of the diaconate in the church, to its scriptural and historical foundations, to a theology of the diaconate, to the rite of ordination, to the challenges yet to be faced in firmly establishing this ministry within the experience and life of the Catholic Church. He firmly situates the diaconate within an ecclesiology of the servant church and christology of the self-emptying Christ. Not only deacons, but all the Christian faithful, will benefit from his account of the diaconate as a distinctive vocation."

—Susan K. Wood, SCL
Professor of Theology, Marquette University

"Continuing his outstanding leadership in the field of diaconal theology William Ditewig presents the church with an ever-maturing vision of the dignity and mission of the deacon. In *The Emerging Diaconate* Ditewig takes us into the unique identity of the deacon as it relates to both church and culture. Here the deacon is seen to be different from the priest and bishop—*not* a lesser office but one that receives its meaning by receiving a share in the bishop's own ministry. According to Ditewig the church and the diaconate will grow in spiritual maturity together as all members enter the mystery of Christ's own service. It is not surprising that both the restoration of the diaconate and the nobility of lay holiness were clarified together at the Second Vatican Council: now, both laity and deacons have to commit themselves to a mutually interpenetrating mission ordered toward the transformation of culture in Christ. This book inspires such collaboration and gives the needed theology to begin such a common journey."

—Deacon James Keating, PhD
Director of Theological Formation,
Institute for Priestly Formation, Creighton University

"*The Emerging Diaconate* offers us a treasure of diaconal history, theology, ritual, and renewal. William Ditewig, [former] executive director of the secretariat of the diaconate at the United States Conference of Catholic Bishops, writes with assurance, experience, and professional training. Ditewig points out clearly the foci for further diaconal studies and renewal. He emphasizes that a theology of the diaconate is intrinsically related to a theology of a ministerial church, and thus he also indicates the need for a re-thinking of ecclesiology as a basis for the diaconate. This volume, encompassing as it does a rich and wide perspective of ministry, is a major help to bishops, priests, deacons, lay ministers, and theologians as they struggle to comprehend the meaning of church ministry in today's third-millennium society. This book is another major deacon-work from Paulist Press."

—Rev. Kenan B. Osborne, OFM
Emeritus Professor of Systematic Theology,
Franciscan School of Theology, Berkeley

"One of the greatest success stories of Vatican II is the renewal of the permanent diaconate. Just about 40 years old, and with almost 16,000 deacons in the United States, the diaconate continues to seek more adequate grounding in theological reflection and practice. Deacon William T. Ditewig's book, *The Emerging Diaconate: Servant Leaders in a Servant Church*, is an excellent contribution to the renewal of the theology of the diaconate. Using the resources of Scripture, systematic and historical theology, Canon Law, as well as his own rich pastoral experience, Deacon Ditewig both informs and challenges. The major challenge is this: the permanent diaconate cannot make sense in the church until the entire church is diaconal in its life. This excellent book should find a place in the library of every permanent deacon, and should enrich the discussion about the diaconate in every parish and diocese, across the nation, and throughout the English-speaking world."

—Deacon Owen F. Cummings, DD
Regents' Professor of Theology,
Mount Angel Seminary

"A valuable and visionary work, *The Emerging Diaconate* is a singular achievement: comprehensive, insightful, and astonishing in its scope. Deacon William Ditewig has given us a groundbreaking work that simultaneously validates, illuminates, and celebrates the diaconate—a ministry that is proving to be increasingly important and necessary to the church of the 21st century."

—Deacon Greg Kandra, Diocese of Brooklyn,
CBS Evening News with Katie Couric

"William Ditewig's unique background as a trained theologian, an ordained deacon, and former executive director of the secretariat of the diaconate at the USCCB makes him an ideal person to author a comprehensive study of the order of the deacon in the church today. Ditewig displays his immense knowledge of the topic with a light but sure touch. He masterfully synthesizes historical scholarship and uses that scholarship as a foundation for developing a constructive theology of the diaconate appropriate for the church today. Ditewig's erudition is obvious yet he is able to write in a style that is accessible to the non-specialist. His work is sure to serve as a benchmark for future explorations of the theology of the diaconate."

—Richard R. Gaillardetz, PhD
Murray/Bacik Professor of Catholic Studies,
University of Toledo

"Deacon Ditewig's study of the way the renewed permanent diaconate is now and will be in the future is rooted in deep consideration of the diaconate's scriptural and historical roots. He has presented the continuum of the expression of the deacon-servant from ancient times through Trent and Vatican II, up to the present. His work continues the ongoing discussion of the theological and ministerial place of the diaconate, and will form the locus for continuing investigation of the meaning of kenosis in ministry."

—Phyllis Zagano, PhD
Senior Research Associate-in-Residence,
Hofstra University

Cover design by Cynthia Dunne
Book design by Lynn Else

Library of Congress Cataloging-in-Publication Data

Ditewig, William T.
The emerging diaconate : servant leaders in a servant church / William T. Ditewig.
p. cm.
Includes bibliographical references.
ISBN-13: 978-0-8091-4449-5 (alk. paper)
1. Deacons—Catholic Church. 2. Christian leadership. 3. Service (Theology) I. Title.
BX1912.D54 2007
262′.142—dc22

2007019235

Published by Paulist Press
997 Macarthur Boulevard
Mahwah, New Jersey 07430

www.paulistpress.com

Printed and bound in the
United States of America

CONTENTS

ACKNOWLEDGMENTS

This book represents the culmination of work that has spanned more than two decades. After many years of serving in lay ministry, with a special emphasis on adult faith formation, I became intrigued by questions related to leadership in the Church emerging from the Second Vatican Council, and these formed the basis of serious graduate study. So I wish to acknowledge first the constant support, challenge, and inspiration of the Sisters of Providence at Saint Mary-of-the-Woods College, along with my classmates, who gave shape to my own reflections and study. Special thanks and mention must go to Ruth Eileen Dwyer, SP; Alexa Suelzer, SP; Dr. Ernie Collamati, PhD; and Susie Collamati.

Later, at Catholic University of America, teachers such as Kate Dooley, OP; Joseph Komonchak; Nelson Minnich; Fred McManus; Jim Provost; Seely Beggiani; John Tracy Ellis; and David Power helped refine the questions across a wide spectrum of study. Because questions of leadership and governance refuse to be pigeonholed into a single category, it is necessary to inquire into a variety of sources and disciplines, and this remarkable faculty made that process possible; never easy, but possible!

As always, a special acknowledgment is given to the whole team at Paulist Press and, in particular, my editor, Mr. Kevin di Camillo. Kevin is the captain who has guided all of the books on the extensive "deacon library" skillfully through the publication process and safely into harbor. It is his hard work and dedication to this series that has made it all possible.

And to my family, who has lived through it all, my constant appreciation and love!

For Diann With Love

Introduction

THE CHURCH, MINISTRY, AND THE DIACONATE

The permanent diaconate...a driving force for the Church's service.
—Paul VI, *Ad pascendum*

Out of the Mist into a New Day

This is a book about the contemporary Catholic Church, which continues to emerge from the Second Vatican Council. While some people may consider the Council a distant event whose significance is passed, Pope John Paul II once wrote, "The best preparation for the new millennium, therefore, can only be expressed in a renewed commitment to apply, as faithfully as possible, the teachings of Vatican II to the life of every individual and of the whole Church."[1] The council was a catalyst for renewal that has only just begun to mature. While the principal focus of the project is the diaconate, this particular act of renewal (of the diaconate) must be seen in the broader context of *overall reform and renewal* initiated by that great council. Not only is the diaconate continuing to "emerge" into the imagination and life of the church as a renewed ministry, but the church itself continues to emerge into new contexts and challenges in the new millennium. Our ultimate goal is to examine the implications of the renewed diaconate for the church's own identity and mission.

A few years ago, Paulist Press released *101 Questions & Answers on Deacons* as part of its *101 Questions and Answers* series. In some ways, this current work is a successor to that book. The first book was an introduction to the topic of the diaconate; now I hope we can put more flesh on that outline by continuing to develop an understanding of the diaconate in its proper ecclesial setting. In my opinion, this notion of *ecclesial integration* is critically important at this time in the life of the church; this is certainly true in the case of the permanent diaconate.

I have served as a deacon in the Catholic Church for more than seventeen years; however, I have also been a husband for thirty-five years, a father for thirty-four years, and a grandfather for more than five years. Professionally, I have been a radio newscaster, a high school associate principal, a diocesan official in several different dioceses, and a college professor. And then there were those twenty-two years as a career Navy officer, specializing as a Hebrew and Russian linguist and cryptologist. My point is that in the Catholic imagination, once a person is ordained a deacon or a priest, often that fact seems to subsume many other facets of a person's background. Once, after a number of years, I was able to visit a former college professor, a good friend. In the time since our last meeting, my family had grown, I had been ordained, we had moved overseas, I had retired from the Navy, I had finished a doctorate, and my wife and I had become grandparents. Throughout our visit, my friend kept shaking her head, and I asked her what was wrong. "I just struggle with *why* you did it; *why* did you have to become a deacon?" In my life, I had integrated diaconate into the broader context of our lives; but for my friend, the diaconate stood out as a particular challenge, and she couldn't see past it.

I hope, with this book, to address some of the myths and misperceptions that persist with regard to the renewed diaconate. Even more important, I hope that it will be an aid to integration: that the renewed diaconate, as the church's experience with this ancient order continues to mature, may be seen ever more clearly within its proper ecclesial and social context, integrated more seamlessly into the fabric and *communio* of the church. In short, while much has been learned about the diaconate since its renewal forty years ago, much of its potential remains largely untapped. We have learned to walk, but much remains to be done so we can run. As we shall see, the pioneers of a renewed diaconate, incarcerated at Dachau concentration camp, saw the diaconate as a necessary component of a renewed church transforming the world so that tragedies such as the Second World War and the *Shoah* would not happen again. Unfortunately, the events of the late twentieth century and the first years of the twenty-first reveal only too vividly how acutely such an overall transformation is still needed.

On a personal level, I hope that my friend may come to understand why I became a deacon.

The Diaconate Returns

A Personal and Generational Recollection

Like all disciples, deacons come with widely diverse backgrounds and experiences. I can still remember how I first heard of the diaconate, and it was, frankly, underwhelming. I offer this reflection only to demonstrate how important context can be in our perception of things. Others will, of course, remember this same period of time in their own way and through the lens of their own unique experiences, and I hope that this personal recollection will be a catalyst for their own reflection.

In 1956, when I was six years old and just beginning second grade, I informed my parents and teachers that I was going to be a priest. "Well," Sister Mary Elva said, "you won't be able to be a priest if you're not an altar server." So, by the time I was seven, I was an altar boy, even though it was very unusual in our parish for a third grader to be allowed to serve. However, I was tall enough to fit the cassock and surplice, and I had learned the Latin responses. By sixth grade, a couple of friends and I were going off to St. Henry's Preparatory Seminary in Belleville, Illinois, for a week in the summer, having responded to a brochure inviting us to "Be a Seminarian for a Week!" We did this for a week after sixth grade and again after seventh grade. I didn't go after eighth grade because I'd already been accepted at the seminary for the following fall as a freshman.

From 1963 to 1970, from thirteen to twenty years of age, I was in high school and college seminary for my home diocese. I give the dates in order to highlight the connection between our formation and the most significant and influential ecclesial event of the twentieth century: the Second Vatican Council (1962–65). What a wonderful time to be in the seminary! For the first few years of our formation, the council itself was in session, and our teachers worked hard at keeping up-to-date with the press releases and other information coming from Rome, and the enthusiasm of those years has been unmatched since. Early in our time in the seminary, the Council Fathers were about to release *Sacrosanctum Concilium*, the Constitution on the Sacred Liturgy, and I remember well one of our older priest-teachers (he may have only been in his fifties or sixties, but to us teenagers, that seemed pretty ancient!) telling us how great it was going to be when we could celebrate Mass in the vernacular. "I would give anything to celebrate Mass in English," he would say, "but *I* won't live to see it. But you, gentlemen, God willing, *you* will be able to face your people and offer prayers to God in our own language!" Before the end of that same school year this same priest, with tears in his eyes, was celebrating Mass with us in English.

And then came the first years of the implementation of the council, and still the enthusiasm was great. Nothing seemed impossible, and we seminarians were being asked to look at pastoral life with creativity and dynamism: to preach the Gospel of Christ in new ways to a new world, or as Vatican II had phrased it, "to scrutinize the signs of the times and to interpret them in light of the Gospel" (*Gaudium et Spes* 4). For seminarians of our generation, as for all of us in those years, great moral issues abounded that demanded immediate and courageous attention: many of our classmates had gone off to fight and some to die in a place called Vietnam. The civil rights movement was raising our awareness of the evils of racism in our society, and eventually similar movements matured from these, as our attention was raised to the evils of sexism and other patterns of social injustice. Many of our seminary professors and our parish priests and bishops were taking the lead in speaking out and leading these efforts, and we were inspired to join them. Often these two great movements against the war and social injustice merged in our consciousness, and they became part of the matrix within which we studied philosophy and theology. Not only did it color the way we came to appreciate and understand these subjects; in a very real sense, they were often "two ends of the same thought." For example: we were studying Scholastic metaphysics, using Thomas Aquinas's *Summa Theologiae* (in Latin, of course); after class, the same professor would lead an antiwar rally on the campus quadrangle. Racism and the war were (and remain) the great moral evils of our day, and we were engaged in practical attempts to apply Gospel values in response to them.

Nineteen sixty-eight was a watershed year. Camelot, and innocence, had ended for our generation in 1963, when President John F. Kennedy was assassinated, but 1968 was, if possible, even worse. In January of that year, many of us who had not yet paid too much attention to the war in Vietnam were shaken by the news of the Tet offensive throughout many parts of Vietnam, especially around Khe Sanh. Not only were the military details of the event horrific, but it was also the first great indicator of just how much our elected officials had been misleading the nation about the nature and conduct of the war. By March, public confidence in the administration had deteriorated so much that President Johnson withdrew as a candidate for reelection to the presidency. This was my freshman year in college seminary; at the beginning of the 1967–68 academic year, there had been protests on campus against the war but also efforts in support of our troops. But after Tet, the whole mood changed, and now there was nothing positive about any aspect of our involvement in the war.

Then later in the same year came the stunning impact of the assassinations of Dr. Martin Luther King, Jr., and Senator Robert F. Kennedy. Suddenly, both those charismatic leaders were ripped off the scene, men who had influenced our generation so greatly. One experience from that time is still particularly vivid. A seminary classmate and close friend was from the same city in which our seminary was located, although he was, naturally, living with us in the seminary rather than at home. At the height of the civil rights movement, my friend's father told him in no uncertain terms that if he [the father] ever found out that his son was marching in a civil rights or antiwar demonstration, he would no longer let his son back into their home. Then came Dr. King's assassination. The local diocese, in collaboration with other local churches, coordinated a solemn procession through the center of the city, ending at the cathedral with an ecumenical and interfaith prayer service in honor of Dr. King. We processed silently and solemnly, some of us holding banners that read simply, "Dr. Martin Luther King, Jr., R.I.P." My friend and I were carrying that one, and naturally, that's the one that the media focused on: my friend's father saw him on the TV news, carrying the banner. He called the seminary and left word for the rector (who was, of course, with us at the procession and prayer service) that his son was no longer welcome at home. There was an eventual reconciliation, which involved the rector, our friend's mother, and most of us fellow seminarians, but it took nearly a year.

But 1968 was about more than American politics and secular social issues. In the church, 1968 was also the year of the papal encyclical *Humanae Vitae*. Pope Paul VI, choosing to move in a different direction from the pontifical commission that had been studying the issues of artificial birth control, set off an ecclesial firestorm that is still being felt today. But in 1968, it felt like a nuclear blast had gone off. In the Archdiocese of Washington, D.C., alone, more than fifty archdiocesan priests declared that in good conscience they would not support Pope Paul's teaching on birth control. Cardinal Patrick O'Boyle disciplined many of these priests, eventually suspending at least nineteen of them from ministry; they appealed their case to the Holy See. Eventually, a compromise was reached, but the damage was done. At least twenty-five Washington priests left the church over this issue. This was the experience in just one diocese, and similar turmoil was taking place around the world. *Time* magazine reported an unnamed American scholar in Rome as saying, "Birth control is the Pope's Vietnam."[2]

While the crisis surrounded the question of birth control, the real issue was that of authority in the church. By the end of the 1960s in the United States, according to priest-sociologist Andrew Greeley, 70 percent of Catholic women were using artificial birth control. And, according to Greeley, the belief among Catholics that a family should have as many children as possible was declining: from 41 percent in 1963, down to 18 percent by the mid-1970s. According to Greeley, between the years 1963 and 1973 the belief among Catholics in the United States that Jesus Christ had handed the church to the popes of Rome had dropped from 70 percent to 42 percent.

In 1965, when the Second Vatican Council ended, anything and everything seemed possible; now, a scant three years later, everything seemed to be falling apart. Still, in this social and ecclesial maelstrom, I remember those years as a time of great and boundless possibility. Many of us who were active in the church during those days still speak of the enthusiasm we all felt; nothing was impossible and no problem was unsolvable if we just put our minds, hearts, and hands to addressing it. It wasn't going to be as easy as we had thought, perhaps, but it was still achievable through prayer and hard work; or, in the words of St. Benedict, "*Ora et labora.*"

The Diaconate Enters "on little cat feet"[3]

I have tried to capture a small sense of the time in order to contrast all of this high drama, tumult, and excitement with something that went largely *un*noticed by those of us in the seminary at the time. In 1967, shortly before our graduation from high school seminary, and a year before he would issue *Humanae Vitae*, Pope Paul VI issued a document entitled *Sacrum Diaconatus Ordinem*. In this document, the pope dealt with something that most of us seminarians took at the time to be a very minor event: the renewal of the diaconate as a *permanent* order of ordained ministry. This struck us as a kind of novelty; after all, we were still going to be priests, and being a deacon, for us, was just going to be the last signal that our "real" ordination was getting closer.

There was some interest in the fact that some older *married* men might be ordained deacons, but in the arrogance of youth, that just seemed rather quaint, because becoming something called a "permanent deacon" seemed about as significant as becoming some other kind of church worker who wasn't a priest—nice enough, but not truly and sacramentally significant. Being a "permanent deacon" made about as much sense as being a "permanent" subdeacon, or a "permanent" porter or lector or exorcist or acolyte.[4] It was, as we would say today, something that flew well below our radar screen. By the time the U.S. bishops requested and received permission from the Holy See in 1968 to begin forming and ordaining permanent deacons, we seminarians were focused on issues of far greater moment, like war and racism and the impact of *Humanae Vitae*.

Amid the general cacophony of the time, the diaconate whispered its return upon the ecclesial stage, and in light of the major traumas of the day, this development seemed to draw little initial attention. Certainly not everyone shared these same experiences or this same context, but I believe it is important to remember how different the world was at the birth of the renewed diaconate. The diaconate is not some static reality that may simply be transposed from one time to another: like all parts of the church, it is a living, organic, and dynamic reality. And how things have evolved over the intervening decades! The number of aspirants and candidates for the permanent diaconate in the United States now exceeds the number of men in the seminaries, and the number of deacons continues to rise steadily. There are now thousands of lay ecclesial ministers, with substantial pastoral experience and credentials, often holding advanced degrees which only a generation ago would have been the province of priests.

As I have written previously,

> Sorting out the issues involved in reviving a permanent order of ministry that had been largely dormant for more than a millennium would be challenging enough under the most stable of cultural, social and ecclesial conditions! The challenge increases exponentially, however, when coupled with the two chronologically coincident realities of a veritable explosion in lay ecclesial ministries and a drastic drop in the number of presbyters. The confluence of these three realities—the growth of lay ecclesial ministry and the sacramental diaconate with the decline in numbers of presbyters—has led some commentators to suggest various causal relationships between them which may or may not be accurate. This has only underscored the critical need for continuing scholarly and pastoral discourse on the sacramental identity of all who minister, and the relationships that ought to exist between them.[5]

Charting Our Course

Nature of the Church, Nature of Diaconate

As the great philosopher and educator Bill Cosby likes to say, "I told you that story so I could tell you this one." As mentioned above, this is a book about the contemporary Catholic Church. The relationship between the nature of the church and the nature of the diaconate has been clearly stated in a succession of papal teachings and official documents.

This relationship was made explicit first by Paul VI. In his homily at the last general session of Vatican II on December 7, 1965, Paul summarized the work of the council:

> We stress that the teaching of the Council is channeled in one direction, the service of humankind, of every condition, in every weakness and need. The Church has declared herself a servant of humanity at the very time when her teaching role and her pastoral government have, by reason of this Church solemnity, assumed greater splendor and vigor. However, the idea of service has been central.[6]

It is no coincidence that the same Pope Paul VI who stressed the nature of the church as servant would be the very man to renew the order of the diaconate itself within the church, calling it a "driving force for the Church's *diakonia* and a sacrament of the Lord Christ himself, who 'came not to be served but to serve.'"[7] John Paul II, in a 1987 address to the U.S. diaconate community gathered in Detroit, made the following observation:

> The service of the deacon is the Church's service sacramentalized. Yours is not just one ministry among others, but it is truly meant to be, as Paul VI described it, a "driving force" for the Church's *diakonia*. You are meant to be living signs of the servanthood of Christ's Church.[8]

Benedict XVI, in his first encyclical, *Deus Caritas Est* (2006), reminds his readers that "[b]eing Christian is not the result of an ethical choice or a lofty idea, but the encounter with an event, a person, which gives life a new horizon and a decisive direction."[9] He adds that while love of neighbor is a responsibility of each member of the faithful, "it is also a responsibility for the entire ecclesial community at every level: from the local community to the particular Church and to the Church universal in its entirety. As a community, the Church must practice love. Love thus needs to be organized if it is to be an ordered service to the community."[10] He then goes on to highlight the choice of the seven "deacons"[11] in Acts 6 as "a decisive step in the difficult search for ways of putting this fundamental ecclesial principle into practice."[12] Furthermore, the pope notes, the ministry of the seven was not about a "purely mechanical work of distribution."

> The social service which they were meant to provide was absolutely concrete, yet at the same time it was also a spiritual service; theirs was a truly spiritual office which carried out an essential responsibility of the Church, namely a well-ordered love of neighbor. With the formation of this group of seven, "*diakonia*"—the ministry of charity exercised in a communitarian, orderly way—became part of the fundamental structure of the Church.[13]

The pope concludes:

> The Church's deepest nature is expressed in her threefold responsibility: of proclaiming the word of God *(kerygma-martyria)*, celebrating the sacraments *(leitourgia)*, and exercising the ministry of charity *(diakonia)*. These duties presuppose each other and are inseparable. For the Church, charity is not a kind of welfare which could equally well be left to others, but is a part of her nature, an indispensable expression of her very being.[14]

As ordained ministers, deacons participate in the threefold apostolic ministry of the bishop for Word, Sacrament, and Charity, the duties of which "presuppose each other and are inseparable." In the

National Directory for the Formation, Ministry and Life of Permanent Deacons in the United States, the bishops of the United States teach that there is an "intrinsic unity" to the deacon's ministries, that they "are *not* to be separated; the deacon is ordained for them *all*, and no one should be ordained who is not prepared to undertake each in some way."[15] In short, then, it may be concluded the diaconate sacramentalizes the *diakonia* of the church itself through the integral and balanced exercise of what is essentially servant-leadership.

Edward Kilmartin observed, "Ministries of the Church must be consistent with the nature of the Church, or more precisely, derived from the nature of the Church. The way in which one conceives the nature of Church determines whether a particular form of ministry is acceptable."[16] Applying Kilmartin's insight to the diaconate, one may say that the church has ministers known as "deacons" because the church understands itself to be diaconal; furthermore, it is against that diaconal nature of the church that the particular exercises of the diaconate are to be judged.

The Diaconate on Its Own Terms

The diaconate must be assessed on its own sacramental relationship to and within the nature of the church itself and on the basis of its own unique sacramental identity. A frequent mistake made when discussing the diaconate is to compare and contrast it with the priesthood.[17] This happens on both the popular and the scholarly level. It is not uncommon for deacons to hear, "So, what does the priest *do* that you *can't*?" Or, "This is my friend Bill. He's a deacon; he can do everything a priest does *except* say Mass and hear confessions." Here is an even more subtle example: It is often asserted—incorrectly as we shall see later in chapter 2—that the major impetus behind renewing the diaconate as a permanent order of ministry came from bishops of the third world and mission countries who were suffering from a lack of priests. Then one hears (all too often) the following assessment, "The Council restored the diaconate because they thought it would be useful in countries with a lack of priests; but the diaconate has failed to take root there, while it has been very successful in the developed West where it really wasn't needed!" There are actually two major flaws in this assertion. Leaving aside the incorrect major premise until chapter 2, notice that the relative success or failure of the diaconate is being characterized by *its reference to the presbyterate;* the need for deacons is couched in terms of a shortage of priests. I once received a phone call from a woman who was terribly upset about the ills and scandals afflicting the church. She thanked me for the work that deacons were doing, and then said, "Won't it be wonderful when all these troubles are over, deacon, and then we won't need you guys anymore."

The late James H. Provost once observed, when writing about the diaconate in the 1983 *Code of Canon Law*, that there is "still no coherent treatment of permanent deacons as a 'proper and permanent rank of the hierarchy' comparable to the treatment given presbyters and bishops in the code; rather, they are treated as exceptions to the norms for presbyters."[18] This great insight applies to more than the *Code of Canon Law;* our theology and even popular imagination have failed to grasp this essential point, which is captured quite well in the *National Directory for the Formation, Ministry and Life of Permanent Deacons in the United States:* "the diaconate is *not* an abridged or substitute form of the priesthood, but is a *full order in its own right*."[19]

Contemporary attempts in theology and canon law to define and describe the nature and functions of the diaconate (and other forms of ministry) must be examined critically so that language which may legitimately apply to the priestly orders of bishop and presbyter is not applied inappropriately to the deacon. Terms of theological discourse, and legal expressions flowing from that language, must continue to develop. This book is an attempt to contribute to that effort. It is concerned fundamentally with the sacramental identity of the diaconate: to consider what diaconal ordination *means* in terms of the deacon's sacramental identity, that identity which derives from the reception of the sacrament of orders within a servant church.

It is a central thesis of this work that a significant difficulty exists in understanding the contemporary diaconate as "a proper and permanent"[20] order precisely because much of the theological and canonical language that has developed concerning the ordained ministries emerged subsequent to the decline of the diaconate as a permanent order. While it is sometimes said that the diaconate had *disappeared* by the end of the patristic era, and that it was *restored* by the Second Vatican Council, these characterizations are inadequate in that they miss a shift in paradigm. The diaconate *never* disappeared; rather, by the Middle Ages, it had been transformed from a *permanent* form of official ministry and redefined into a *transitory* stage on the way to ultimate ordination into the presbyterate. The diaconate ceased being described on its own terms and began being defined and described by its relationship to the presbyterate, its ultimate end. The paradigm for discussions of ordained ministry, therefore, became primarily sacerdotal (i.e., the priestly office of presbyters/bishops), and in particular, presbyteral, ministry. Since this transition from permanent to transitional, theological and canonical developments essentially equated the category of "ordained ministry" with "the ministry of presbyters." Consider just one example from the 1917 *Code of Canon Law*, which said that "first tonsure and orders are to be conferred only on those who are proposed for ascending to the presbyterate and who seem correctly understood as, at some point in the future, being worthy priests."[21] In short, under this system, all ministry (even within the ranks of the ordained) found its meaning by and through its relationship with the presbyterate, against which *all* ministry was ordered. James Barnett, himself an Anglican priest, once described this reality as "the omnivorous priesthood" and made a strong claim that this was a "real problem with both lay and diaconal ministry, indeed also of an impossibly overburdened presbyteral ministry."[22] Other ministries, including the episcopate and diaconate (as well as various forms of lay ecclesial ministry), are often still measured against this paradigm.[23] Using such a frame of reference, ministries other than the presbyterate are often described in terms of what they are *not*: the laity are described as "nonordained"; deacons do not "say Mass," do not "hear confessions," do not "give last rites." This method of "negative identification" must be overcome if the diaconate is to develop into the "proper and permanent" order described by the council.

Paragraph 29 of Vatican II's Dogmatic Constitution on the Church *(Lumen Gentium)* changed all this. For the first time in well over a millennium, the church now had a *permanent* order of ordained ministry that was distinct from the presbyteral order. "At a lower level of the hierarchy are deacons, who receive the imposition of hands 'not unto priesthood, but unto service.' For, strengthened by sacramental grace they are dedicated to the People of God, in conjunction with the bishop and his body of priests, in service of the liturgy, of the Word, and works of charity."

The ancient assertion that deacons are ordained not to priesthood but to service has remained consistent throughout the history of the diaconate, while the cultural, canonical, and theological contexts within which this claim has been made have varied greatly. For the purposes of this study, however, the statement is taken at its word: deacons are not ordained to priesthood. With Vatican II, and in particular after Pope Paul VI implemented the council's decision in 1967 with *Sacrum Diaconatus Ordinem*, a person again could be ordained into a "proper and permanent" order that did not lead inevitably to the presbyterate.

The significance of the council's decision to renew the diaconate as a permanent order of ordained ministry lies in the recognition that ordained ministry can contain an order that is not destined, defined, or described in terms of priesthood. I am not at all suggesting that the ordained ministries are not related, and intimately so, with the ministry of Christ and with each other; just the opposite is true. However, it is in Christ that we find the model of ministry, and that model is not exclusively presbyteral. This conciliar insight has yet to catch fire in the popular imagination, which often still sees the presbyterate as the center of the ministerial universe, measuring all ministry against it. Nearly every deacon (and lay ecclesial minister) has stories of this struggle in the popular understanding of ministry. The wife of one deacon was once asked whether, after her death, the deacon "would become a *real* priest." Another deacon was asked when his "*real* ordination" (meaning his ordination to the presbyterate) would take place, and still another once worked with a pastor who referred to the deacon's wife as the deacon's "beautiful impediment" (to priestly ordination).

This book is divided into two parts. Part 1 is entitled "The Present Diaconate and How We Got Here." The rediscovery or restatement of the church's diaconal nature did not emerge out of a vacuum, and the desire for a particular sacramental expression of this diaconal nature by renewing the order of deacons as a permanent sacrament of ministry did not simply fall from the heavens. This first part will consider the historical trajectory of the diaconate: from its scriptural roots and its "golden age"; the history of the contemporary renewal and its influence on the deliberations and decisions of the council vis-à-vis the renewed diaconate; and finally, the initial stages of the renewal following the council until 1998.[24] Part 2, "Toward a Theology of the Diaconate," attempts to situate the contemporary diaconate within the larger ministerial context of the church today. It also attempts to suggest possibilities for realizing the untapped potential of a renewed diaconate in the contemporary church.

Part One

THE PRESENT DIACONATE AND HOW WE GOT HERE

Strengthened by sacramental grace, in communion with
the bishop and his group of priests, deacons serve the
People of God in the ministry of the liturgy,
of the word, and of charity.

—*Lumen Gentium* 29

1

THE DIACONATE TODAY

As a community, the Church must practice love. Love thus needs to be organized if it is to be an ordered service to the community.
—Benedict XVI, *Deus Caritas Est* 20

Introduction

Before we roll the clock back and examine how we have arrived at this point in time with the diaconate, we should first describe where we are. Those who spend time working with the diaconate learn very quickly that there are probably more misunderstandings, myths, and misperceptions about the diaconate than about any other group in today's church! So let us try to paint a picture of where we are existentially, especially here in the United States.

Consider some of the following observations that are made frequently about the diaconate, sometimes by deacons themselves, but also by their bishops and pastors or by the people with whom they serve. For example, one often hears that "the number of deacon candidates has fallen off" and that the diaconate is no longer growing in numbers. Yet another consistent story is that the diaconate is not really needed in the United States "because the bishops at Vatican II intended it for use in the third world and mission territories." A recent book on the priesthood by a highly respected author reports that deacons are present and serving in about half of the dioceses of the United States. ("What's the problem with that?" you may ask. The problem is that the readers of this assertion will presume its veracity, when actually, we have deacons serving in all but a handful of our 195 dioceses and eparchies in the United States. This information has been available for many years.) Another frequent assertion is that deacons, as a rule, are not very well educated men. Still another is that most deacons work in the secular workplace. Finally, I have even heard it said that divorce is on the rise among deacons owing primarily to the pressures of ordained ministry; therefore, married men should no longer be ordained. Every one of these assertions is false or inaccurate—and yet they persist.

For much of the data that follows I am indebted to the fine work of the Center for Applied Research in the Apostolate (CARA) located on the campus of Georgetown University. We will be using five broad sets of data: (1) a special CARA report on the diaconate from June 2000;[1] (2) a CARA Profile of the Diaconate from January 2004;[2] (3) the 2005–2006 CARA report on ministry formation;[3] (4) a CARA 2007 post-formation survey;[4] and (5) the 1996 national survey on the diaconate conducted by the Bishops' Committee on the Diaconate of the United States Conference of Catholic Bishops.[5]

This chapter is divided into three sections. First is a section focused on quantitative data (number of deacons, number of candidates, where deacons serve, and so on). Second is a section more qualitative in nature (how deacons have been accepted by others, ministries deacons are involved in, and levels of ministerial satisfaction they report). Third is a section addressing a number of issues raised by the data.

Quantitative Issues

Number of Permanent Deacons

The March 2007 CARA study estimates a total of 16,661 permanent deacons in the United States. As of the CARA report published in 2000, only seven dioceses in the country did *not* have deacons serving.[6] Figure 1 shows the growth in numbers of the deacons and deacon candidates between 1971 and 2007. Over the past ten years, the average rate of increase each year has been about 3 percent.[7]

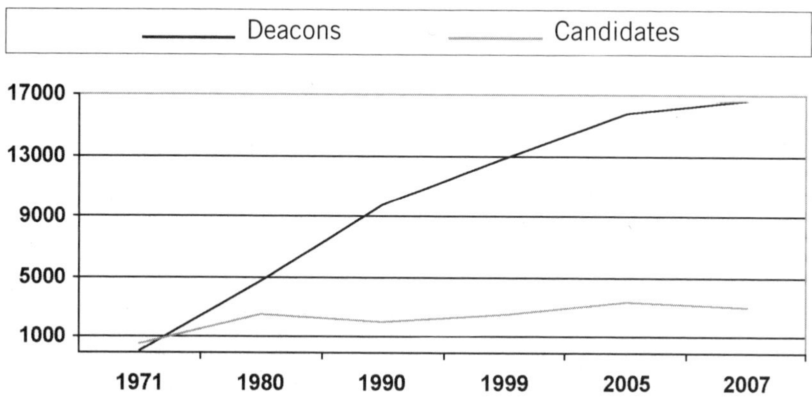

Figure 1. Deacons and Candidates, 1971–2007
Sources: CARA 2000; CARA 2007; *Official Catholic Directory*

A word of background is in order about the unique nature of diaconate formation. Unlike formation for the priesthood, in which seminarians are sent by their bishops to seminaries, which are often regional institutions serving a number of dioceses around the country and the world where the curriculum is established under close scrutiny by the Holy See and the United States Conference of Catholic Bishops, diaconate formation is quite different. Each diocese establishes its own policies and procedures, following standards identified by the Holy See and the USCCB.[8] These formation programs use a variety of delivery methods, schedules, and content, based on the needs and resources of the local diocese and respecting the fact that most candidates are working people with family responsibilities that make full-time formation, especially in a resident institution like a seminary, impossible.

While there was a *slight* fall-off in the number of candidates in the 1980's, those numbers have long since reversed. A number of informal conversations with diocesan bishops and diocesan directors of diaconate suggest—at least anecdotally—that when numbers have dropped in the formation of deacons, it has been the result of a change of diocesan or national requirements rather than a decline in vocational interest or response. For example, a diocese may have simply not admitted new candidates for a period of time while the formation program was being evaluated. Figure 2 reflects the number of diocesan formation programs around the country, with formation programs currently in place in all fifty states and in the District of Columbia.

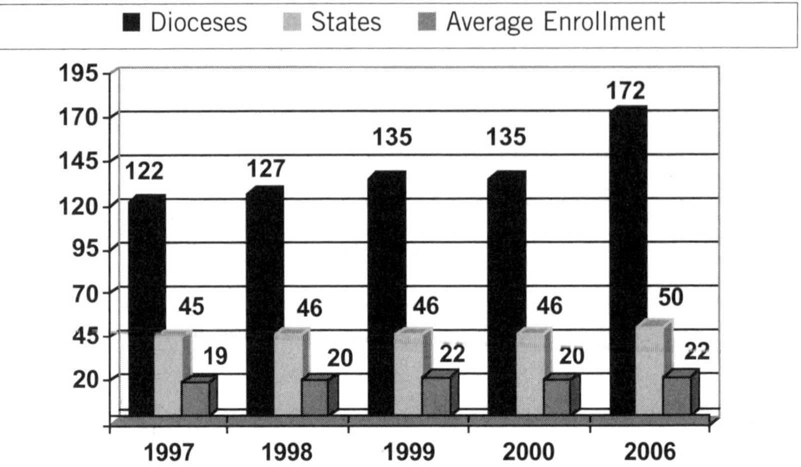

Figure 2. Diocesan Diaconate Formation Programs, 1997–2006
Sources: CARA 2000; CARA Formation 2006

Active programs are found in 172 of the 195 dioceses and eparchies of the United States. In the latest survey of formation programs (2006), five directors reported that their diocesan programs are on hold at this time, most often because of a change in bishops. Ten programs have been reactivated or newly formed, and six programs will be under way within another year. Many of these programs report that they are in the process of being redesigned in light of the 2004 *National Directory*. It is reasonable to assume that additional dioceses will be initiating or redesigning formation programs as a result of this document as well.

In short, overall experience, reflected in these data, indicates that the permanent diaconate has been in a constant state of numerical growth from the time of its renewal.

Distribution of Deacons

In 2000, CARA reported eleven dioceses with more than 200 deacons each. By 2007 that number was up to nineteen dioceses.

Chicago was still in the lead with 632 deacons (although the number of Chicago deacons in 2000 was 817). In 2000, the top three dioceses included Chicago (817), New York (340), and Hartford (319). The population was shifting by 2007, with Chicago (632) now followed by Galveston-Houston (454), Trenton (418), Washington (398), and New York (385). Figure 3 lists the nineteen dioceses that report more than 200 deacons.

Arch/diocese	Number of Deacons
1. Chicago	632
2. Galveston-Houston	454
3. Trenton	418
4. Washington	398
5. New York	385
6. Hartford	330
7. San Antonio	324
8. Los Angeles	300
9. Boston	284
10. Baltimore	276
11. St. Louis	271
12. Rockville Centre	264
13. Phoenix	261
14. Cleveland	256
15. Joliet	224
16. Santa Fe	223
17. St. Paul and Minneapolis	217
18. Philadelphia	213
19. Newark	210

Figure 3. Arch/dioceses with Largest Number of Deacons
Source: CARA Post-Ordination 2007

Figure 4 depicts the distribution of deacons throughout the country by region, with 21% of deacons serving in the South, 29% in the West, and 33% in the Midwest; in other words, half of the deacons in the United States are in the South and West.

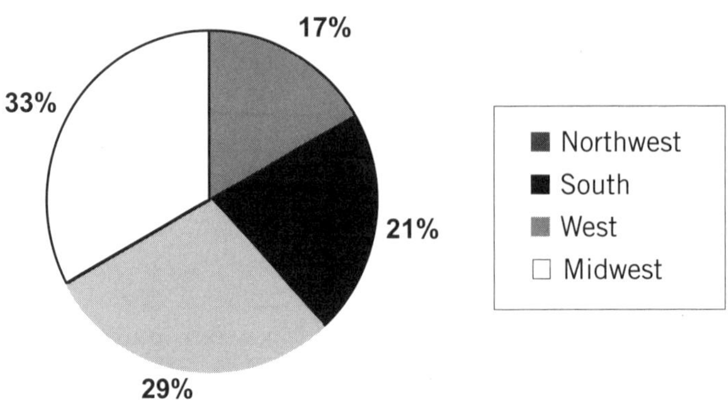

Figure 4. Regional Distribution of Deacons as of 2004
Source: CARA 2004

Race and Ethnicity

Deacons are not as racially diverse as the overall Catholic population in the United States—although they *are* more racially diverse than the Catholic priesthood. The Catholic population is about 65% Caucasian, 28% Latino, 4% African American, 3% Native American, and 1% Asian. Catholic priests, on the other hand, are about 94% Caucasian, 2% Latino, 1% African American, 3% Asian, and less than 1% Native American. In view of this, now consider figure 5, which provides the data on the diaconate.

It should be borne in mind that these are national averages; various regions will exhibit great variation in these numbers.

Age

The aging of the diaconate is a significant issue, which will be discussed later. Before reviewing the statistics, one should bear in mind that the canonical age for married men to be ordained is thirty-five, and that the average age of deacons in nearly every other part of the world is about forty-one. Now consider the data for the United States (figure 6).

The average age of deacons in the United States as of the 2007 data is now 62. The data reveal that in the 1970s the average

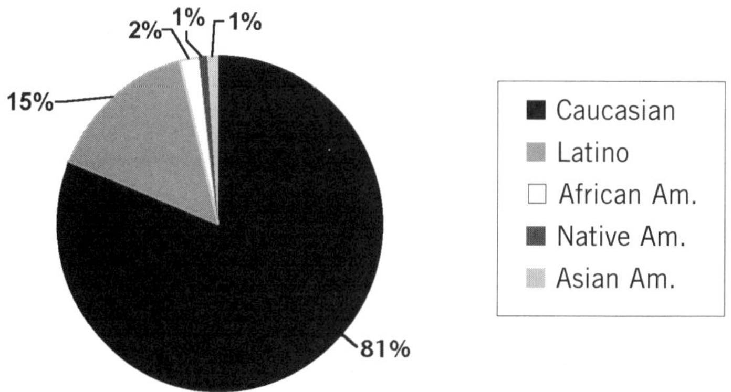

Figure 5. Race and Ethnic Background
Source: CARA Post-Ordination 2007

age of deacons was about 49 years; throughout the 1980s the average rose to 59; and throughout the 1990s and into the new century, it has continued to rise to 62. This aging of the diaconate is matched by a similar rise in the average age at which deacons are being ordained: in the 1970s, the average at ordination was 46; in the 1980s it was up to 49; in the 1990s it was 53.

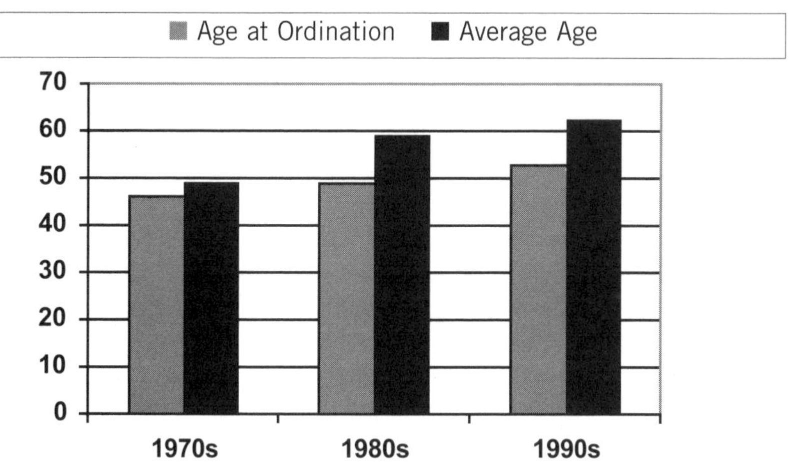

Figure 6. Average Age at Ordination and Average Age
Sources: CARA 2004; USCCB Study 1996

Figure 7 below summarizes the trends since 1996. Notice that only 1% of deacons in the United States are under the age of 40, and only 16% were under the age of 50 in 1996; now only 10% are under the age of 50. At the other end of the spectrum, nearly 40% of all U.S. deacons are over the age of 70. Sixty-eight percent of deacons, nearly 7 out of 10, are between the ages of 50 and 70.

Year	35–39	40–49	50–59	60–69	70–79	80+
1996	1%	15%	35%	32%	16%	
1999	1%	10%	32%	35%	18%	4%
2007	1%	9%	29%	39%	39%	

Figure 7. Age Distribution for Deacons, 1996–2007
Sources: CARA 2000; CARA Post-Ordination 2007

In the 2004 survey, CARA decided to break the number of deacons into four generations according to the era of their birth: the World War II generation, born between 1901 and 1924; the so-called Silent generation, born between 1925 and 1942; the Vatican II generation, born between 1942 and 1960; and the post–Vatican II generation, born after 1960. Figure 8 records the results: 61% of deacons are from the Silent generation, 30% from the Vatican II generation, 9% from the World War II generation, and 1% from the post-Vatican II generation.

The phenomenon of an aging diaconate appears to be a rather unique feature of the diaconate in the United States. Although scientific documentation is not available to make a definitive comparison, sufficient anecdotal evidence has been obtained from members of the International Diaconate Center (IDC, headquartered in Rottenburg, Germany) that indicates an average age of about 41 for deacons in most of the rest of the world. As part of my assignment with the United States Conference of Catholic Bishops, I frequently represented the USCCB at various international meetings and gatherings. It was not uncommon for my international deacon colleagues to suggest that the diaconate in the United States has been turned into a "retirees' club." The issue of the age of deacons will be examined at greater length in chapter 4, when we cover the history of the contemporary renewal of the diaconate.

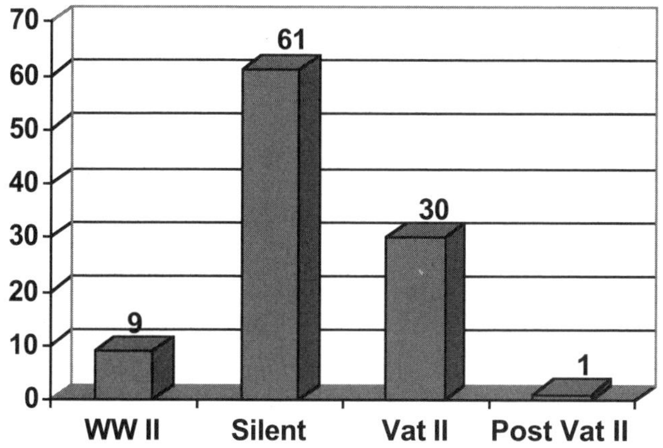

Figure 8. Deacons by Generation of Birth
Source: CARA 2004

Education

The general education level of deacons and candidates continues to rise. Figure 9 shows the overall education level of deacons based on the latest research.

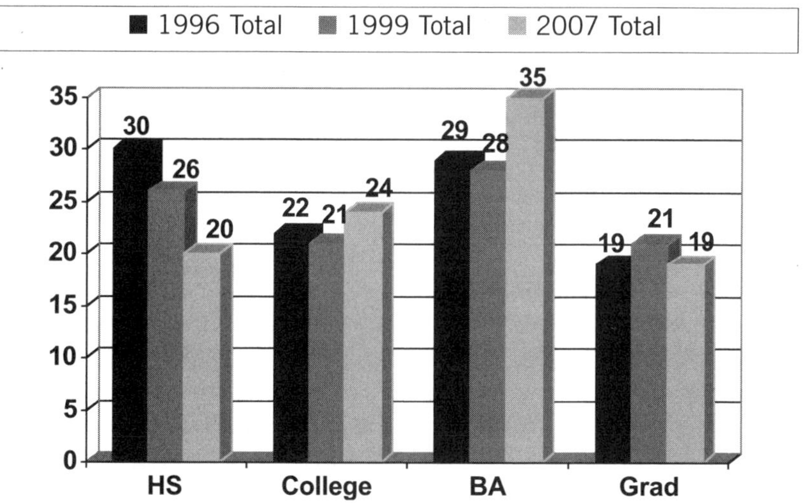

Figure 9. Diaconate Education Levels, 1996–2006
Sources: CARA 2004; CARA Post-Ordination 2007

The trends are clear: the number of deacons with a high school education or less continues to decline. The vast majority of deacons have at least some college (78%), with 31% holding bachelor's degrees, 25% holding graduate degrees (20% with master's degrees, and 5% with doctorates). Figure 10 compares these results with other parts of the general population.

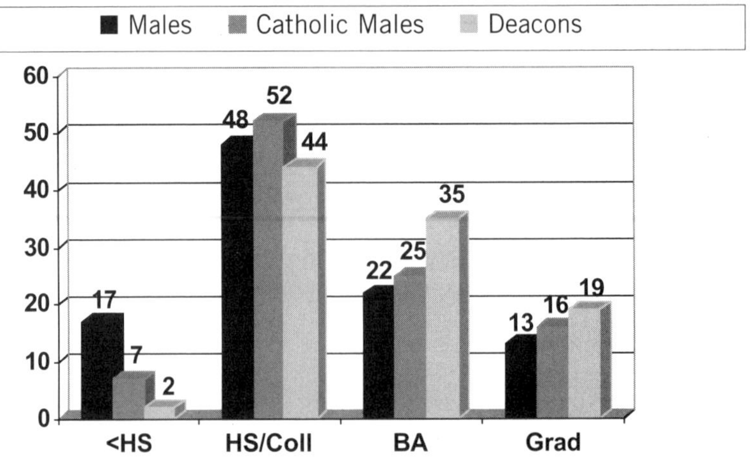

Figure 10. Deacon Education Levels Compared with Other Catholic Males and with Males in General over the Age of 35
Source: CARA 2004

CARA focused on graduate education levels by generation, and an even more striking fact emerges: Vatican II and post-Vatican II generations are reflecting significantly higher education levels, perhaps paralleling the levels of that generation as a whole (figure 11).

One final fascinating fact is that men entering formation for the permanent diaconate and men entering the final four years of formation for the priesthood are arriving with similar educational backgrounds. Deacon candidates generally have completed their formal education prior to entering formation. In a 2004 survey of the priesthood ordination class of that year, 28% of those men had begun their final four years of formation with a graduate degree of some kind. As can be seen from the data above, in general, 25% of deacon candidates already have graduate degrees; this percentage is notably higher (as high as 36%) for candidates of the Vatican II generation.

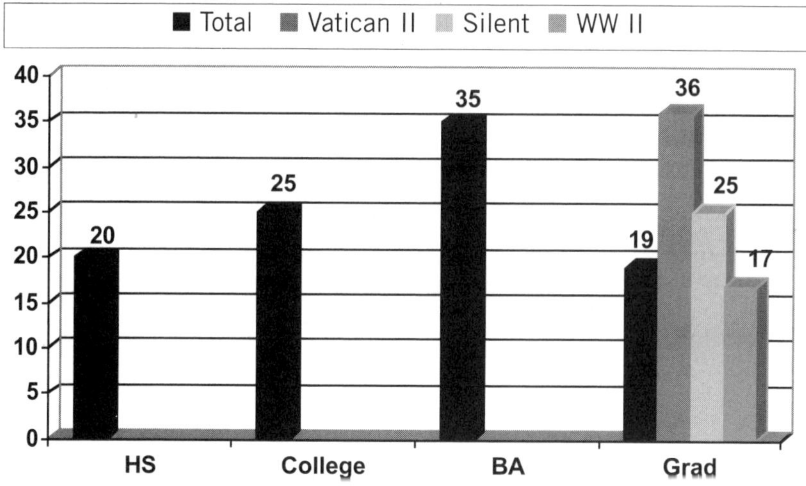

Figure 11. Deacon Graduate Education by Generation
Source: CARA 2004

It is clear that deacons—including today's deacon candidates—are a highly educated segment of the Catholic population.

Marital Status

Figure 12 tells the story: 93% of deacons are married; 4% are widowed; 2% are single and never married. Fewer than 1% are divorced, and some of these divorces predated ordination. A small percentage of deacons (0.3%) have received a dispensation from the "impediment of orders" and have remarried following the death of their spouse and have remained in ministry.

Two major issues leap from the data. The first is the exceptional need for theological work on the relationship of the sacraments of matrimony and orders. While there is great overall appreciation of the relationship of celibacy to orders, because of the centuries of celibate clergy in the Latin West, there is no such parallel appreciation of *matrimony* and orders. This having been said, however, another need is discernible, and that is the danger of associating the diaconate almost *exclusively* with marriage. I once received a phone call from a gentleman who told me that he thought he might have a vocation to the diaconate, but that he felt he couldn't apply because he wasn't married! This was a concern of some of the bishops at the Second Vatican Council, one of whom remarked that he was concerned that a two-tier clerical structure might emerge: a celibate priesthood and a married diaconate. It is useful to remember that there are married priests (in the Eastern Catholic Churches as well as married former Protestant ministers who have been received into the church and have subsequently been ordained into the priesthood), and that there are celibate deacons. Marital status is *not* an inherent part of the orders themselves.

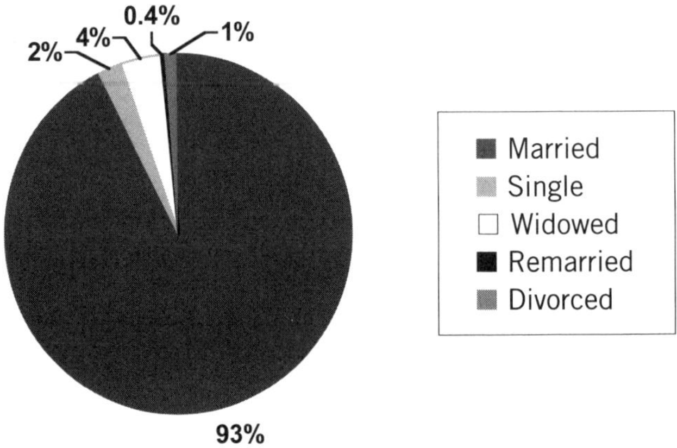

Figure 12. Marital Status of Permanent Deacons, 2006
Source: CARA Post-Ordination 2007

Ministry and Compensation

Theologically, of course, deacons are always "full-time" ministers, and John Paul II observed that the diaconate is a "ministry, not a profession." Still, in the popular imagination, deacons are often perceived as "part-time" ministers who serve as other commitments (family, secular job) permit. This will be discussed in greater detail a bit later, but for now we must deal with the notion of the deacon and his relationship to public ministry.

In the 2004 CARA survey, only 38% of deacons reported working in a secular job or occupation (figure 13). Responding to the question, "Are you currently employed in a secular job?" only 38% answered affirmatively.

These figures may represent another dimension of the aging of the diaconate. "Deacons of the Vatican II/Post-Vatican II Generations are much more likely than Pre-Vatican II Generation deacons to report that they are employed in a secular job (65 percent compared to 28 percent of Silent Generation deacons and 7 percent of World War II Generation deacons)."[9] Furthermore, "deacons ordained in 1990 or later are more likely than those ordained earlier to report that they are employed in a secular job (49 percent compared to 34 percent of deacons ordained in the 1980s and 20 percent of those ordained in the 1970s)."[10] Nonetheless, even if this is the case, the existential reality is that the vast majority of deacons today do not hold secular jobs.

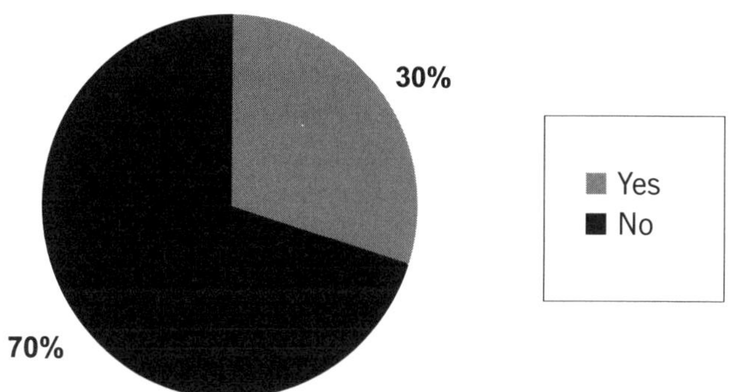

Figure 13. Deacons Employed in Secular Occupations
Source: CARA 2004, CARA 2007

Closely related to questions of this type are issues of compensation. It is not uncommon to hear, at least popularly, that deacons are an "all-volunteer" force, and that they are not paid for ministry. Referring again to the 2004 CARA survey, respondents were asked, "Are you paid for ministry?" The responses are represented in figure 14.

An examination of these last two sets of data is particularly revealing with regard to Vatican II–generation deacons. If 65% of deacons of that generation are holding secular jobs, 35% are not. Since these are men still of "working age," it would appear that at least 32% of them are now "working" and being compensated by church employment.

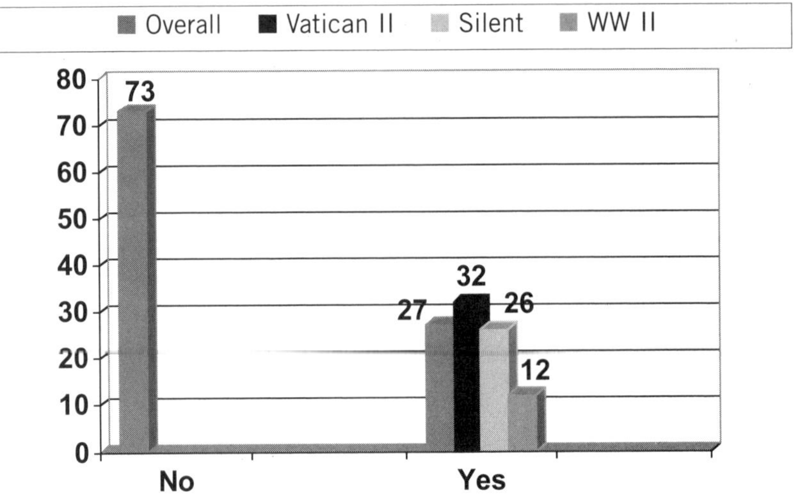

Figure 14. Deacons and Financial Compensation
Source: CARA 2004

We can look at another question from the 2004 survey for further confirmation that roughly a third of deacons are involved in full-time ecclesial ministry. Respondents were asked to characterize the time spent in ministry.

Not surprisingly, 30% of deacons report serving in ecclesial ministry on a full-time basis. Looking at the updated survey results from 2005, we find that 33% of deacons report working full-time in a secular occupation, and 6% working part-time. 13% of deacons report working in full-time ministry; 47% report working in part-time ministry.

Clearly the data indicate that an increasing number of deacons are serving in full-time, compensated ecclesial ministry. This is happening as increasing numbers of deacons "retire" from the secular work force (but *not* from active ministry); in some cases, deacons are taking advantage of "early retirement" options from secular employment with a view to entering full-time ecclesial ministry.

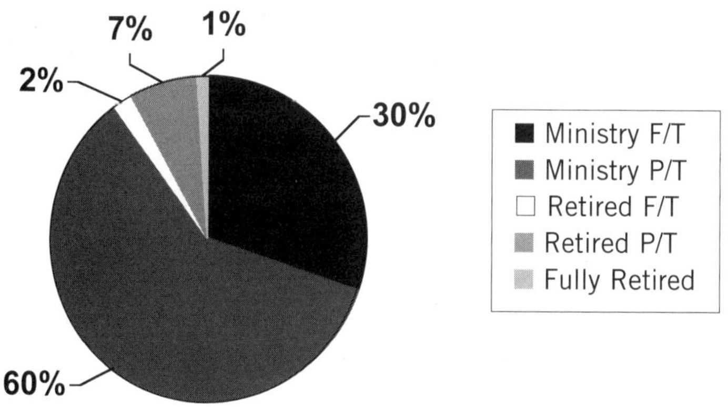

Figure 15. Percentage of Time Spent in Ministry
Source: CARA 2004

Qualitative Issues: Identity, Ministry, Challenges

In 1993, the bishops of the United States approved an extensive examination of the permanent diaconate. Throughout 1994, the data collection and initial analysis took place. Phase I focused on the experience of deacons themselves; phase II, on the wives of deacons; phase III, on the supervisors of deacons; and phase IV, on parish and diocesan lay leaders. The final report was issued in 1996. In effect, this USCCB report was an amalgam of four distinct but related surveys.

Three sections of the study offer particularly fruitful material for subsequent examination: "Who Are the Deacons?," "Family Life and Diaconal Responsibilities," and "What Do Deacons Do/ What Will They Do?"

Who Are the Deacons?

Two points stand out in this category of the study. First, by 1996, 60% of deacons reported "professional or managerial careers that usually followed at least a college education."[11] It further notes that this reveals higher levels of education than "the already high levels" of an earlier 1981 study. Given the data collected subsequent to this study, it seems clear that this trend is continuing. The vast majority of deacons have college educations and significant leadership experience in their secular occupations and professions. This experience, expertise, and education—when put to optimal use within the context of ecclesial ministry—can be a unique contribution of the diaconate. The challenge is for bishops, directors of diaconate formation, and deacons themselves to recognize the diverse gifts and talents already possessed by deacons in virtue of their secular backgrounds, and how these gifts may be best adapted to official ministry.

The second point reports that "a little over one-half" (52.4%) of the deacons surveyed reported that they had in the past considered a vocation to the priesthood. However, "only about one-third" claimed that this earlier interest had any significant influence on their becoming deacons. Far more influential was a "need to deepen the service(s) I was already giving to the church" (61%).[12] This insight draws our attention to the critical question of vocational discernment. A consistent concern in diaconal formation programs is to ensure that candidates demonstrate a proper disposition for the vocation of deacon—not for that of presbyter. The diaconate is not a "back door" for entering ordained ministry for men who, for whatever reasons, cannot respond to a priestly vocation.

It is also important to realize that a vocation to the diaconate does *not* mean a man has a vocation to the priesthood. This fact is obscured, of course, because we still have the practice of requiring that all seminarians for the priesthood be ordained deacons first. Still, a vocation to one order is not a vocation to another. This fact is important because many people make the assumption that, if the deacon had the chance, he'd become a priest. It is not unusual for a deacon who has been widowed to be asked by parishioners or even pastors if he will now become a priest! The *National Directory* correctly notes that the permanence of the order of deacon needs to be respected as a significant theological characteristic.

Underlying the restoration and renewal of the diaconate at the Second Vatican Council was the principle that the

> diaconate is a stable and permanent rank of ordained ministry. Since the history of the order over the last millennium, however, has been centered on the diaconate as a transitory stage leading to the priesthood, actions that may obfuscate the stability and permanence of the order should be minimized. This would include the ordination of celibate or widowed deacons to the priesthood. "Hence ordination [of a permanent deacon] to the Priesthood...must always be a very rare exception, and only for special and grave reasons.[13]

A personal experience may illustrate the concern on this point. The day before I was ordained deacon, I had a final interview with the cardinal. When I went into his office and sat down, he gestured to the various stacks of files and papers on his desk. "This is your record, Bill. This stack covers the eight years, high school and college, that you spent in the seminary studying for the priesthood. Before we talk about anything else, we need to come to grips with this." I admit to being taken aback; of all the things I thought he would want to discuss, this had not even entered my mind. He continued, "So, Bill, have you discerned in yourself a call to priesthood or to diaconate?" For the cardinal, this was the most fundamental question to be addressed. The diaconate cannot be a haven for people who are, in reality, frustrated priests. Clearly, since the cardinal ordained me the following day, I must have assured him sufficiently!

Family Life and Diaconal Responsibilities

Considerable concern over the deacon's ability to balance his various obligations of family life, secular occupation, and ecclesial ministry has been a feature of most formation programs since the earliest days of the renewed diaconate. In the 1996 study, all four groups surveyed reported very positively on the mutuality of family life and the deacon's ministries. Not only did the deacons' supervisors and parish and diocesan lay leaders report minimal conflict on this issue, but the wives of deacons and the deacons themselves reported overwhelmingly (85.5%) that the blend of family life and ministry was mutually beneficial, and that their family lives had been deeply enriched by the diaconate.

What Do Deacons Do and What Will They Do?

The 1996 study found that most deacons were particularly involved in—and were reported by their supervisors and lay leaders as quite effective and successful in—the traditional liturgical and sacramental roles. While the frequency of preaching by deacons varies considerably around the country, more than half the lay leaders reported that deacons' preaching was "about the same in quality" as priests'. In a good summary statement, the study reports:

> From these data (and, later, the written comments) it appears that the vast majority of supervisors and lay leaders regard their deacons as clearly necessary for their parishes, judge them effective in their parish ministries, and find them satisfactorily trained for these responsibilities. However, both their supervisors and their parish lay leaders are just about evenly divided about whether the deacons' ordination is important for the actual ministries they characterize as ably performed.[14]

From this section, three points are raised for further examination. First, deacons are being well received *as parish ministers.* On the surface, perhaps, this may not seem significant; however, upon closer examination this is a very important concern. Priests, for example, are perceived by parishioners *as diocesan ministers* who are currently serving in a particular parish; deacons, on the other hand, are perceived largely as parish ministers, and usually parish ministers at the same parish they've lived in for years before they were ordained. Second, the role for which the deacons are being affirmed seems to be that of simply extending the ministry of the pastor. As lay leaders look to the future, they anticipate that, because of a shortage of priests, the deacon's role will continue to "supply," to the extent of their faculties and authority, the ministries previously provided by priests. The third issue is the rather functional understanding of ordination revealed in the responses of some of the supervisors and lay leaders, who question the need for ordination for the deacons to do the things they're doing.

In summarizing the study, the bishops had this to say as their "Central Finding":

> The restored Order of Diaconate, largely parish-based, has been successful and increasingly important for the life of the Church. The primary challenges of the diaconate for the future are to broaden its ministries beyond its largely successful and increasingly indispensable adaptations to parish life and to emphasize more strongly that deacons, through ordination, are called to be model, animator, and facilitator of ministries of charity and justice within the local church.[15]

Furthermore, the bishops posed a number of questions for reflection on the future, including: "How are the issues of the deacon's identity and acceptance to be resolved in light of the tendency of many to use the deacon to address the present shortage of priests?"[16]

The bishops recommended measures that would encourage greater ministry by deacons outside parish boundaries, exercising ministry on a diocesan basis as well as within a parish. By the time of the 2004 CARA study, 62% of deacons reported serving in a blend of parish/nonparish ministries, with only 36% serving only in parish ministry.[17] The most frequent "nonparish" ministry was that of counseling (37%), usually at a hospital or other health care facility (37%). Other types of non-parish ministry include serving as chaplains (35%), spiritual direction/retreat work (31%), social work or social service (30%), and teaching (25%). Nearly a quarter of deacons (22%) report working at the diocesan offices. Some dioceses adopted assignment policies in which deacons received a *dual* assignment: to a parish for ministries of Word and Sacrament, and to another agency or institution for additional service and leadership responsibility. It seems that the bishops' efforts to expand the role of deacons outside the parish is working.

Issues Raised by the Data

The data, of course, raise any number of issues, but I wish to highlight two of them here.

The Aging of the Diaconate

This is a most significant issue, and its impact can be seen in several others as well. As noted above, this appears to be a rather unique characteristic of the diaconate in the United States, and the reasons for this will need to be explored. Because the average age of deacons in the United States is now up to 62, this may be contributing to the rather significant increase of deacons available for *full-time* ministry; they are men who have retired from secular occupations in order to serve the church on a full time basis. While this has positive dimensions in that it provides additional full-time ministers for the church, it adds its own challenges as well, as we shall see.

On a practical level, there is concern that ordaining older deacons limits the length of time (in years) that they will be able to serve, not to mention concern over health and injury-related issues. An interesting tidbit that will be described in greater detail in chapter 4 when we discuss the Second Vatican Council, concerns the various proposals that were made at the council concerning age and the diaconate. A number of bishops, when recommending the renewal of the permanent diaconate, suggested that mature married men might be ordained, and the age suggested was 40. When the topic of the diaconate was brought to discussion by the full council, this age was rejected *as being too old*, and the final proposal was to lower this "mature" age to 35.

"Employment" versus "Assignment"

The increase in the availability of deacons as full-time ministers has led to an additional challenge. Deacons are generally not paid for standard parish ministries, and they are responsible for earning a living to care for themselves (and their families, if married). Unlike priests, deacons do not draw a salary from the church, *unless* they hold some additional diocesan or parish position. For example, if a deacon is assigned to a parish, he does not get a salary from the church, but if he heads a diocesan office, he draws the salary associated with that office.

Now here's the scenario:. Deacon Tom, whose secular job is Director of Training for a local corporation, is assigned by his bishop to Holy Family Parish. Holy Family is a thriving parish, with K-8 parish school. A year after Deacon Tom arrives at the parish, the principal of the school decides to retire, and the pastor and board of education begin the selection process for a new principal. Deacon Tom and his family discuss the situation. The deacon has a master's degree in education and has had some school experience earlier in his career. They decide that he should take early retirement from the local corporation and apply for the position of principal. In this way, he can be serving in full-time ministry, something he has always wanted to do. So Deacon Tom applies for the job and is hired.

A year goes by. Although the deacon is a fine man, he is out of his depth as principal. The pastor and board meet to consider the teacher and administrator contracts for the coming year, and when they get to the principal, they are in a quandary. Certainly they will need to remove the deacon-principal; but the pastor points out that this will mean that a fired parish employee is still going to be present in the parish as an assigned member of the clergy! In other words, the deacon has been serving both as a parish employee (as school principal) and as a cleric assigned to the parish by the bishop.

This potential for conflict has led some dioceses to establish policies precluding deacons from seeking employment within the same parish to which he is assigned by the bishop. In other words, using the example above, Deacon Tom would not have been able to apply for the school position at Holy Family. If a similar position opened up at St. Stephen Parish across town, that would be acceptable.

Deacons as Parish Life Coordinators (c. 517 §2)

According to CARA, the number of deacons being assigned to provide the day-to-day leadership of parishes without a resident pastor (sometimes referred to as "canon 517.2 parishes" since this is the canon governing such assignments) is on the rise. Between 1993 and 2004, the number of parishes with Parish Life Coordinators rose from 268 to 566. In 1993, 36 deacons held such an assignment; by 2004, the number had risen to 148. "In 2004, 26 percent of parishes were entrusted to deacons and another 26 percent to lay men and women."[18]

Certainly many deacons possess the necessary gifts, background, experience, and education to serve effectively in such assignments. Still, this increases the pressure and potential to further transform the diaconate into a form of ministry derived from a shortage of priests, rather than offering a particular diaconal ministry to and for the church. The ministry associated with c. 517 §2 is an exceptional ministry, one that canonists call "extraordinary" for both deacons and laypersons who exercise it. If there were sufficient numbers of presbyters available, there would be no need for this ministry; this can lead to the gravely mistaken view that "once we have enough priests" there won't be a need for deacons or for lay ecclesial ministers, since they were just needed as a stopgap, filling in until we had enough priests. This is a most dangerous misunderstanding, and one that needs careful attention.

Issues such as these are not insurmountable, but my point in raising them is simply to highlight the fact that as the demographics of the diaconate evolve, the church is experiencing new challenges and tensions that will need to be addressed. Furthermore, given the tendency of many (as highlighted in the 1996 study) to use the diaconate as part of a solution to the shortage of priests, this all combines to distort the reasons for the renewal of the diaconate by the Second Vatican Council. More deacons serving on a full-time basis means, in the eyes of some, more deacons available to compensate for a shortage of priests. "The challenge of the next decades will be to make these developments more theologically rich and thus to expand the deacon's sense of ministry, evangelization, and service continually, even beyond the parish."[19]

Conclusions

Let us conclude this chapter with four observations. First, the renewed diaconate is not simply a restoration of the ancient diaconate. It is a new expression of this ministry in the church. It is important to examine how this particular ministry relates to other ministries in the church. The contemporary diaconate has emerged during a time of rapid, and some would say explosive, growth in lay ministry, coupled with a drastic decline in the number of presbyters. In light of these factors, it is important to discern the proper areas of ministry for the diaconate, so that it does not develop into a kind of substitute for sacerdotal ministry, on the one hand, or a clericalized form of lay ministry, on the other. The *Directory for the Ministry and Life of Permanent Deacons* states:

> In every case it is important, however, that deacons fully exercise their ministry, in preaching, in the liturgy and in charity to the extent that circumstances permit. They should not be relegated to marginal duties, be made merely to act as substitutes, nor discharge duties normally entrusted to non-ordained members of the faithful. Only in this way will the true identity of permanent deacons as ministers of Christ become apparent and the impression avoided that deacons are simply lay people particularly involved in the life of the Church.[20]

Second, since much of our theology of orders has been developed in terms of the sacerdotal orders (i.e., of bishops and especially priests), there is a need to examine the unique and nonsacerdotal sacramental identity of deacons.

Third, a number of official documents have dealt with the renewed diaconate, and these will be examined in greater detail in the following chapters. It must also be recognized, however, that a far greater number of significant official documents have either minimized or ignored the role of the deacon.[21] It is important, therefore, to attend to this silence. Are the documents silent because there is no proper role for the deacon in a particular instance, or, as seems even more likely, because the diaconate has simply not been thought of in that role? In the study that follows, we shall have occasion to consider whether silence betokens a lack of applicability to the diaconate, or whether a silence is a lacuna that ought to be addressed.

Fourth, as an ordained ministry, the diaconate shares in the one sacrament of orders. However, that one sacrament is expressed in both sacerdotal and diaconal ways. For over a millennium, pastoral leadership has been described and defined in sacerdotal terms. However, ordained "not unto priesthood but into service," deacons exercise a form of ordained pastoral leadership that is *not* sacerdotal. The precise nature of diaconal pastoral leadership, distinct from but related to leadership as exercised by other members of the church, especially in light of the long absence of a permanent diaconate from the daily life of the church, remains to be developed.

2

SCRIPTURAL ROOTS

Religion that is pure and undefiled before God, the Father, is this: to care for orphans and widows in their distress, and to keep oneself unstained by the world.
—James 1:27

In examining the origins of the diaconate, one is often referred to the standard "deacon" passages, those passages which, accurately or not, seem to be referring to early Christian officeholders known as deacons. Probably the most famous of these would be Acts 6:1–6, the selection of "the Seven." There is the First Letter to Timothy (1 Tim 3:8–13), in which Paul outlines for Timothy the qualifications to be sought in new deacons (following a similar listing of qualifications for new bishops). We also find several references to deacons on other Pauline letters, such as the reference to "our sister, Phoebe," who is described as *diakonos* of the church at Cenchreae (Rom 16:1). However, we are not interested in the origins of the diaconate simply as a specific order of Christian ministers. As I have said from the beginning, the diaconate as an order can find its proper meaning only within the broader fundamental reality of the Church-as-Deacon. In other words, Christians *have* deacons because Christians *are* deacons. This is similar to the understanding first expressed so well in the First Letter of Peter (2:9), that we are a "priestly people": we *have* priests, because we *are* priests. This "priestly-diaconal" nature of the followers of Jesus Christ flows directly from our baptism into the life of the Trinity and our sacramental connection with Christ himself.

Therefore, this chapter surveys notions of *diakonia* found in both Hebrew and Christian scriptures, and with that foundation firmly in place will we turn to the specific category of deacons as Christian officeholders. The goal at this point is not to attempt an exhaustive treatment of the subject; that far exceeds the scope of the current project. Our goal is much more pragmatic: to suggest certain biblical themes that describe *diakonia* as a constitutive element of a covenant *communio*.

If this *still* sounds more theoretical than practical, consider the tendency in many communities to compartmentalize the many functions of the parish or diocese. If a parishioner is asked, "Does your parish sponsor any outreach programs for those in need in your community?" the answers might very well be, "Sure! I don't know much about it, but we have a social concerns committee and *they* do something." After all, we often adopt this sort of attitude about many other dimensions of life—why not at church? In a diocese in the Midwest, the bishop was approached by a group of representatives from a small rural parish who were concerned that their parish might be closed. They told the bishop they had come up with a solution to the problem. They explained to the bishop that the parish would sponsor a priest to come to the parish and diocese from an African country. He would then be available to say Mass on Sunday at the parish, and for the rest of the week, the bishop could assign him to any other tasks the bishop wanted. When the bishop asked why they wouldn't want the priest to be present and to serve them throughout the rest of the week, they responded, "We don't really do anything else; after all, all we need is Mass on Sunday." In this particular small, rural community, worship on Sunday was the sole aspect of parish life that was of concern.

What makes a parish a parish? Expressed more negatively, what elements must be present without which the community cannot consider itself a Catholic parish? Certainly the ability to worship together on Sunday is an essential element, within the broader context of a full sacramental life. To this must be added the ministries of Word and Mission: to evangelize, catechize, and educate the community, to spread the good news of Jesus Christ. Paul VI referred to evangelization as the "essential mission" of the church itself.[1] As we saw in the introduction, however, the church also has a servant character, which is essential to its very nature:

> We stress that the teaching of the Council is channeled in one direction, the service of humankind, of every condition, in every weakness and need. The Church has declared herself a servant of humanity at the very time when her teaching role and her pastoral government have, by reason of this Church solemnity, assumed greater splendor and vigor. However, the idea of service has been central.[2]

Therefore, in this chapter we will look for evidence of this essential element of our nature in scripture. In addition, we will also consider the earliest scriptural evidence of deacons as Christian officeholders, especially in light of broader themes such as Christ's teaching on the nature of servant leadership and indeed the whole notion of Christ's *kenōsis* itself.

Themes from the Hebrew Scriptures

In his comprehensive *Reading the Old Testament: An Introduction*, Lawrence Boadt concludes with a chapter entitled "Themes of Old Testament Theology," in which he observes,

> The final chapter of an Old Testament Introduction has the task of pulling together many of the themes studied in the individual books of the Bible....It is very important for us to be able to discover some unifying themes which make this a single Testament of *and* which enable us at the same time to treasure its many different voices expressing the breadth and beauty of the human experience of God over the ages.[3]

Boadt concludes that "the only fair candidate for a single dominant theme in the Old Testament would be the *person of God*,"[4] and he then develops ten additional themes that flow from this one. Within this thematic framework, I believe we can develop a *biblical* sense of the servant nature of God's covenant people. So, with thanks and appreciation to Boadt and the thematic categories he proposes, the following section will attempt just that.

God Is One

Most of the religions of the ancient world were polytheistic, with massive variations in how people were to relate to the gods. Into this mix came the radical monotheism of the Israelites. The message was straightforward: the Israelites were describing a new "kind" of God, and a new way of relating with God. "Above all, this God ruled human history and actively guided, protected, cared for and was involved in human affairs—the whole Bible tells this story."[5] This insight serves to underscore the fundamental belief that everything flows from this God, all of creation and the people God has chosen. This is what makes "church" fundamentally distinct from a mere social gathering of like-minded individuals. So, if we are to come to some understanding of what it means to be church, we are involved in a proper theological endeavor: the church is *God's* community; to understand the church, we must struggle as best we can to understand God.

Within this theme, I propose a particular subtheme: that *God's Creation is an ongoing event of diakonia.* It is the nature of God to be generative—more specifically, to generate. God is constantly pouring forth, or in John Macquarrie's nicely turned phrase, "letting-be."[6] In Christian scriptures, John will describe this generativity of and by God as love, but already in the Hebrew scriptures it is clear that creation is seen by the ancient Hebrews as the act of a loving and providential Yahweh. Paul will speak of the self-emptying *(kenōsis)* of Christ, showing us another divine attribute. Thus, the Christ who came "to serve, not to be served," in his divine nature is essentially *diaconal.* Perhaps this contributed to the insight from St. Ignatius of Antioch, who connected the ministry of the bishop with that of God the Father and the ministry of the deacon with that of Christ. "Correspondingly, everyone must show the deacons respect. They represent Jesus Christ, just as the bishop has the role of the Father, and the presbyters are like God's council and an apostolic band. You cannot have a Church *(ecclesia)* without these."[7] Therefore, from the beginning of the Judeo-Christian tradition, in the opening lines of the scriptures themselves, we can find an insight into the notion of self-giving love in the very nature and activity of God.

God Is Active in History

On this theme Boadt offers this fine summary:

> Above all, this insight into divine activity declares that God was a *Liberator and Savior*. He delivers the patriarchs Abraham, Isaac and Jacob; he saves Moses and the slaves at the Red Sea; he hears the cry of the poor and listens to them in the psalms; he frees his servant who gives witness through suffering in the Book of Isaiah; he pleads with Israel to return and change its heart and be liberated in Hosea and Jeremiah. There is perhaps no stronger theme anywhere in the biblical tradition than this one. It forms the background for understanding the New Testament proclamation of Jesus; it is the *central motif* of the later themes of *messiah* and *hope*. And it certainly has vital ramifications for our world today.[8]

Not only *is* there a God; this is a God who is *involved*, and involved in very specific and concrete ways. It is important to recognize that this liberating, saving activity of God is always for a further purpose: people are saved *so that they themselves may do something:* to fulfill a mission, to offer thanksgiving and praise to God. It is through this saving activity that God reveals. Boadt writes, "God not only *cares about* humans but operates in a carefully *ordered* and *loving* way for the good of humans—and always has."[9]

Personal Response and Prayer

While thus far we have focused on God's initiative in Hebrew scripture, we turn now to personal, human response to God's action.

> The Old Testament never accepts that a worship of God can be adequate which is grateful only for the preservation and daily working of nature. Ours is a personal God

> who demands from us a *personal* response of friendship, loyalty, obedience, and communication.[10]

One of the earliest chroniclers of the renewed permanent diaconate, Norbert Brockman, observed: "In the Old Testament there was a real connection between service to neighbor *(diakonia)* and cultic worship *(leiturgia)*. In early Christian writings *leiturgia* was used to indicate both worship and service to neighbor."[11] Although this may be discerned in an almost limitless number of passages, consider one striking example from the Second Book of Samuel:

> They brought in the ark of the Lord, and set it in its place, inside the tent that David had pitched for it; and David offered burnt offerings and offerings of well-being before the Lord. When David had finished offering the burnt offerings and the offerings of well-being, he blessed the people in the name of the Lord of hosts, and distributed food among all the people, the whole multitude of Israel, both men and women, to each a cake of bread, a portion of meat, and a cake of raisins. Then all the people went back to their homes. (2 Sam 6:17–19)

Notice again the understanding that David, and indeed all people of the covenant, act in very concrete and practical ways, and always their actions flow from a sense of prayer and praise for God. Boadt points out that, regardless of various specific literary genres to be found in the Bible, "*all of the biblical text* tells the glory of God....The Bible teaches us something about our continual need to struggle for what is right while proclaiming that only God can accomplish it."[12]

This connection between the worship of God and our practical response that flows from it has particular application in the contemporary church. A friend of mine who is pastor of a large parish was approached by a small group of parishioners who wanted him to establish a perpetual adoration chapel in the church. Although certainly not opposed to the idea in principle, the pastor did have some concern with the rationale being offered by the people involved. They seemed to be approaching this in a very "detached" way, with no apparent desire to connect their worship with practical application. So he decided to try something. He prepared a list of various outreach ministries sponsored by the parish and the diocese. He asked that those who wished to participate in perpetual adoration also sign up to help out in one of the areas of ministry on the list. Sadly, the members of this particular group refused to do so. The pastor eventually established the perpetual adoration chapel, but he continued to insist that parishioners find concrete ways to live out the implications of that worship and praise. In doing so, he was recognizing this ancient biblical marriage of prayer and action.

Covenant and Tradition

Throughout the tradition, this creative, loving, providential God has reached out to God's creation, and in a special way to humanity, to establish a covenant bond: "I will be your God and you shall be my people." This "people called out by God" is brought into existence through the initiative of God, and the Old Testament is full of reference to God doing everything possible to get the people to "be all they can be" in responding to God's call.

Therefore, from the beginning, being a people of God has involved relationship and responsibility for God's creation. The people are called, among other things, to steward God's gifts; this is seen in many areas of the Hebrew scripture, but consider just a few examples: In the creation accounts, Adam and Eve are told by God to "name" the animals: a sure sign of stewardship and responsibility. There is, if I may borrow a word that Cardinal Leon-Josef Suenens would use during the Second Vatican Council, a "co-responsibility" of humanity and God for tending God's creation. Boadt observes, "It is our task now to recognize how this [bond of loyalty and responsibility between God and humanity] formed and preserved the true *inner bond* of Israel as a *community* that maintained a profound respect for the worth and love of neighbor—as Leviticus 19:18 points out so strongly when it demands *love of neighbor* as much as of oneself."[13]

In terms of tradition, Boadt refers to Israel as a people of *torah*, which, although frequently translated as "law" is more accurately rendered by "teaching" or "way of life."[14] *Torah* as a way of life, as a set of traditions, helps to preserve the community despite all threats and hardships:

> The greatness of biblical revelation is that it uses the structure of society to help a community function religiously, but at the same time moves beyond those structures....The Scriptures themselves are written so that Israel can be freed from any single human social structure or government or land and continue to meditate and proclaim the *enduring covenant* through time.[15]

Once again we see the concreteness expected in the people's response to God's initiative. In response to God's love, providence, "letting-be," the people respond, not simply through a set of sterile "laws" but through a full *way of life* based on a "dedicated love" (*chesed,* an almost untranslatable Hebrew word; "dedicated love" is an acceptable but still ultimately inadequate attempt to capture its richness and depth) of God and neighbor, a love that cannot (or at least should not) be separated. Even the content of the Decalogue underscores this reality, by offering terms of our relationship to God (the first through third commandments) and to others (the fourth through tenth commandments). Not only are the Ten Commandments the "terms" of the covenant; they are signposts in this complex set of relationships and way of life.

The Prophets and Justice

"God does indeed make demands on the community, demands that they be *like* God." If the claim of Genesis 1:26 means anything when it says that humans are made in the image and likeness of God, it means that we too have moral choice and moral responsibility."[16] It is the role of prophets to hold up to the community the choices that should be made in light of the *way of life* to which they are called. A prophet—literally, one who speaks on behalf of another—calls the people to accountability and responsibility.

Since human beings are created in the image and likeness of God, they are called to be as "God-like" as they can be. Because we are human, this is an impossible goal this side of heaven, but we must stay the course, and this is the message of the prophets. Furthermore, we are called to see creation as God sees it, and, when sinfulness distorts and abuses that creation (including human relationships), proper biblical justice demands that we attempt to put things right again. Biblical justice is unlike some contemporary views of justice that demand "people get what they deserve"; rather, biblical justice calls for creation to be the way God wants it to be.

Hope and the Future

The Bible also "brings comfort and hope in times of trouble and loss."[17] From the beginning, creation is described by God as being "good," *not* evil. There is a general optimism about the future, because, after all, it is ultimately the One God who is in charge, and who will provide for his people. While the path we are on at the moment may be dark and full of danger, this will eventually be swept away in God's plan. The message of the prophets continues in this regard: they do not simply call the people to return to the covenant out of a blind obedience, but because by remaining faithful to the covenant, the future will be better.

The people, then, are called to be a people of hope, who see the ultimate goodness of God's creation and God's loving plan.

Wisdom

Boadt concludes his themes with the observation that "the Bible is wisdom." "Wisdom books are not just appendages but form a very important layer of tradition that affirms that God made humans *rational and free*, with divine powers of *searching* and *choosing* and behaving ethically."[18]

It is my contention that these various themes from the Hebrew scriptures all, in various ways, underscore a *diaconal* component to the human response to God's call to covenant intimacy. Properly understood, as we shall shortly see in the New Testament evidence, *diakonia* is a much broader category than simple menial service performed on behalf of another. Rather, *diakonia* involves a mind-set, a way of life, and a perspective on life that serve to *connect* people together. It is the connection of a messenger taking vital information from one person to another, an angel caring and tending for a person in the desert, a waiter bringing food and drink from one person to another. The themes from the Old Testament that have been examined here seem to convey this need for practical ways to nurture this bond of covenant and communion, and this is, ultimately, *diakonia.*

New Testament Themes on *Diakonia* and the Diaconate

Many studies have been done on the scriptural origins of Christian ministry. In particular, those ministries eventually described as "ordained" have been closely examined.[19] The deacon as an ecclesial officeholder emerges in the New Testament, but great care must be exercised because specific references to what may be considered an early "office" of deacon are quite rare. Furthermore, "the origins of the permanent diaconate cannot be seen in isolation, but must be discovered within the development of the apostolic ministry of bishop, presbyter, and deacon."[20] In addition, these scant specific references to the diaconate appear within a much broader matrix of diaconal terminology and concepts.

Scripture reveals several levels of meaning concerning *diakonia* and its exercise.[21] As early as 1976, Norbert Brockman provided this succinct overview:

> English translations tend to obscure the fact that the words *diakonos* and *diakonia* are commonly used throughout the New Testament. The latter is the term generally used to indicate service or ministry in the New Testament in the wide sense. Apostleship itself was a *diakonia* for St. Paul, as was the ministry of angels, and that of the women who tended Jesus. Nevertheless, it is possible to isolate instances already in the New Testament, in which the term *diakonia* was used in a technical or quasi-technical sense. By the time of 1 Timothy, the usage in 3:8–13

> seems clearly in the technical sense of a specific order or office in the priesthood.[22]

Understanding the nature of *diakonia* and its several levels of meaning is a complex issue. As most frequently translated into English, *diakonia* is *service*. This English word is so nebulous, however, that it is most difficult to develop with any specificity what this service entails. John N. Collins has continued and expanded the effort of earlier writers to expand our understanding of *diakonia*. Through his detailed word analysis of *diakonia* and its cognates, he provides valuable confirmation of the point that other writers had been making for some time, but without the same level of documented precision: that diakonia means much more than simple "menial service." Collins observes:

> *Diakonia* and its cognates occur about a hundred times in the New Testament, and they have generally been translated into English by words of the "ministry" group, although in today's Bibles it is very often by words of the "service" group....The word "service" with which "diakonia" is frequently alternated has many uses in English and usually we have no trouble understanding what people are talking about....Take the word into a theological setting and other meanings appear, but here replace the English word with "diakonia" and the statements at once become less precise.[23]

At least four levels of meaning have been identified:

1. the everyday sense of "serving a meal or waiting on tables"

2. a more general sense of "assisting or attending to" another

3. a sense of "mediator, emissary, go-between"

4. a technical (or perhaps semitechnical) use that refers to a recognized church officeholder

This point is critically important, and the danger of not appreciating this diversity of meaning has more than theoretical implications; it can distort the potential and the future of the diaconate itself. Consider just one example. During diaconate formation, in addition to other studies and activities, candidates are often asked to take part in a variety of pastoral assignments. In one diocesan formation program, candidates were asked to identify four areas of ministry that they had not experienced before, and then arrange to learn more about these ministries and exercise them over the summer. The only other stipulation was that the ministries had to be "truly diaconal," and this was defined exclusively in strictly charitable terms. One candidate came to the director of formation and asked if he could do some work in adult faith formation; he was told that this "was not really diaconal" and he would have to find something else. This response was also given to other requests involving tribunal ministry, RCIA (Rite of Christian Initiation of Adults) and even marriage preparation!

To reduce *diakonia* to activities only related to menial service misses the richness and the potential of the concept. Even more, it seriously distorts and restricts the paths of future development of the diaconate itself. As will be seen in chapter 4, the bishops of the Second Vatican Council described the entire apostolic ministry as a *diakonia*, involving ministries of Word, Sacrament, and Charity. The biblical heritage that undergirds such a broad-based understanding of *diakonia* is fertile indeed.

We have seen in our review of Old Testament themes the link in the Hebraic tradition between God's call and ethical human response, between the worship of God and care of those in need. This link is maintained in the New Covenant. For example, the Letter of James calls the service of widows and orphans "religion that is pure and undefiled before God" (Jas 1:27). In reviewing the Pauline correspondence, Kenan Osborne observes:

> Paul uses the term *diakonos* and its cognates both in its ordinary meaning as servant and service, but also as a particular service, the service of the gospel, the service of ministry to the church, the service which is a grace given by God in Christ....All ministry in the church is *diakonia*.

> [It] is seen as coextensive with the state of discipleship. *Diakonia* was not seen in the early Church as something one did, but as something one was.[24]

The New Testament texts that allude to a specific office of deacon must be studied against this backdrop of *diakonia* discipleship.

Diakonia: The Ministry of Christ

Mark's use of deacon terminology is rare; most significant are Mark 9:35; 10:43; and 10:45, in which Christ refers to his own ministry as one of service, and that those who would be leaders in the community should also be servants of others. The Matthean parallels also stress the role of Christ as deacon, and Matthew grounds discipleship and judgment on acting *in persona Christi Diaconi*. "In Matthew's well-known passage on the final judgment, one is ultimately judged on whether or not one has been a deacon: 'when did we see you hungry, naked, etc.…and not come to your help?' In this sense, to be a 'deacon' is to be a 'Christian.'"[25] Luke uses "deacon" terminology more than Mark or Matthew,[26] but yet again we find the emphasis on Christ's self-identification as deacon: "In the three synoptic gospels it is obvious that the image of Jesus the servant, Jesus the deacon, has made a tremendous impression on all three of these Jesus communities."[27]

While John uses "deacon" terminology less frequently than the other New Testament writers, it is most significant that *only* in the Gospel of John is found the scene of Jesus washing the feet of his disciples (John 13:2–17). With the dramatic emphasis given to this event by John, and placed in the eucharistic context of the Last Supper, the importance of *diakonia* in the life of the disciples and their leaders is clearly stressed. More than simply an example of charitable hospitality, the foot washing points to Jesus' death.

> The clearest indication that the evangelist means the footwashing to symbolize Jesus' death is found in Peter's misunderstanding of what Jesus is doing. Peter thinks that Jesus is performing a simple act of humble service such as a slave might perform. He refuses, therefore, to

> let Jesus wash him. Peter's misunderstanding is confirmed by Jesus' words: "What I am doing you do not know *now*, but *afterward* you will understand."[28]

Raymond E. Brown has written:

> In demeaning himself to wash his disciples' feet Jesus is acting out beforehand his humiliation in death....The footwashing is an action of service for others, symbolic of the service he will render in laying down his life for others; that is why Jesus can claim that the footwashing is necessary if the disciples are to share in his heritage and that it will render the disciples clean.[29]

The implications of this passage for the identity of Christ as well as the identity and ministry of the apostles are profound, since it links the kenotic self-sacrifice of Christ to the life of the disciple. Just as Christ is willing to give himself completely "to the end" for the sake of others, so too must his disciples. "To 'have part with Jesus' through washing means to be part of the self-giving love that will bring Jesus' life to an end, symbolically anticipated by the footwashing."[30] Furthermore, those who would be leaders in the community of disciples are to be identified by their own self-sacrificing love in imitation of the *kenōsis* of Christ.

> The theme of death is behind the use of the word *hypodeigma* [v. 15]. This expression, found only here in the NT, in well-known Jewish texts (cf. LXX 2 Macc 6:28; 4 Macc 17: 22 – 23; Sir 44:16) is associated with exemplary death. Jesus' exhortation is not to moral performance but to imitation of his self-gift....Entrance into the Johannine community of disciples meant taking the risk of accepting the *hypodeigma* of Jesus, a commitment to love even if it led to death.[31]

How the significance of this passage applies to the specific nature of the diaconate will be developed in more detail in chapters 4 and 5.

Deacons as Officeholders: Linked to Apostolic Ministry

While the New Testament describes all Christian ministry as *diakonia*, some of the churches began to designate certain leaders of the community as *diakonoi* in a more technical sense. It is impossible to determine the precise nature or the comprehensive functions of these ministers, but it is clear that these deacons were collaborators with *apostoloi* or *episkopoi*. In at least two of the three passages referring to deacons in some sort of technical sense (Rom 16:1; Phil 1:1; and 1 Tim 3), the ministries described are found in conjunction with *apostoloi* or *episkopoi*. It seems reasonable to conclude that the deacon-as-officeholder is to be understood in the deacon's relationship to the bishop, however those offices would develop over time.

Deacons' "Qualifications" for Service

Several decades after Paul wrote to the Romans, the author of 1 Timothy describes the kinds of persons who should be serving as *diakonoi*.

> Deacons likewise must be serious, not double-tongued, not indulging in much wine, not greedy for money; they must hold fast to the mystery of the faith with a clear conscience. And let them first be tested; then, if they prove themselves blameless, let them serve as deacons. Women likewise must be serious, not slanderers, but temperate, faithful in all things. Let deacons be married only once, and let them manage their children and their households well. (1 Tim 3:8–12)

1 Timothy emerges from the final period of New Testament history (approximately AD 100–400), a period that sees the growing institutionalization of the church:

> To survive and function in the world the movement also requires an organizational structure, a decision-making apparatus, and a definition of the function of its officers

> and servants. To meet these needs the Christian church at the end of the New Testament period was rapidly establishing a creed, a canon, and an organized ordained ministry."[32]

The organization of ministry required a list of "formation standards," which the author of 1 Timothy provides.[33] Whatever their specific functions might have been, deacons were to be mature persons of integrity and dedication, not motivated by greed, and able to manage their own affairs well: all possible early indications that deacons were emerging as administrators of the community's resources. Further, those who would serve as deacons were to be tested (and perhaps investigated: "if there is nothing against them"); such a process of testing is absent from the description of the *episkopos*, as is the injunction that the deacon is to "hold the faith with a clear conscience" (1 Tim 3:9). Although the specific functions of the deacon were not addressed, they were certainly matters of serious concern for the overall well-being of the community.

A number of points may be made about the implications of this passage. First, deacons are presented as co-workers with the bishops. Second, deacons are to be serious persons of integrity and dedication; this may be an early indication that as community leaders deacons were already emerging as administrators of the community's resources. Third, the overall seriousness of diaconal duties suggests a period of testing that is notably absent from the description of the bishop, further suggesting the need for a high level of overall public trust in the deacon, and possibly suggesting a fiduciary responsibility by the deacon for the welfare of the community. Fourth, there is the presumption that both deacons and bishops serve with the context of marriage and family, thus revealing in their personal "states of life" the kind of integrity, dedication, and love that is to be brought to the community at large. Fifth, there is the unique mention of women in the passage related to deacons. Robert Wild writes, "Since the qualities required of the 'women' (or 'wives' [i.e., of the deacons—the Greek *gynaikas* is ambiguous]) are virtually identical to those listed in vv. 8–9, and since there is no similar reference to the wives of bishops or elders, the author probably refers here to women deacons."[34]

Therefore, whatever particular ministries the deacons are exercising at Ephesus do not appear to be gender-specific. "Whatever a male deacon did, presumably a woman deacon did also."[35]

Deacons and Acts 6:1–6

The classic text that, from the second century, has been associated with the diaconate is the famous passage in Acts 6 that describes the selection, election, and ordination of the seven members of the Jerusalem Hellenist community. Irenaeus, writing in the late second century, is the first known writer to refer to "the Seven" as "deacons." "More careful scholarship, however, has brought into question such an identification of the seven chosen to minister to the Hellenistic Christians with those otherwise called 'deacons.'"[36] Nonetheless, the text is important for this study in its perspective on apostolic ministry and because it is possible to see the early church responding to pastoral needs through the discernment, selection, and official installation of these ministers in a public and prayerful (i.e., liturgical) way. "What makes the ordering of the seven so important is that it demonstrates how the apostolic Church responded to the 'need for a structure of the community.'"[37]

Again in this passage is found the grounding of official ministry in the ministry of the apostles. "Nowhere do we see more clearly the unique role of the Twelve maintaining the wholeness of God's renewed people. They preserve the *koinōnia* by their solution, for the Hellenists are to remain as fully recognized brothers and sisters in Christ."[38] If this passage is to be applicable to the diaconate, it must begin here, with the grounding of the ministry in that of the apostles, a ministry of communion, reconciliation, and wholeness.

Conclusion

A number of scriptural insights regarding *diakonia* and deacons have been identified in this chapter:

1. *Diakonia* is a constitutive element of the Judeo-Christian covenant tradition. In particular, *diakonia* is

linked with the worship of the Triune God, with *diakonia* serving as the bond of *koinōnia. Diakonia* is *never* reducible to simple charity; it is, in fact, the self-giving love of God.

2. Christian discipleship revolves around this dimension of *diakonia*. Modeled by Christ, *diakonia* becomes the cornerstone of Christian life.

3. Leadership in the Christian community infers leadership in *diakonia*, again as exemplified and taught by Christ as he washes the feet of the Twelve. Apostolic ministry, therefore, is servant leadership that is iconic of the diaconal character of the community of disciples itself.

4. Deacons emerge from the scriptural evidence as associated with apostolic ministry, either through direct service with an apostle (e.g., Paul or Peter), or through association with the *episkopoi* serving as "successors to the apostles."

5. While specific functional evidence is minimal, deacons are recognized as part of the ministerial leadership "team" and appear to have been responsible for matters critical to the support and life of the community, possibly focused on the administration of the resources of the community on behalf of the *episkopos*.

In the next chapter, we turn our attention to the experience of deacons in the first centuries of the church's life, often referred to as the "golden age" of the diaconate.

3

THE RISE AND FALL OF THE ANCIENT DIACONATE

Deacons must be respectable men whose word can be trusted, moderate in the amount of wine they drink and with no squalid greed for money. They must be conscientious believers in the mystery of the faith. They are to be examined first, and only admitted to serve as deacons if there is nothing against them.
—1 Timothy 3:8–10

Introduction

Contrasted with the sketchy biblical data available on the diaconate, the evidence from the first through sixth centuries is particularly extensive. This chapter reviews two broad sources of testimony: (1) the writings of the patristic authors themselves; and (2) the conciliar and juridical record from the period. Following the earliest record of deacons in the apostolic and postapostolic church, the diaconate entered a so-called golden age from the time of Ignatius of Antioch to the Council of Nicaea. Following Nicaea, however, the diaconate began its decline into the largely ceremonial and transitional form in which it existed until the Second Vatican Council (1962–65).

As we prepare to review the patristic, canonical, and juridical sources on the diaconate of the patristic era, the following caution remains an appropriate way to begin:

> The difficulty comes really from forgetting that the early Church was an organic growth: we are apt to expect to find already precisely formulated at a very primitive stage structures and offices that only developed gradually in response to circumstances and needs. It seems safer to start from the assumption that the diaconate developed gradually.[1]

Not only did the diaconate develop gradually, it developed with great regional variety as well.

In reviewing the sources, I will not spend much time on the various liturgical functions of the deacon; rather, the existence of specific liturgical functions by the deacon is stipulated and acknowledged. My emphasis will be on the range of extraliturgical functions to get a sense of the scope and variety of diaconal ministry throughout the period. The reason for this is simple: if we can gain an appreciation of the creative uses to which the ancient diaconate was put, we might get a sense of its untapped creative potential in our own age.

Patristic Sources[2]

Ordinary Diaconal Functions

Table 1 summarizes diaconal functions throughout the period under review, beginning with scriptural citations and extending until the sixth century. The original data in the table were developed by James M. Barnett in *The Diaconate: A Full and Equal Order*, revised in 1995. Barnett's work has been a valuable resource for scholars and those in formation for many years. Following the table, each of the sources will be examined in turn.

Table 1. Historical Summary of Diaconal Functions
Source: Barnett, *Diaconate*, 124–25, adapted, revised, and expanded by W. T. Ditewig.

Synoptics	*Diakonia* constitutive of all discipleship; leadership in *diakonia* constitutive of apostolic ministry. (Mark

	10:43–44; 23:11, 12; Luke 22:26; 14:11; 18:14; Matt 20:26–27; 25:31–46)
Acts	Not limited to *diakonoi:* official ministry flexible in response to pastoral needs, linked to apostolic ministry. (Acts 6)
John	Apostolic ministry more than simple Christian charity; kenotic, total self-sacrifice in imitation of Christ. (John 13:2–17)
Paul/ Pastorals	*Diakonos* as co-worker with *apostolos* or *episkopos;* emissary, messenger. Proven spiritual, community leaders. (Rom 16:1; Phil 1:1; 1 Tim 3)
ca. 95	Ministry of teaching and prophecy; linked with *episkopoi. (Didache)*
ca. 95	Possibly constitute with the bishops the ruling council in some churches. (*Didache,* also Ignatius and Polycarp)
ca. 96	Part of divinely ordered structure; overall community leadership in support/collaboration with bishop. (Clement, Ignatius)
ca. 115	Symbolize Jesus Christ; linked with *episkopoi* and *presbyteroi;* act as an agent or ambassador of the church; serve with bishops and presbyters as part of the community's ruling council; minister the chalice; proclaim the gospel; announce parts of the eucharistic service; serve the entire *ekklēsia.* (Ignatius)
ca. 140	Administer the distribution of alms to the poor and needy. *(Shepherd of Hermas)*
ca. 150	Serve as part of the community's ruling council. (Polycarp)
ca. 185	Administer the eucharistic bread and wine to all present at the eucharistic assembly and to those absent; minister of church's *communio.* (Justin Martyr)
ca. 200	The apostolic roots of church order; initial association of deacons with the Seven. (Irenaeus)
ca. 200	Be the "eyes" of the bishop in all matters but especially in discovering the pastoral and moral needs of the people; keep order in the assembly; report the sick to the congregation for their visits and help. *(Pseudo-Clementines)*

Continued

Table 1 Continued

ca. 200	Baptize on a par with presbyters (both need bishop's authorization). (Tertullian)
ca. 215	Instruct the people at weekday *agapē* assemblies; bless bread at Christian fellowship meals in the bishop's absence; *leitourgia* reason for ordination; the servant of the bishop; identify the sick to the bishop; instruct clergy and others; be responsible for the cemetery. (Hippolytus)
ca. 235	"Shepherd the people" with the bishop; the bishop's "hearing, mouth, heart, soul"; bishop and deacon as father and son; deacons and presbyters serve with bishop in administration of justice; guard the doors and keep order among the people at the Eucharist; announce a bidding to the people at the Eucharist. *(Didascalia Apostolorum)*
ca. 250	City of Rome divided into seven administrative regions, each assigned to a deacon (and subdeacon) for overall administration. (Fabian)
ca. 250	Extraordinary ministers of reconciliation; overall dispensation of church's goods, especially to the poor. (Cyprian)
ca. 300	Encourage contributions for those in need; maintain good order and discipline: "instruct, persuade, admonish, rebuke." *(Apostolic Church Order)*
ca. 306	On occasion, head small, rural congregations; baptize when in charge of such a congregation; distribute communion to the dying *with presbyter or bishop's permission.* (Elvira)
ca. 314	Prior to Arles, some deacons may have presided at the Eucharist, probably under extraordinary circumstances and in the absence of a bishop (or presbyter?) (Forbidden at Arles); deacons now to do nothing "without the presbyter's knowledge." (Arles)
ca. 325	Deacons not to preside at Eucharist; deacons subordinate to presbyters. (Nicaea)
ca. 380	Announce various stages of the Eucharist; proclaim the Gospel at the Eucharist; bid the prayers of the people at the Eucharist; announce the kiss of peace; represent

	their bishop at synods in latter's absence; preside with other ministers when quarrels among Christians were adjudicated; investigate and welcome newcomers; assist at Baptism (notice change in role from ca. 200) *(Apostolic Constitutions)*
ca. 400	Responsible for catechesis. (Augustine)
ca. 475	Counselor of the whole clergy; minister to "sick, stranger, widow, orphans, those in need"; responsible for catechesis; responsible for burying the dead (as in Hippolytus) *(Testament of Our Lord)*
ca. 475	Subordinate to bishops and presbyters; ordained *non ad sacerdotium sed ad ministerium* (note change from Hippolytus's *non ad sacerdotium sed in ministerio episcopi). (Statuta Ecclesiae Antiquae)*
ca. 506	Head parishes (as at Elvira); authority in fiscal management of parish identical to that of presbyters. (Council of Agde)
ca. 597	Head parishes (as at Elvira and Agde); practice in decline. (Council of Toledo)

An examination of these functions reveals that, while deacons always served in an assisting capacity, they had authority in many areas, either through their participation in the order of deacons or because of particular delegation by the bishop. Several sources reveal that deacons in some areas served in a variety of roles related to judicial functions, in this sense understood as part of the governing body of the community—that is, an entity empowered to make decisions on behalf of the community for its efficient and orderly functioning. This is suggested in Ignatius, Polycarp, the *Didascalia Apostolorum*, the *Apostolic Constitutions*, and possibly the *Apostolic Church Order*. Some deacons served in various functions of administration, as emissaries, as administrators of church property and goods, and as leaders of remote communities.

Ignatius, the bishop-martyr of Antioch, was concerned with "order" and unity in the Christian community.[3] Written toward the end of Trajan's reign (98–117), the letters of Ignatius "witness to a unique understanding of the office of bishop."[4] From his letters we see the emergence of a monoepiscopate and a clearly defined tripartite hierarchy of bishop with priests and deacons assisting, according to their proper roles. Ignatius compares the bishop to God the Father, presbyters to the College of the Apostles, and the deacons to Jesus Christ: "Correspondingly, everyone must show the deacons respect. They represent Jesus Christ, just as the bishop has the role of the Father, and the presbyters are like God's council and an apostolic band. You cannot have a Church *(ecclesia)* without these."[5] "Let the deacons (my special favorites) be entrusted with the ministry of Jesus Christ who was with the Father from eternity and appeared at the end of the world."[6]

Ignatius is interested in promoting the unity and harmony of the church; his call for the respect to be shown the community's ministers should be seen in this light. In his letter to the church in Smyrna, Ignatius writes:

> Flee from schism as the source of mischief. You should all follow the bishop as Jesus Christ did the Father. Follow, too, the presbytery as you would the apostles; and respect the deacons as you would God's law. Nobody must do anything that has to do with the Church without the bishop's approval.[7]

Such a reference leads James Barnett to assert, "It is because of the high esteem in which the deacon was held that he may have been included in the governing council."[8] Although I am *not* persuaded that this assertion is readily sustainable, clearly deacons are seen as ministers exercising an important responsibility for the governance of the community.

Ignatius also spoke of the deacon as a legate of the community. In his letter to the Philadelphians he wrote:

> I feel that you ought, as a Church of God, to choose a deacon to go there [Antioch] as an ambassador of God, for the glory of the Name and to congratulate them when they assemble together. Blessed in Jesus Christ is the man who is to be found worthy of this ministry. All praise to you, too, who send him. You can do this for the Name of God if only you choose to; just as the Churches

> which are near neighbors sent deacons or priests and, some of them, bishops.[9]

The deacon's leadership role in the community becomes increasingly clear. Polycarp, an *episkopos* of Smyrna martyred ca. 156, refers to presbyters and deacons in his letter to the Philippians (ca. 117). "Polycarp makes no mention of a bishop of Philippi but he does speak of the obedience due to presbyters and deacons."[10] He writes:

> Likewise the deacons should be blameless before his righteousness, as servants of God and Christ and not of men; not slanderers, not double-tongued, not lovers of money, temperate in all matters, compassionate, careful, living according to the truth of the Lord, who became a 'servant of all'....It is necessary...to be subject to the presbyters and deacons as to God and Christ.[11]

Kenan Osborne notes a tone reminiscent of 1 Timothy in this description, and, consistent with Ignatius, the deacon is compared with Christ, specifically, Christ the Servant.[12] No precise information is given concerning the functions of deacons, but the people are to be subject to the authority shared by presbyters and deacons, which suggests to some that deacons were part of the ruling church council at Philippi.[13]

The *Didascalia Apostolorum* was composed in Syria during the early to middle years of the third century.[14] Probably no other ancient source is more descriptive of the relationship of bishop to deacon and of the source of the deacon's authority.

> Let the bishops and the deacons, then, be of one mind; and do you shepherd the people diligently with one accord. For you ought both to be one body, father and son; for you are in the likeness of the Lordship. And let the deacon make known all things to the bishop, even as Christ to His Father. But let him order such things as he is able by himself, receiving power from the bishop, as the Lord did from His Father....But the weighty matters

> let the bishop judge. Yet let the deacon be the hearing of the bishop, and his mouth and his heart and his soul; for when you are both of one mind, through your agreement there will be peace in the Church.[15]
>
> Let the deacon be ready to obey and to submit himself to the command of the bishop. And let him labor and toil in every place whither he is sent to minister or to speak of some matter to anyone. For it behooves each one to know his office and to be diligent in executing it. And be you [bishop and deacon] of one counsel and of one purpose, and one soul dwelling in two bodies.[16]

According to the *Didascalia* deacons participate in a variety of functions associated with the good order, discipline, and administration of the community: among them, the deacon assists in the administration of justice. The author exhorts bishops: "Let your judgments be held on the second day of the week....Let also the deacons and presbyters be ever present in all your judgments, to judge without acceptance of persons, as men of God, with righteousness.[17]

One other function the deacon performs will be echoed in later developments: namely, the welcoming and "certification" of new members of the community.

> If anyone come in from another place, bringing recommendatory letters, let the deacon be the judge of the affair, inquiring whether they be of the faithful, and of the Church, whether they be not defiled by heresy, and besides, whether the party be a married woman or a widow. And when he is satisfied in the things of the Lord, let him conduct everyone to the place proper to him.[18]

The deacon does all this because of the power received from the bishop, both through the laying on of hands and also by specific assignments given to him by the bishop. The *Didascalia* echoes Ignatius in describing the deacon in terms of Christ: "The bishop sits for you in the place of God Almighty. But the deacon stands in place of Christ; and do you love him."[19] Similarly, "If then our Lord did thus, will you, O deacons, hesitate to do the like for them that are sick and infirm, you who are workmen of the truth, and bear the likeness of Christ."[20]

The *Apostolic Constitutions*, dated between AD 375 and 400,[21] repeats several points already noted above: that deacons were to be a part of the bishop's "judgments" on the second day of the week; that the deacon was responsible for welcoming new members (at least laypersons and other deacons) into the community after assessing their "references." Finally, the *Apostolic Church Order*, most probably written in Egypt at the beginning of the fourth century,[22] directs that three deacons were to be appointed for legal reasons: "There shall be three deacons for 'by three shall every matter be established.'"[23] These deacons are appointed "in order that they may be able to bear an effective witness in cases of complaint before the disciplinary judgment."[24]

Deacons served a variety of administrative or executive functions, whether as a representative of the bishop (or the entire community), or in supervising the care of those in need. As seen in the letter of Ignatius to the Philadelphians above, there is evidence that some deacons served as emissaries or legates of bishops and their communities. The *Shepherd of Hermas*, dated ca. 140, "consists of a sermon on penance, apocalyptic in character, and, all in all, curious in form and subject."[25] Deacons are referenced in one of the visions, in which the growing church is described in terms of a tower under construction, and in one of the parables, which identifies sinners in need of repentance. In the vision is this description:

> The stones that are square and white and fit their joints are the apostles and bishops and teachers and deacons who have lived in the holiness of God, and have been bishops and teachers and deacons for God's chosen in purity and reverence.[26]

In the parable, however, among the sinners in need of repentance are found "deacons who served badly and plundered the living of widows and orphans, and made profit for themselves from the ministry they had accepted to perform."[27] Deacons are identified through their direct care of the poor, in this case widows and orphans.

Written in Rome, the *Apostolic Tradition* is the only surviving order of the Western church. While the exact dating of the document remains disputed it has most often been dated ca. 215 and is frequently (but not definitively) attributed to Hippolytus of Rome.[28] The document begins with directions for the ordination of bishops, presbyters, and deacons. A deacon is to be ordained after he is selected "after the fashion of those things said above,"[29] referring back to the instructions concerning the ordination of the bishop, who is chosen by all the people.

Unlike the ordination of a bishop, in which *all* bishops present lay hands on the new bishop, and the ordination of a presbyter, in which *all* presbyters present "touch the one to be ordained," *only* the bishop lays hands on the deacon.

> When the deacon is ordained, this is the reason why the bishop alone shall lay his hands upon him: he is not ordained to the priesthood but to serve the bishop and to carry out the bishop's commands. He does not take part in the council of the clergy; he is to attend to his own duties and to make known to the bishop such things as are needful. He does not receive that Spirit that is possessed by the presbytery, in which the presbyters share; he receives only what is confided in him under the bishop's authority.[30]

The text describes the following duties that might be assigned to the deacons. "Let each of the deacons with the subdeacons attend upon the bishop; and let it be reported to him who are sick, that if it seem good to the bishop he may visit them."[31] In addition, deacons are part of a daily "staff meeting": "Let the deacons and presbyters assemble daily at the place which the bishop shall appoint for them. And let not the deacons especially neglect to assemble every day unless sickness prevents them."[32] This passage is significant, especially in light of the earlier observation that deacons do not share in the "council of the clergy." Yet in this passage, both presbyters and deacons are present, with a special emphasis on the participation of the deacons. Easton concludes, "At these gatherings the clergy received assignments for their duties of that day;

in these latter the deacons were more important than the presbyters and their absence a more serious fault."[33]

Fabian, the bishop of Rome who was martyred in 250, divided Rome into seven districts, with each district assigned to one of the seven Roman deacons, who exercised administrative governance over their respective "deaconries."[34] The well-known legend of the deacon Lawrence (d. 258) gives an insight into the role of the deacon in Rome during this period.[35] After the arrest and martyrdom of his bishop, Lawrence himself was arrested and ordered to hand over the treasures of the church. At the appointed time, Lawrence reported to the authorities and brought the poor of the Christian community. He was summarily martyred, according to legend, burned on a gridiron. Again the deacon is linked with his bishop in his service to the poor, and the deacon is the Christian official who was expected by the authorities to be responsible for the goods of the Christian community.

Extraordinary Functions

There are three additional functions which we might term *extraordinary* that are documented in the literature: (1) the deacon as an extraordinary minister of reconciliation, (2) the deacon leading remote communities in the absence of presbyters or bishops, and (3) the office of archdeacon.

1. The Deacon as Extraordinary Minister of Reconciliation

The *episkopos* Cyprian, writing from exile during the Decian persecution of AD 250, devotes considerable effort to the matter of reconciliation of those who have lapsed from the faith as a result of the persecutions of the time. In *Epistle XII* we find that although Cyprian sees the reconciliation of the lapsed as primarily his own responsibility as *episkopos*, the presbyters and deacons should assume this responsibility when the penitent is in danger of death. In such a case:

> If they should be seized with any misfortune and peril of sickness, [they] should, without waiting for my presence, before any presbyter who might be present, or if a pres-

> byter should not be found and death begins to be imminent, before even a deacon, be able to make confession of their sin, that, with the imposition of hands upon them for repentance, they should come to the Lord with the peace which the martyrs have desired, by their letters to us, to be granted to them.[36]

While Cyprian clearly gives precedence to a presbyter over a deacon in the sacramental reconciliation of a penitent in danger of death, *both* presbyters and deacons are extraordinary ministers of reconciliation, which would normally be the function of the bishop. Nonetheless, because of the gravity of the situation, in a context of death in a time of persecution, the needs of the people had to be met, and "even a deacon" could serve as a minister of sacramental reconciliation.

2. *The Deacon as Community Administrator*

The Council of Elvira (AD 306) addressed the administration of a community by a deacon: "If a deacon in charge of a people without a bishop or presbyter has baptized some members of the community, the bishop must complete their initiation through his blessing" (can. 77). The pastoral care of a community by a deacon is assumed, although he is not competent to initiate newcomers fully into the community; that role is reserved to the bishop. The Council of Agde (506) referred to deacons in charge of local churches, and indicated that their authority in fiscal matters is the same as that of presbyters in charge of churches.[37] The Council of Toledo (597) also referred to this possibility, although the practice appears to have died out at approximately this time.[38]

Beyond this, specific diaconal functions are unknown. Deacons serving in any community held ordinary responsibility for the goods of the church and the care of those in need. A deacon in charge of a community not served by a bishop or presbyter had to see that the revenues and offerings were duly applied to the care of the church and its property, the needs of the poor, support for himself as well as any other clerics, and the treasury of the bishop's house.[39]

Augustine wrote one of the earliest known treatises on catechesis when he responded to a request from the Carthaginian deacon Deogratias for advice and guidelines on the catechesis of new Christians.[40] He writes, "You have informed me that in Carthage, where you hold the position of deacon, persons who have to be taught the Christian faith from very rudiments are frequently brought to you by reason of your enjoying a reputation of possessing a rich gift in catechizing."[41] The evidence suggests that at least some deacons shared in the responsibility for the catechesis of the community, although Deogratias may have had a unique role in that regard (because of his "rich gift in catechizing"). At least one commentator has found evidence for catechesis as a function of the deacon as early as 1 Timothy;[42] certainly catechesis would remain a part of the deacon's responsibilities if he was serving in a community without presbyters or bishop.

However, there were limits beyond which the deacon could not go. In the most noteworthy example, some deacons—presumably serving in charge of communities without presbyters or bishops—had become involved in "offering" the eucharistic celebration. Canon 15 of the Council of Arles (AD 314) has, "Concerning deacons, whom we know to offer *(offerre)* in many places: it is determined that this must never happen."[43] Put simply, the deacon was competent to guide the pastoral life of the community to the extent that ordination and specific delegation by the bishop allowed.

3. The Archdeacon

The office of archdeacon emerged late in the fourth century, with the archdeacon serving as a kind of executive assistant to the bishop. Consider the following précis of the archdeacon's role:

> Beginning with the fourth century this specialized activity of the *diaconus episcopi* takes on gradually the character of a juridical ecclesiastical office....Thus, in the period from the fourth to the eighth century the archdeacon is the official supervisor of the subordinate clergy, has disciplinary authority over them in all cases of wrong doing,

> and exercises a certain surveillance over their discharge of the duties assigned them. It was also within the archdeacon's province to examine candidates for the priesthood; he had also the right of making visitation among the rural clergy....The archdeacon was, moreover, the bishop's chief confidant, his assistant, and when it was necessary, his representative in the exercise of the manifold duties of the episcopal office. This was especially the case in the administration of ecclesiastical property, the care of the sick, the visitation of prisoners, and the training of the clergy.
>
> The authority of the archdeacons culminated in the eleventh and twelfth centuries. At that time they exercised within the province of their archdiaconates a quasi-episcopal jurisdiction. They made visitations, during which they were empowered to levy certain assessments on the clergy; they conducted courts of first instance, and had the right to punish clerics guilty of lapses; they could also hold synodal courts....In the thirteenth century numerous synods began to restrict the jurisdiction of the archdeacons....Moreover, by the creation of the diocesan office of vicar-general, there was opened a court of higher resort than that of the archdeacon, and to it reverted the greater part of the business once transacted in the court of the archdeacon.[44]

The archdiaconate was an exceptionally powerful and influential office throughout its existence.[45] This is especially evident in the archdeacon's exercise of governance. However, this study will not focus on this particular office. The archdiaconate was not an office linked to the ordinary functions of the diaconate. Very few deacons served as archdeacons and, in its later form, it was almost always an office held by a presbyter! The exercise of the archdiaconate was not based exclusively or uniquely on ordination to the diaconate but on the appointment of a person to the office by the bishop. Therefore, while the nature and role of the archdeacon is a curious chapter in the history of ordained ministry, especially given its powerful exercise of governance, the current study hopes to focus on the ordinary effects of diaconal ordination upon the deacon's exercise of governance.

The Decline of the Diaconate: The Rise of *Cursus Honorum*

"The decline of the diaconate springs more from the development of the idea of *cursus honorum* than from any other single factor."[46] During the fourth century, Christian life underwent significant transformation. Partly as a result of Christianity's new relationship with the empire, Christian public life gradually took on the trappings and structures of the state. It is during this period that the "minor" orders appeared (porter, exorcist, acolyte, and lector, all suppressed by Paul VI in 1972), along with supraepiscopal offices such as "metropolitan." "Such a structure easily gives rise to the idea of a succession of grades onto which one moves from lower to higher, traditionally called *cursus honorum*."[47] Certainly this process of "rising through the ranks"—new to the church—paralleled the experience of Christians in the civil and military aspects of their lives. In this system a person demonstrated potential for higher office by first performing and mastering the responsibilities of a lower. Such an understanding has obvious and profound implications for the ordained ministry.

The process by which the diaconate became understood as subordinate to the presbyterate was quite gradual. In the fourth-century council of Elvira (306), we read in canon 32: "However, if constrained by illness, if it is necessary, a presbyter *[presbyter]* may give him communion...or even a deacon, if the priest command him *[si ei iusserit sacerdos]*.[48] John J. McCarthy observes, "The requirement that the deacon receive permission from the priest to give communion, even in extreme circumstances, suggests that, even in his ministry to the sick, the deacon's power to distribute the Eucharist was, according to the council, to be narrowly circumscribed and his position, with respect to this task, was to be subordinate to that of the presbyter."[49] This conclusion seems valid, although it is not absolutely clear from the text if *sacerdos* refers *only* to presbyters or if it intends or includes the bishop. Since both *presbyter* (used specifically to identify presbyters) and *sacerdos* are used in this passage, it is possible that the terms are distinguishing between presbyters and bishops, in which case the passage would be indicating that the deacon may give communion in this case only "if the bishop command him." Regardless of the meaning of *sacerdos* in this passage, the actual subordination of deacon to presbyter may be indicated more concretely by the use of the phrase "even a deacon."

The Council of Nicaea clarifies the emerging relationship between presbyters and deacons even further: "The deacons are to keep within their proper bounds, knowing that they are the servants of the bishop and that they are less than presbyters."[50] Legislation and exhortations abound in which the deacon is enjoined from sitting among presbyters or in any way being seen as superior, or even equal, to the presbyters.

This clerical stratification, while frequently noted as presbyter *over against* deacon, eventually extends to bishop over presbyter as well. Consequently, while the pre-Nicene deacon was clearly identified as the bishop's assistant, by the fifth century the deacon was the presbyter's assistant, with the presbyter clearly subordinate to the bishop. This is seen in the *Statuta Ecclesiae Antiqua* (ca. 475) wherein Hippolytus's declaration that the deacon is ordained *non ad sacerdotium sed in ministerio episcopi* is modified. Now the deacon is ordained *non ad sacerdotium sed ad ministerium*, since the deacon is to be the servant of all in the sacerdotal orders. To remove any doubt on this point, the *Statuta* states, "Thus the deacon shall know he is the presbyter's minister as well as the bishop's."[51]

Several points suggest themselves. First is the remarkably consistent connection between bishop and deacon. Even as the deacon gradually and increasingly became associated with and subordinate to the presbyters, *the connection with the bishop never disappeared*. It is the bishop who ordains the deacon, not the presbyter, and it is on behalf of the bishop that the deacon acts. A particularly telling historical fact that underscores the close connection between deacon and bishop is that in many documented instances, it is the deacon who is elected to succeed the bishop. "The selection of deacons rather than presbyters oftentimes to fill vacancies in the bishop's office was logical, since many of the bishop's duties were administrative, as were the deacon's, following the emergence of the monoepiscopate and later the monarchial episcopate."[52] The diaconate was perceived as a powerful administrative ministry that worked intimately with the bishops, so intimately that the deacon was often the most qualified successor to the bishop. As vicars of the bishop, deacons exercised a share in his responsibilities in governance as the bishop deemed proper. In short, the deacon in this period seems to have exercised significant administrative governance functions, clearly a participation in the bishop's own administrative responsibilities.

Second, while the diaconate is described as a rather flexible order that takes on a variety of functions in diverse pastoral settings, the diaconate remains essentially distinguished from the sacerdotal ministries. In fact, it is when deacons appear to move into more sacerdotal functions that the patristic and canonical sources stress the fact that deacons are ordained *not* for priesthood but for *service*. During this time of the flourishing and eventual decline of the diaconate, the deacon's identity as nonsacerdotal is consistently maintained.

Third, just as there is a unique sacramental relationship with the bishop, there is a unique relationship of the deacon with the community itself. Throughout this period, writing and legislation stress the responsibility of the deacon for the welfare, good order, and discipline of the assembly. Although this responsibility is not exclusive to that of the deacon, it is the deacon who appears to have a particular focus or emphasis on the care of the people.

However, references to the diaconate largely disappear after the fifth century, and by the eleventh century it was largely a transitional and, worse, ceremonial stage of preparation for the presbyterate.

> During the Middle Ages the main function of the deacon, as he still existed at all, was to assist the president at the Eucharist. Once the helper of the bishop, the deacon had become the helper of the presbyter. One must understand that by the Middle Ages, the presbyterate had come to be recognized as the only order, with all the minor ministries subject to it....Peter Cantor (1191) put

> this role in perspective by calling the deacon "a secretary at the altar" and denying the common assertion that the assistance of the deacon was necessary for the celebration of the Eucharist.[53]

Conclusion

This survey has probably not been the most exciting material to read, but it is important to get a sense of the great diversity of the ancient diaconate, for two reasons:

First, it is important to underscore the fact that *the renewed diaconate was never intended to recreate the patristic diaconate*, even if it could. The patristic models of the diaconate offer us valuable insights into the maturing Christian communities of that era, but they are not some kind of template against which the contemporary diaconate should be restricted. Just as other forms of ministry, such as that of bishops and priests, have evolved gradually into their contemporary forms, so too the diaconate will need to continue to evolve.

Second, perhaps the best model from the patristic era for the contemporary diaconate lies in its very creativity and diversity. Within the cultural pluriformity of the time we find deacons acting in a wide variety of ways, from representing their bishops, leading communities, assisting at the Eucharist, administering the church's property, and caring for newcomers. In subsequent chapters we will have the opportunity to explore equally creative and diverse responses in the pluriformity of our own day and time.

In the next chapter, we move on to the contemporary renewal of the diaconate by examining the Council of Trent, which hinted at the possibility of a renewal of the order, and the 1917 *Code of Canon Law*, which provided the legislation on the diaconate that was operative at the time of the Second Vatican Council.

4

PREPARING FOR RENEWAL: THE COUNCIL OF TRENT AND THE 1917 *CODE OF CANON LAW*

You know how it goes: You go into a class or a lecture and the teacher says, "In order to understand our topic, we have to turn back the clock and examine what led up to it." Sometimes this means looking at topics, issues, and history that at first blush seem to have little to do with the matter at hand. But such a process *is* necessary so that a contemporary issue may be understood in its proper context, or as part of a larger trajectory of meaning. By doing this, the teacher hopes that students will more fully appreciate the contemporary issue in question.

In speaking of the renewal of the diaconate in the contemporary church, we must do the same thing, and so we begin our look at the modern diaconate not simply by looking at paragraph 29 of Vatican II's Dogmatic Constitution on the Church *(Lumen Gentium)*, or even at the council itself, but by looking back at the first hints of a renewed diaconate at the Council of Trent (1545–1563). We will then jump forward to consider how the diaconate was dealt with in the 1917 *Code of Canon Law*, which was the legal framework out of which the bishops of Vatican II were operating. With these two major pieces in place, we will then be ready to move on to the more proximate influences on the proposals to renew the diaconate, and the work of the Second Vatican Council itself.

The Council of Trent (1545–1563)

Background of the Council

There is much more that separates these two great councils of the church than the passage of four hundred years. The Council of Trent was called to respond to the challenges presented by the Protestant reformers of the sixteenth century, amid European wars, intrigue, and political maneuvering. No stranger to wars, intrigue, and political maneuvering, the Second Vatican Council (1962–1965) emerged in response to the worldwide challenges posed by two world wars, economic collapse, the rise of totalitarian regimes, the beginning of the nuclear age and the cold war. Ultimately, despite numerous differences in scope, method, and content, *both* councils were concerned with reform and renewal in the church. And, as part of their respective programs of reform and renewal, both of these councils turned to the question of the diaconate in the church.

Considering that the Council of Trent was intended to address the problems and issues raised by Martin Luther (1483–1546) and other reformers, it may strike us as strange that the council did not begin for nearly thirty years *after* Luther made his ninety-five theses a matter of public debate. This delay was due to the almost unbelievably complex political situation of the time. One of the classic texts on this matter is Philip Hughes's *The Church in Crisis: A History of the General Councils, 325–1870.*[1] Hughes offers this summary:

> The general attitude towards the plan of a General Council may thus be summed up: the man who was pope through the greater part of the period, Clement VII (1523–34), was at heart consistently hostile; the cardinals and other officers of his Curia were, for quite other reasons, still more hostile; the German Catholics were eager for a council, but a council in which they would really matter, a council fashioned rather after the pattern of a parliament than General Councils have usually been; the Catholic kings who enter the story are Charles I of Spain (just lately become the emperor Charles V), the

> life-long champion of the council idea, and Francis I of France, its bitterest opponent. And the history of Europe during the crucial twenty-five years, 1520–45, is little more than the history of the duel between these two princes. In their wars Clement VII, as often as he dared, sided with the King of France, for purely political reasons—it was, invariably, the side that lost.
>
> The council problem comes to this, that a General Council was absolutely necessary, and that, for political reasons, it was just not possible to summon one.

The longer the delay, the worse the problems became. During the interval, in addition to the wars and other political struggles of the time, ecclesial realities were changing, too. The doctrines of the Reformers, especially Lutheranism, became more solidified. Catholic responses to the reformers varied greatly as individual critics offered their own solutions for the situation. Hughes refers to the fact that liturgical practices were already changed, that "those clergy who wished had already married," and, in short, that the positions of the reformers had matured, and the relative positions of each side had hardened. All of this made the tasks of the council, when it finally got under way, all the more necessary and complex.

The council was finally scheduled to begin on November 1, 1542, in Trent. Three papal legates (one of them Cardinal Reginald Pole, a respected papal diplomat from England, who was a deacon) arrived on November 2, and there were essentially no bishops present. By the following May (1543), there were still only about a dozen bishops! This was due, yet again, to the outbreak of war, so in July 1543, the opening of the council was delayed yet again, and the legates returned to Rome. Finally, after the end of the war and with all negotiations completed, the legates returned to Trent on March 13, 1545, and the council celebrated its solemn opening on December 13, 1545. There were only thirty-one bishops present, with forty-eight theologians and canonists present as advisors.

The council would eventually cover some eighteen years (1545–1563), but it was not in session all that time. Because of the deaths of popes and political, military, and even medical crises (the plague struck Trent in 1547, for example), there was one postponement of four years, and a second of *ten* years. Therefore, the work of the council may be divided into twenty-five "sessions" spread across three major time periods:

- Sessions 1–10 were held from December 13, 1545, to June 2, 1547.
- Sessions 11–16 were held from May 1, 1551, to April 28, 1552.
- Sessions 17–25 were held from January 17, 1562, to December 4, 1563.

The number of bishops in attendance was also quite varied. During the first period (1545–1547) the number of bishop gradually grew from thirty-one to sixty-eight. In the second period (1551–1552), there were forty-four bishops for the first half of the period, and fifty-one for the second half. The third period (1562–1563) was the best attended, with 105 bishops present at the opening of the period. That number grew to 228 at one point, and then went back down to 176 at the closing session.

As we now prepare to discuss the diaconate at the Council of Trent, we can point out that the major discussion on the sacrament of orders took place during the third and final period of the council.

The Diaconate and the Council of Trent

The 90th General Congregation of the Second Vatican Council approved the restoration of the diaconate in the Latin Rite of the Catholic Church on September 29, 1964.[2] With the appearance of the *motu proprio Sacrum Diaconatus Ordinem* on June 18, 1967, Pope Paul VI provided the implementing directive for this restoration. But for a similar implementing document after the Council of Trent, the diaconate might well have been restored in the sixteenth century, for during the twenty-third session of that council, the council fathers decreed "that the functions of holy orders from the deacon to the porter, which have been laudably received in the Church from the times of the Apostles...may again be restored to use in accordance with the canons."[3] Whether the council fathers at Trent had in mind a "permanent diaconate" such as that restored by Vatican II is doubtful; however, it may be said with some confidence that they fully intended a richer and more pastoral expression of the diaconate than that which prevailed at the time of the Reformation. The purpose of this section is to examine the *Acta* of the Council of Trent in an attempt to discover its view of the diaconate within the structure of the sacrament of order.

As the Council of Trent convened, the diaconate may have seemed a most unlikely candidate for discussion. The diaconate in the Western church had already become, in most areas, little more than a ceremonial phase of a man's journey to the priesthood. In a curious twist of history, however, it is well established that English Cardinal Reginald Pole, one of the papal legates who served as presidents of the council, was in deacon's orders throughout the council and was only ordained bishop much later in his life.[4] With the grave issues of doctrine and reform of primary concern to the council, including the very nature of the episcopate and presbyterate, the place of deacons probably seemed of relatively minor importance. On the other hand, one may say that it was precisely *because* of the council's concern over the episcopate and presbyterate that made a consideration of the diaconate necessary. Whatever the case may be, as Edward Echlin observes:

> The question of the diaconate *did* emerge. If the council was to reform the Church of Rome this could be done not by returning to the Middle Ages but by conformity to scripture and the early Church. And an active diaconate was evident in scripture and the early Church. There were, moreover, pressing needs for the Church's charity as Europe urbanized.[5]

On September 23, 1562, as the council fathers and their theologians began their discussions on the sacrament of order, the door was opened to a reformed and renewed diaconate as part of the ordained ministry of the church.

Raising the Question

Having concluded its monumental twenty-second session, which dealt with the Mass, the council turned its attention to the sacrament of order. This is a most logical progression, for, as the opening words of the Decree of the Twenty-third Session proclaim,

> Sacrifice and priesthood are by the ordinance of God so united that both have existed in every law. Since therefore in the New Testament the Catholic Church has received from the institution of Christ the holy, visible sacrifice of the Eucharist, it must also be confessed that there is in that Church a new, visible and external priesthood.[6]

The first point to be stressed in Trent's understanding of the sacrament of order was its complete linkage to the sacrifice of the Mass. The council had just defined the Mass as an extension of the sacrifice of Christ on the cross, the central event of salvation. Thus, theological reflection on Eucharist and all ranks of ordained ministry (the minor and major orders) was focused on the Mass, and the various orders were viewed from the perspective of their relationship to the sacrifice of the altar.

The nature and position of the diaconate within the sacrament of order was included early in the discussions. A congregation of "minor theologians"[7] met with the bishops on September 23, 1562, to begin the council's examination of the subject. The first speaker, the young Jesuit biblical scholar Alfonso Salmeron, referred to the various orders that had been evident in the church from the very beginning: "Truly, the Sacrament of Order is received in diverse ways....Each way is an acknowledged grade in the church of God; the priesthood is distinguished from the diaconate, and the presbyterate is distinguished from the episcopate."[8] This thought was refined later the same day when subsequent speakers, such as Francesco Sanchez, specifically cited the diaconate as one of the major orders (of presbyter, deacon, and subdeacon) because they were called primarily for service at the Eucharist.[9] The other orders, known as minor orders, were *not sacraments*, according to Sanchez, because they were not chiefly concerned with the Eucharist. This distinction, while useful, was incomplete for some of the council fathers, since it omitted the bishop from the discussion. Therefore, on September 24, Benedict of Mantua declared the episcopate, presbyterate, and diaconate to be a sacrament.[10] The evidence indicates clearly that it was the understanding of Trent that the diaconate was indeed part of the sacrament of order because of its scriptural roots and because of the diaconate's ancient and long-standing association with the Eucharist.

On the other hand, the diaconate was *not* universally praised or affirmed, especially in some kind of expanded role. One might point to comments such as that made by Diego Laynez, "The devil induces the legislation of those things which destroy the priesthood under pretext, that a deacon should preach and other things of this kind."[11]

The focus of these initial discussions was on the deacon's ministry at the altar, and the deacon's sacramental identity was to be found in his eventual ordination to the presbyterate. In the words of one bishop:

> There are many diverse ministries in the church which serve the priesthood either by preparing the faithful for the reception of the Eucharist, such as porters, lectors, and exorcists; or for the preparation and execution of the sacraments, such as acolytes, subdeacons, and deacons, which are orders so arranged from the minor orders ascending through the middle ones to the major orders until they are consummated in the priesthood.[12]

Toward the end of the council, however, discussions seemed to move toward a perspective more grounded in the patristic tradition. A text was reviewed that included the following description of the diaconate:

> Deacons are the eyes of the bishops and special ministers of the church whose works, whether in the celebration of the sacred mysteries or in the administration of the church, should always be present.[13]

On June 2, 1563, the bishop of Ostuni took the floor of the council and offered a comprehensive intervention on the sacrament of order. He spoke of his vision of the roles of the diaconate in the context of the entire sacrament:

> I desire that the functions of subdeacon and deacon, diligently culled from the sayings of the holy Fathers and conciliar decrees, be restored, especially those of deacons. For the church has always used their services, not only in ministering at the altar, but also in baptism, in the care of the sick, of widows and the suffering. Finally, all the needs of the people are placed before the bishop by deacons.
>
> I also desire...a longer period between orders, at least three or four years, in which he may minister in his order and serve well in his office, and then be allowed to proceed to a higher order.[14]

Given the reference to a longer interstice between the various orders, Echlin refers to this recommendation as a call for a "temporary permanent" diaconate.[15] But nowhere in the *Acta* is there a more comprehensive list of diaconal functions than in the statement on the ministry considered by the council on July 6, 1563.

> It is fully apparent that many necessary and sacred services were committed to the order of deacons, which is distinct from other ministries of the church and next to the priesthood. They are the eyes of the bishops and special ministers of the church whose works, whether in the celebration of the sacred mysteries or in the administration of the church, should always be present. In the holy sacrifice they offer at the altar the gifts received from the subdeacon, they care for the altar of the Lord, proclaim the Gospel to the people, assist the consecrating priests, and admonish the people on the solemn rites to be observed in church. They also should exhort that [the people] raise their hearts and prepare their souls for

> prayer. They should warn those who intend to be present at the sacrifice to have no adversity between themselves, no hatred, no wrath or ill will, but mutual love. The ministry of deacons should be assiduous in governing the church. Their office is to guard the preaching bishop lest he be threatened by vicious enemies or the divine word be reviled by insults and be despised. When the bishop directs, deacons may baptize and preach, and to reconcile, without solemnity, public penitents to the church in the case of necessity and in the absence of the bishop or priests. They should seek out and diligently care for whatever pertains to the corporal needs of widows, students, orphans, the imprisoned, the sick and all the afflicted and provide for the spiritual help of the faithful. They have loving concern for all the faithful in works of mercy, especially for those in whom they observe a greater need for such charity.[16]

There is no indication in the *Acta* or in the decrees and canons of the Council that this statement was ever officially promulgated; certainly the proposal that the diaconate be restored to its former functions was never implemented.

In summary, Trent enumerates the following diaconal functions:

1. Assisting at the altar, specifically by receiving the gifts,
2. Assisting the priest,
3. Proclaiming the Gospel,
4. Exhorting the people, and
5. Caring for the altar.

Preaching is allowed with special permission of the bishop, as are baptizing and simple reconciliation. Outside the Eucharist, deacons are to be conscientious in "governing" the Church, although specific examples of this governance are not described. They are extraordinary ministers of baptism and, echoing Cyprian, deacons may "in case of necessity" reconcile penitents in the absence of the bishop or priests. Finally, deacons are to be diligent in meeting the corporal and spiritual needs of all the faithful.

One may only speculate how the history of the contemporary diaconate may have developed had the possibility of a renewed diaconate contemplated by the Council of Trent been implemented. Although a restored diaconate was never fully implemented after Trent, the fact that the council had discussed the diaconate at all became an influential factor for some of the bishops at Vatican II. While it is true that even after Trent the diaconate remained transitional, subordinate, and mainly liturgical, some of the groundwork for a fully renewed order had been done.

The Pio-Benedictine Code of Canon Law (1917)

Canon law, in addition to providing rules for ecclesial living, emerges out of a theology of church. In other words, how we understand ourselves as church will be reflected, usually in very concrete and practical terms, in our system of law. James A. Coriden, in speaking of the development of canon law, writes, "the church's rules were shaped by its internal needs, the surrounding cultures, and the pressures of changed circumstances."[17]

Although the church has had rules from the beginning, how these rules, laws, and policies were assembled has taken many forms. Pope Pius X initiated the preparation of the first codified legal system of canon law, which because of the First World War, finally appeared in 1917 with the promulgation of the *Codex Iuris Canonici* by Pope Benedict XV. Coriden notes that the new Code "brought relative order out of the chaotic state of canon law at the beginning of the twentieth century. The promulgation of the Code marked the opening of a new canonical epoch."[18] For our purposes, it also provides a window into ecclesial understanding and praxis on the threshold of the Second Vatican Council. Unfortunately, but not surprisingly, this will not take long to review.

The Diaconate in the 1917 Code

Canon 108 of the 1917 Code addresses the identity of clerics:

> §1. Those who are taken into divine ministries at least by the reception of first tonsure are called clerics.
>
> §2. [Clerics] are not all of the same rank, but among them there is a sacred hierarchy in which some are subordinated to others.
>
> §3. By divine institution, the sacred hierarchy in respect of orders consists of Bishops, priests, and ministers; by reason of jurisdiction, [it consists of] the supreme pontificate and the subordinate episcopate; by institution of the Church other grades can also be added.[19]

According to Stanislaus Woywod's commentary on this canon:

> The Code repeats the dogmatical teaching of the Council of Trent on the hierarchy of orders and jurisdiction. It leaves unsettled the question as to what is meant by the "ministers" in the above enumeration of bishops, priests and ministers. The common teaching of theologians is that the deacons only are meant by the term "ministers," and that the subdeacons are not included.[20]

Canon 118 directs: "Only clerics can obtain powers, whether of orders or of ecclesiastical jurisdiction, and benefices or ecclesiastical pensions."[21] All this is well and good, but how does the 1917 Code treat the order of deacons? What are they described as doing? What are their functions?

The following table contrasts the 1917 Code with the 1983 Code as they apply to diaconal functions. The current code will be examined in much greater detail in a subsequent chapter; its inclusion here is simply to contrast the two codes.

Table 2. Diaconal Functions in the 1917 and 1983 Codes of Canon Law

Sources: James A. Coriden, Thomas J. Green, and Donald E. Heintschel, eds., "Table of Corresponding Canons: 1983 Code with 1917 Code," in *The Code of Canon Law: A Text and Commentary* (New York/Mahwah, NJ: Paulist Press, 1985), 1047–92. Stanislaus Woywod, *A Practical Commentary on the Code of Canon Law* (London: Herder, 1926). John P. Beal, James A. Coriden, and Thomas J. Green, eds., *New Commentary on the Code of Canon Law* (New York/Mahwah, NJ: Paulist Press, 2000). William H. Woestman, *The Sacrament of Orders and the Clerical State: A Commentary on the Code of Canon Law* (Ottawa: St. Paul Université, 1999), 387–88.

FUNCTION	1917 CODE	1983 CODE	ROLE OF DEACON
Proclaim Gospel	N/A	757	Not included in 1917 Code, although so designated in the liturgical books; specifically included in 1983
Preaching	1327, 1337	764	Included under "clerics" in 1917; specifically included in 1983
Catechesis	1333	776	Included under "clerics" in 1917; specifically included in 1983
Baptism	738	861, §1	1917: Extraordinary minister; 1983: Ordinary minister
Minister of Communion	845	910, §1	1917: Extraordinary minister; 1983: Ordinary minister
Eucharistic Benediction	1274, §2	943	1917: Exposition/ reposition allowed to deacon, blessing

FUNCTION	1917 CODE	1983 CODE	ROLE OF DEACON
			reserved to priest; 1983: ordinary minister for exposition/ reposition *and* blessing
Matrimony	1094	1108	1917: presiding at matrimony reserved to priests; 1983: with delegation of ordinary or pastor, deacon, and other presbyters are ordinary ministers
Power to dispense	N/A	1079–1081	1917: Deacons have no power to dispense from impediments; 1983: under specific conditions, deacons may dispense
Blessings	1146, 1147, §4	1168, 1169, §3	1917: Deacons may bless when expressly authorized; 1983: Deacons bless according to the appropriate liturgical books
Funerals	N/A	1176–1185	1917: No mention of deacons as ministers of funerals; 1983: deacons officiate as expressly cited in the ritual.
Liturgy of the Hours	N/A	1173, 1248, §2	1983: Deacons may preside, even solemnly, at celebrations of the Hours and other services

Continued

Table 2 Continued

FUNCTION	1917 CODE	1983 CODE	ROLE OF DEACON
Pastoral Care in Absence of Priest	N/A	517, §2	1917: Deacons could be "given" a parish in anticipation of imminent ordination to priesthood; 1983: deacons given precedence in absence of presbyters
Tribunal Officials, including Judge	N/A	1421, 1428, 1435, 536	1917: no mention of deacons; 1983: deacons as judge, promoter of justice, defender of the bond, auditor, chancellor, notary, pastoral councils

In comparing the functions of deacons as described in the Pio-Benedictine Code of 1917 and the revised Code of 1983, one may make the following observations: In every case, the deacon of the 1917 Code was either not permitted certain functions later allowed in 1983, or he was an extraordinary minister of those functions. In the 1917 Code, the deacon was not specifically authorized to preach; however, there seems to have been some latitude on this matter since bishops and pastors could assign "other suitable men" to preach and to catechetical ministry if the need arose. The deacon was specifically included as an extraordinary minister of baptism and an extraordinary minister in the distribution of communion. Deacons could expose the Blessed Sacrament, but benediction itself was reserved to a presbyter. *At no time* was the deacon listed as even an extraordinary witness of matrimony, nor was he capable of granting dispensations. "Deacons and lectors" were permitted to bless as described in the liturgical books. They were not included as celebrants of funeral rites. They could not serve as judges in any capacity. There were no comparable canons discussing deacons as presiders at the Liturgy of the Hours, or leading a parish in the absence of a presbyter.

Not surprisingly, we may conclude that the 1917 Code *describes a deacon only in light of his eventual ordination as a presbyter.* The deacon was a cleric, surely, but a cleric with little or no legal function, and the few functions available to him were extraordinary. Essentially, when the Second Vatican Council and Pope Paul VI renewed the diaconate, it was going to be necessary to provide for changes to the law. This was accomplished initially by Paul with his promulgation of *Sacrum Diaconatus Ordinem* in 1967, which contained the first legal norms for the renewed diaconate.

Conclusion

Collectively, the last two chapters have covered two thousand years of history, if only in a cursory manner. We have seen the deacon emerge as an officeholder in the ancient church, a person who shared in the responsibility of good order in the Christian community; a person who, on behalf of the community and in the name of the bishop, had a particular role in being responsible for those in need. Needs take many forms, and the deacon also took on various roles as catechist, reconciler of sinners, member of the community's ruling council, and legate. Always closely associated with his bishop, the deacon was often the bishop's successor, and some deacons served in the extremely powerful office of archdeacon, with responsibilities over the rest of the clergy (including presbyters), with fiscal and judicial oversight. However, in the restructuring of ordained ministry beginning in the fourth century, the deacon as a proper and permanent minister began to fade from the scene, becoming a minister identified with his ultimate goal of priesthood. Gradually, the sacramental identity of the deacon was subsumed into that of the presbyter. This was the paradigm in place on the eve of the Second Vatican Council.

5

VATICAN II AND THE RENEWAL OF THE DIACONATE

Introduction

An earlier version of this chapter appeared recently in James Keating's *Deacon Reader*.[1] The purpose of this chapter is to outline the contemporary renewal of the diaconate up to and including the work of the Second Vatican Council. Long before the council took up the question of renewing the diaconate as a permanent state of ordained ministry, there had been growing interest in the subject by theologians, bishops, and others involved in pastoral ministry through the first half of the twentieth century. Having a sense of how their work contributed to the ultimate decision of the council helps situate the council's work in context.

After teaching a three-part parish seminar on the history of Vatican II and its documents in a neighboring parish, I was approached by the young pastor, who thanked me for the presentations, which had been very well received. Then he added, "But I don't know why you bother with this. After all, Vatican II is history; we need to move on." One may suppose that others share his unfortunate view. In order to understand the council's actions with regard to the diaconate (or anything else, for that matter) it is critically important to appreciate the dynamics of the council and how it accomplished its tasks. As we shall see, many of the myths that often surround the renewed diaconate may be dispelled by an examination of the record of the council itself. In short, it is one thing to report the fact that the bishops of the council voted to renew the diaconate; it is quite another to try to understand *why*.

Appreciating the catalysts leading to the council's decision and Paul VI's eventual implementation of that decision is a necessary first step in developing a contemporary theology of the diaconate.[2] Developing a theology for a newly renewed, ancient order of ministry that had not been exercised on a permanent basis (with a few notable exceptions) for well over a millennium would be challenging enough.

> The challenge increases exponentially, however, when coupled with the two chronologically coincident realities of a veritable explosion in lay ecclesial ministries and a drastic drop in the number of presbyters. The confluence of these three realities—the growth of lay ecclesial ministry and the sacramental diaconate with the decline in numbers of presbyters—has...has only underscored the critical need for continuing scholarly and pastoral discourse on the sacramental identity of all who minister, and the relationships that ought to exist between them.[3]

Roots of Renewal

At least four streams of influence converged at the council:

1. the German experience prior to the Second World War,
2. the Dachau experience and postwar developments centered in Germany and France,
3. pastoral developments related to the *missio ad gentes* and catechetics, and,
4. significant papal teachings.

The German Experience Prior to World War II

Josef Hornef, in a classic text on the restoration of a permanent diaconate, traced the written record suggesting a renewal of the diaconate to an 1840 letter from a Frankfurt physician, J. K.

Passavant, to a friend who would become the future cardinal archbishop of Breslau, Melchior van Diepenbrock. Passavant observed that the priesthood was too divorced from the daily life of people, and he proposed two possible solutions:

> The Church can either permit priests to marry in the manner in which the Greek Uniates are permitted to do, or she can expand the sphere of activity of deacons, so that these men, who would be allowed to be married, could carry out in part the teaching office and other ecclesiastical functions, while the priest (who would therefore have to be senior) would exclusively administer the sacraments, especially confession. If in the considered opinion of the bishops, then, several deacons (archdeacons) could be drawn from the best educated ranks of the so-called laity, then the Church would have excellent ministers at her disposal.[4]

The letter hints at the possibilities of a renewed diaconate as a sacramental sign of an expanded ministry. There is no indication that Passavant's suggestions were considered beyond this exchange of letters. While Hornef identifies similar suggestions outside Germany, it is generally acknowledged that the German experience was to be the most influential voice in the call for a renewed diaconate. One reason for this may be found in the growth of the idea in the context of the German *Caritas* movement.

The history of the *Deutscher Caritas Verband* began in 1897 when the Catholic bishops of Germany directed its establishment to carry out a ministry of charitable outreach to those in need.[5] Following the devastation of World War I, *Caritas* expanded its efforts into every German diocese. Training centers were established, and many of the country's leading churchmen supported its work. Articles in the *Caritas* journal proposed and developed the notion of a renewed diaconate, especially after Hitler's rise to power in 1933.

For example, in 1934 *Caritas* director G. von Mann wrote of a renewed diaconate of charity which, rooted in the sacramental life of the parish community, would be charged with "the stimulation of charitable activities by the parish community."[6] Although he does not specifically propose an ordained diaconate as such, he stresses the importance of diaconal ministers operating as a kind of diaconal team. In 1936, Hans Schütz published "Diakonie der Liebe" in *Caritas*. Schütz reported on a meeting of Caritas workers in Cologne in September 1935 in which von Mann's notion of a diaconal association developed even further. During the meeting, the participants discussed the possibility of a restored permanent diaconate with a threefold ministry "of liturgy, charity, and catechesis." There would need to be specific formation for this diaconate, and the ordination of such deacons would include a "missioning" by the bishop.

> The restoration of this office was at that time a necessity, if charitable service was to survive in both the deeds and consciousness [of the people], given the current maelstrom of national events (the "Third Reich" and the domination of the National-Socialist Peoples' Welfare Association).[7]

Four points may be noted from this early "German period." First is the realization that leadership in providing charitable service, sacramentally linked to the ministries of Word and Sacrament, is a constitutive element of the life of the church. Second is the understanding that this service, various functions of which may be exercised by laypersons, is deserving of sacramental recognition and empowerment by the church. Third is the insight that this development was needed as part of an overall renewal of the church in a contemporary world in need of creative responses to extraordinary needs. Fourth is the emphasis that the deacon's authority is derived sacramentally through the deacon's ordination, which links him in a special way to the apostolic ministry of the bishop.

The Dachau Experience and Postwar Developments

The journey toward a renewed diaconate took on added urgency during and after the Second World War. In 1933, Nazi Germany opened its first concentration camp at Dachau. A large number of clergy and religious were apprehended and, in accordance with Nazi policies, they were not given any preferential treatment in the camp. Incarcerated with the general prison population, they continued to minister secretly. Eventually, the Nazis relocated the clergy to Cell Block 26, which became known by the guards as *der Priesterblock*.

During discussions while incarcerated, especially later in the war, several prisoners raised a number of possibilities concerning the renewal of the church following the war. One of these possibilities was the restoration of the diaconate as a permanent state. Fr. Wilhelm Schamoni kept notes of these discussions while still interned in the camp, and he was able to save these notes after the collapse of the Third Reich. After the war, Schamoni and another former prisoner, Fr. Otto Pies, wrote about their experiences and in particular about a renewed diaconal order.

Pies was seriously ill after his incarceration in Dachau, and it was not until 1947 that he was able to document his experiences. In October, he published "Cell Block 26: Experiences of Priestly Life in Dachau."[8] He described discussions on the future of ministry after the war, suggesting that the Holy Spirit was calling new ministries into existence, including the diaconate. Wilhelm Schamoni, finally responding to pleas from Pies and others to publish his own reflections on the question, published *Married Men as Ordained Deacons* in 1953.[9]

Grounding his work in a historical study of the ancient diaconate, Schamoni drew parallels to the postwar world, the devastation of the war having caused massive relocations of peoples, increased missionary activity, and the need for the traditional duties of deacons in administration, liturgy, and sacrament. He also cited the value of deacons in teaching, liturgy, sacrament and Catholic Action. What is perhaps most significant about his work is that, while prescinding from a desire to counteract the growing shortage of priests that resulted from the war, his suggestions were *not* merely to supply more ministers to "fill in" for priests; rather, it was to extend the church's ministry even further, including ministry to priests themselves. He moved beyond the traditional functions of deacons to suggest that they could even counter "the fact that the clerical state has become a profession, a fact that has been allowed to become a cause for resentment, of estrangement from the church and of anti-clericalism"; and that deacons could serve as a sign of "assimilation to the practice of the Eastern Church that can be traced back to apostolic times."[10]

Responding to this call for a renewed ordained diaconate was a young forestry worker named Hannes Kramer, who had already been associated with *Caritas* and its ministry.[11] He dedicated himself to a diaconal ministry. In 1951 he formed the first *Diakonatskreis* (diaconate circle) in Freiburg, West Germany. In addition to providing direct charitable service, members of this group also dedicated themselves to exploring the possibility of a renewed ordained diaconate. The question of the ordained diaconate began to spread outside Germany, largely through the work of the growing number of diaconate circles (Munich, Cologne, Trèves, Essen, and Lyons) and the contributions made by theologians considering the question. Although the diaconate was envisioned in slightly different ways from country to country, one idea remained constant: "In each case liturgical involvement is necessary. Even for the deacon, liturgy should be the center of his life."[12]

Eventually the diaconate circles organized into an association known as the International Diaconate Circle and, eventually, the International Diaconate Center. The deacon circles became so well-versed in the question of the renewed diaconate that they opened an office in Rome during Vatican II to serve as a resource for council fathers interested in researching the question. At about the same time, Karl Rahner and Herbert Vorgrimler edited a text containing a variety of articles on the history of the proposal, the general lines of theological inquiry that had already been pursued, and how the diaconate might be developed in a variety of different countries and cultures.[13] This now-classic text was made available to the world's bishops in advance of the council.

Pastoral Developments in Mission and Catechetics

A clear sign that the idea of a renewed diaconate was reaching far beyond the borders of Western Europe took place in 1956, at the First International Congress on Pastoral Liturgy held from September 18 to 22 in Assisi, Italy. Dutch bishop Willem van

Bekkum, serving in Indonesia, suggested the restoration of a permanent diaconate for mission countries, pointing out that he was speaking not for himself alone but in the name "of countless colleagues" in the missions.[14]

This event takes on added significance because this is the first time a bishop had spoken publicly about the possibility and desirability of a restored diaconate. As Johannes Hofinger would write several years later,

> This is the first time that a missionary bishop had spoken out so clearly and urgently for the restoration of the diaconate, and at such a large and illustrious gathering. Bishop van Bekkum's words have special importance in view of the fact that he had been requested by the organizing committee not so much to give his own personal wishes as an objective picture of the missions today and their needs.[15]

It was Hofinger himself who would next take up the cause of a restored diaconate. Among the duties deacons might perform in the absence of priests (bring communion and Viaticum to the sick and dying, conduct worship services, administer solemn baptism, marriages, and funerals), Hofinger highlighted the deacon's preaching role and service in administration.[16] The powerful combination of van Bekkum and Hofinger added to the growing chorus of voices rising from around the world for a restored diaconate.

Under Hofinger's leadership, a series of six International Catechetical Study Weeks on Mission and Liturgy were organized between 1959 and 1968. These Study Weeks have been referred to as "key moments in the evolution of catechetics,"[17] and they have proved critical in related fields as well, including the development of the proposal to restore the diaconate. During the 1959 Study Week, held September 12–19 in Nijmegen, Holland, Archbishop Eugene D'Souza of Nagpur, India, spoke on "Permanent Deacons in the Missions."[18] In his talk he said, "We respectfully submit that nothing short of the restoration of the permanent diaconate will be of any practical value and permanent advantage to us in the missions."[19] He also referred to the Pope Pius XII's comment in 1957 that "the time was not yet ripe" for restoration, but he suggested that certain parts of the world may be more ready than others, and he urged restoration in those places immediately.

Finally, mention must be made of the French movement toward a permanent diaconate. In 1957, Rev. Michel-Dominique Epagneul published "On the Role of Deacons in the Church Today,"[20] in which he proposed the restoration of the diaconate as a permanent order primarily as assistance to overworked priests. He suggests that since priests would now have qualified assistance in ministry, even greater numbers of men may be attracted to the priesthood. What is most significant about this article, however, is that Epagneul forwarded a copy of it to Pope Pius XII. The Holy Father acknowledged receipt of the article in April;[21] his comments on the diaconate at the Second World Congress of the Apostolate of the Laity (discussed below), took place in October 1957.

Papal Statements

An important development in the contemporary renewal of the diaconate is the Apostolic Constitution *Sacramentum Ordinis* of Pius XII (November 30, 1947). The purpose of the document was to establish clearly the matter and form of the sacrament of order. Among other concerns, the question persisted whether orders other than the presbyterate were sacramental. The pope resolved the matter by declaring that for ordinations to diaconate, presbyterate, and episcopate, the matter and form are the laying on of hands and the prayer of consecration. By including the diaconate in this document, the pope affirmed the sacramentality of the diaconate.[22]

Pope Pius XII provided another significant impetus to the renewal of the diaconate through an address on October 5, 1957, to the Second World Congress of the Apostolate of the Laity in Rome. The pope remarked:

> We know that there is thought these days to introduce the order of the diaconate conceived as an ecclesiastical function independent from the priesthood. The idea, at least today, is not yet ripe. If one day it becomes such, nothing of what we have said would change, except that

> this diaconate would take its place with the priesthood in the distinctions which we have indicated.[23]

Following the pope's remarks, theological and pastoral activity concerning the diaconate rose dramatically.[24]

These four streams of influence: the early German experience, the Dachau experience, the growth of the proposal in mission and catechetical fields, and the interventions of Pius XII, all converged on January 25, 1959, when Pope John XXIII declared his intention to convene the Second Vatican Council.

Vatican II and the Diaconate

While *Lumen Gentium* 29 is the principal conciliar text on the diaconate, the renewal of the order was also strongly encouraged for those Eastern Churches in which "it has fallen into disuse" (*Orientalium Ecclesiarum* 17). The diaconate is referred to as well in the Decree on the Missionary Activity of the Church (*Ad Gentes* 16), the Constitution on the Sacred Liturgy (*Sacrosanctum Concilium* 35), and the Dogmatic Constitution on Divine Revelation (*Dei Verbum* 25).

In this section three conciliar sources will be surveyed:

1. The *Antepraeparatoria series*,[25] which contains the tabulation of topics submitted by the world's bishops for discussion during the council
2. The *Praeparatoria series*,[26] which traces the formulation of the initial drafts of the council documents
3. The *Acta*[27] of the council itself, which contain the actual debate surrounding the proposal to restore the diaconate

The Antepreparatory Stage

One hundred and one specific proposals were made concerning the restoration of the diaconate during the initial consultations for the council; of these, eleven were against the restoration. The proposals fall into four categories: (I) thirty-seven proposals on the restoration in general,[28] (II) another thirty-seven proposals on the requirement for celibacy,[29] (III) sixteen proposals on the requirements and functions of deacons,[30] (IV) the eleven proposals against restoration.[31] Table 3 summarizes these categories, showing the number of proposals in each category and the number of bishops supporting each category.[32]

Table 3. Antepreparatory Proposals on the Diaconate
Source: ADA, Appendix, II/II

CATEGORY	TITLE	PROPOSALS	SUPPORTING SEES
I	*On Restoring the Order of the Diaconate*	37	283
II	*On the Diaconate without the Obligation of Celibacy*	37	138
III	*On the Prerequisites and Functions of Deacons*	16	71
IV	*On the Inadvisability of Restoring of the Diaconate*	11	21

Category I: On the Restoration of the Order of Deacon[33]

Of the thirty-seven proposals in this list, by far the most strongly supported was the second; namely, that deacons should be restored to the offices and in the form of previous ages *(ad officia et in forma priorum saeculorum)*. While the majority of proposals relating to the diaconate were suggested by only one or two bishops, this one lists over 135 individual bishops as well as all 51 bishops from the Congo and Rwanda (voting as a bloc), for a total of 186. This constitutes nearly two-thirds (65 percent) of all the proposals in this category alone, and well over one-third (36 percent) of all the proposals received across all four categories.

Of particular interest is the great geographical distribution of these proposals. A common perception maintains that the impetus behind the diaconate's restoration came from the bishops of the so-called third-world or mission countries. Many of the proposals came from the bishops of Latin America and Africa (well over one hundred of the total number were from these two areas). However, a significant number of proposals were received from bishops from Europe (especially Spain, Germany, France, the Netherlands, and the countries of Eastern Europe) and Asia (especially Micronesia, Indonesia, India, and Pakistan). In light of the historical development of the proposal to restore the permanent diaconate that originated in Germany and France and spread outside Europe in the 1950s, these numbers indicate that by the time of the council, the proposal had significant support from bishops around the world.

Category III: On the Requirements and Functions of Deacons[34]

The sixteen proposals in this category, while they reflect the thoughts of only seventy-one of the bishops, offer some insight into the areas of ministry deacons might be assigned. Table 4 outlines the proposals in category III; while many of the functions listed reflect the practices of the early diaconate, two of the bishops even recommended that deacons might anoint the sick—a function not previously assigned to deacons.

Table 4. Antepreparatory Proposals, Functions in Category III

PROPOSAL	TEXT	SUPPORTING SEES
1	*Deacons should be forty years old, and their doctrine and morals investigated.*	2
2	*Deacons should be forty years old and exemplary catechists.*	1

PROPOSAL	TEXT	SUPPORTING SEES
3	*The following offices are the deacons': preaching, administration of baptism, even solemnly, distribution of holy communion, exposition of the Blessed Sacrament and eucharistic blessing, and taking of Viaticum to the sick.*	3
4	*Deacons may be installed, especially in mission areas and where there is a shortage of priests for the following offices: solemn administration of baptism, valid assistance of matrimony, to administer the Holy Eucharist, even as Viaticum, to preach the word of God in the church, and to administer the goods of the church.*	2
5	*Deacons should be of mature age; of evident Christian spirit; of sufficient knowledge of dogmatics, morals, scriptures, and liturgy. Their offices may be: to be devoted to catechesis, to assist the parish priest in the Eucharist, and to distribute holy communion to the faithful, upon the prudent judgment of the parish priest.*	25
6	*They are bound by the law of residency, under the supervision of the parish priest, sustained by the faithful or by the curia.*	1
7	*Deacons may assist at marriages.*	5
8	*The faculty to preside at Solemn Benediction with the Blessed Sacrament may be granted to deacons.*	3
9	*The administration of the temporal goods of the church may be transferred by the parish priest to the deacon so that the parish priests may focus on spiritual care.*	1

Continued

Table 4 Continued

PROPOSAL	TEXT	SUPPORTING SEES
10	*Deacons attend to the administration of goods.*	1
11	*In accordance with can. 938, the deacon may be the extraordinary minister of extreme unction when there are not enough priests or in urgent necessity.*	1
12	*Deacons may confer extreme unction in the absence of priests.*	1
13	*[Deacons] may bring solace to the faithful in extreme situations.*	21
14	*Deacons may conduct burials.*	2
15	*The order of the diaconate may be conferred on catechists and assisting laity.*	1
16	*Deacons may be named as professors of religion.*	1

The Preparatory Stage

A total of 8,972 proposals were received in Rome from the world's bishops, including the 101 described above. "From this mass of very diversified interests the themes were chosen which seemed to be of the greatest importance, and put before various commissions for a preliminary investigation."[35] The overall topic of the possible renewal of the diaconate was assigned to the commission *De disciplina Sacramentorum* under the leadership of Cardinal Benedetto Masella. Two other commissions also drafted materials on the diaconate: the Commission for the Oriental Churches and the Commission for the Missions.

On Wednesday, January 17, 1962, Cardinal Masella presented the draft *De Sacramento Ordinis*[36] to the third meeting of the Central Preparatory Commission, at which time the first general debate *De diaconatu permanente seu stabili instaurando* took place.[37]

Masella began the discussion by reviewing the four questions considered by the commission:

> 1. Should the minor orders and the diaconate be restored?
>
> 2. In what way should they be restored?
>
> 3. At what ages should the major orders be conferred?
>
> 4. What should the intervals be between the various orders?

The question that caused the greatest debate, according to Masella, was whether the diaconate should be restored in the Latin church. He referred to the 1957 allocution by Pius XII, which emphasized the ordained character of the diaconate (as opposed to a so-called lay diaconate) and encouraged continued study on the subject of restoration. Masella pointed out that the question had now been examined from every aspect: theological, juridical, pastoral and social. Lastly, Masella reported that his commission had prepared the schema from the analysis of the many desires of bishops from around the world during the antepreparatory stage.

Masella offered the following points for discussion:

> 1. That the permanent diaconate, according to ancient practice, should be restored immediately in the Latin church, especially in those dioceses and regions with a shortage of priests;
>
> 2. That this restoration may not take place without the approval of the Holy See;
>
> 3. That permanent deacons are ordained into the clerical state; and,
>
> 4. That permanent deacons should also be restored in various religious communities, with the approval of the superiors and the Holy See.

Masella concluded his remarks by addressing the issue of admitting married men. He pointed out that there was considerable support for the proposal, driven in large part by the great shortage of priests in mission territories. Nonetheless, he also pointed out that, while the majority of the commission's members approved the ordination of married men to the diaconate in certain areas with the approval of the Holy See, the commission also unanimously emphasized that this in no way suggested that the law of celibacy for priests be altered.

In the discussion that followed, ten bishops presented their views on the proposal.[38] Six cited serious problems with ordaining married men to the diaconate, most frequently because of the effects they see this having on the law of priestly celibacy as well as the possible impact this could have on the number of vocations to the priesthood. As Archbishop Marcel Lefebvre put it, "there is the certain danger of a lessening of vocations to the priesthood in favor of a married diaconate."[39]

Cardinals Josef Frings and André-Damien Jullien were concerned over the impact a restored diaconate might have on the lay apostolate, although Frings supported the notion of a restored celibate diaconate as long as the deacon had no desire to ascend *(ascendendi)* to the priesthood.[40] There was an appreciation that many of the functions formerly assigned to deacons were already being performed by laypersons, and that this renewed lay apostolate should not be thwarted by the restoration of another hierarchical order.

Fifty-six fathers on the commission voted on the draft *De Sacramento Ordinis.* Thirty-one voted *non placet,* most objecting to the proposal to restore the diaconate in general or objecting to the possibility of ordaining married men. (Ironically, Cardinal Giovanni Battista Montini of Milan was among this number; as Paul VI he would ultimately implement the renewal.) Eight more fathers voted *placet* on the overall schema, while specifically rejecting the diaconate proposal. One father abstained, leaving only sixteen who voted *placet* without reservation. At the end of this meeting, the commission began the task of redrafting the document to reflect the observations of the Central Commission.

Two days after Cardinal Masella's presentation to the Central Commission, on January 19, 1962, Cardinal Amleto Cicognani presented the draft *De Ecclesiae Sacramentis* prepared by the Commission for the Oriental Churches. The draft affirmed the ancient roots of the diaconate, and, citing the shortage of priests, called for the revitalization of the office.[41] Cicognani reminded the Central Commission that, while the diaconate continued to exist in some Eastern churches, it had ceased in others. Since there were many favorable reasons to restore the order, and since the *Code of Canon Law* for the Eastern Churches already provided for a permanent diaconate, the council should mention the diaconate's value in a general way for the East.[42]

On March 28, 1962, Cardinal Gregorio Agagianian presented the Commission for the Missions' draft to the Central Commission. Among the functions that might be assigned to deacons: they could preach the gospel, have a liturgical ministry, and be responsible for charitable works.[43] The presbyteral and diaconal vocations are distinct, and many who could not or would not become priests, for whatever reason, could become deacons.[44] Deacons could be married, and this marriage would not detract from priestly celibacy.[45] The schema proposed further that the church not grant diaconal functions to those who do not seek ordination, since the diaconate has its own proper functions that should not be performed by the laity. In a point later stressed by Cardinal Leon Josef Suenens during the conciliar debate, ordination gives a special grace with a sacramental character.[46] Finally, the commission proposed that episcopal conferences be given the authority to allow local bishops to confer the permanent diaconate upon those who may even be married.[47]

The First Session and the Schema **De Ecclesia** *(1962)*

The schema *De Ecclesia* consisted of eleven chapters and an appendix on Mary. Chapter 3 was a mere two paragraphs of some thirty-one lines, with no mention of the diaconate.[48]

But there were far greater problems with the document. Various speakers cited a lack of cohesion between the chapters, which reflected a much deeper issue; namely, the document presented no coherent vision of the church. Many fathers were troubled by the highly juridical and legalistic tone of the schema. Given these foundational concerns, the schema was sent back to committee for rewriting prior to the 1963 session.

The Second Draft: Lumen Gentium *(1963)*

The second draft, now known as *Lumen Gentium*, was presented at the Thirty-seventh General Assembly, Monday, September 30, 1963. The council focused largely on this document for the next month. The organization of the schema was completely revised. The eleven dogmatic essays were replaced by four chapters, with the hierarchy (now including the diaconate) included in chapter 2, *De Constitutione Hierarchica Ecclesiae et in specie: De Episcopatu*. But even more significant were the changes in style and content. The chapter on the hierarchy, for example, opens with a pastoral statement on the people of God and the nature of ministry as something good given to nurture the entire body. The fathers accepted this draft for discussion on October 1, 1963, by a vote of 2,231 to 43.[49]

This draft describes deacons as "in a lower level of the ministerial hierarchy." Deacons, who serve in celebrations of sacrifice, as extraordinary ministers of baptism and holy communion, and who perform various public works of charity, proclamation, and administration as assigned by competent authority, assist the bishop and priests. The draft continues by noting that today the diaconate is primarily a step toward the priesthood, but that in the future, in places where the church discerns the pastoral necessity, it will be possible to establish the diaconate as a proper and permanent level of the hierarchy. It is up to the church to decide whether or not such deacons ought to be bound by the law of celibacy.[50]

Reports and Speeches

Cardinal Michael Browne, the vice-president of the Commission *De Doctrina Fidei et Morum*, provided an overview of the revised draft to the assembly, focusing on three significant issues. First, he stated that a major objective of the text was to complete the work of Vatican I, which had declared and affirmed the pope as the successor of Peter, by declaring Catholic doctrine on the bishops as successors to the other apostles. Second, this objective was met through nine paragraphs, one of which was "On the divinely instituted assistants of the bishops, i.e., on presbyters and deacons."[51] This is significant, since the text itself did not specify the divinely instituted nature of the diaconate in those terms. In addition, all nine paragraphs were considered part of the first objective, which was to talk about the bishops; as noted above, the presbyterate and diaconate are defined in terms of their relationship to the episcopate, and Browne emphasized this. Third, he said that the text, after dealing specifically with hierarchical ministry, moved into other forms of ministry, with specific paragraphs on the threefold functions of the church: the functions of teaching, sanctifying, and governing.

Finally, Cardinal Frings and Bishop Joseph Gargitter recommended that the chapters be reordered, with the second chapter becoming *De Populo Dei*, and the third chapter becoming *De Hierarchica*.[52] With the acceptance of these recommendations, the structure of *Lumen Gentium* was close to its final form.

The Conciliar Debate: October 4–16, 1963

The principal conciliar debate on the subject of restoring the permanent diaconate in the Latin church occurred during the Forty-first to the Forty-ninth General Assemblies (October 4–16, 1963). In reviewing the interventions, the climax of the debate occurred on October 8 with the intervention of Cardinal Suenens.

Cardinal Francis Spellman of New York opened the debate on the diaconate on October 4.[53] He objected to the proposal on three grounds. First, while acknowledging that the diaconate had once flourished in the West, he urged further study into the reasons why it became obsolete, since these reasons might indicate the difficulties inherent in its restoration. Second, he cited the difficulties with regard to training deacons, since seminaries (for candidates for the priesthood) were already hard enough to maintain, and distinct houses of formation would need to be established for deacons, since he believed it would be improper to train married men in the same institution as celibate men. Third, he stated that a reason why the diaconate had faded in the West was that deacons were unable to provide the necessary sacred ministries for the care of the faithful. Spellman concluded by asking whether it would not be better to encourage vocations to the priesthood. He felt that the diaconate would result in fewer vocations to the priesthood, leading him to pose the question: is it better to have fewer priests along with permanent deacons, or to have no deacons but more priests?[54]

Cardinal Spellman's objections were echoed by Cardinal Antonio Bacci, who thought the diaconate, especially if opened to married men, was not necessary and was perhaps even dangerous to priestly celibacy and priestly vocations. He went so far as to indicate that any young man would prefer to enter a ministry that allowed him a much easier way to serve the church (without celibacy), and that therefore vocations to the priesthood would fall drastically. He strongly urged the council to delete the notion of a married diaconate. Bishop Alonso de Mello, in a written animadversion, observed that in his opinion the restoration of the diaconate *in any manner, in any place*, was extremely dangerous. He claimed that in today's world, it was not possible to find "men of good repute, filled with the Holy Spirit and wisdom" as Peter called for in Acts 6:1–6. Bishop de Mello asserted: "There are no people like this today, not even among Catholics" *(Non sunt, nec inter catholicos)*.[55]

The first speaker in favor of restoration was Cardinal Julius August Doepfner.[56] He strongly urged acceptance of the draft and addressed the concerns already raised. He supported the inclusion of the diaconate in a dogmatic document because the issue of the orders of the hierarchy of the church is a dogmatic issue, a part of the divine law and therefore an essential part of the nature of the church. He pointed out that the diaconate, ever since Trent, had been seen as part of the sacramental priesthood. Looking to the present situation in many parts of the world, Doepfner pointed to the fact that there are many persons, many of them married, who are serving the church in diaconal roles. He asked, "Why should these people be denied the grace of the sacrament?"[57] The law of celibacy is sacred, but it should not become an obstacle for the evolution of beneficial ways to serve that may be necessary in our times.

Cardinal Landazuri Ricketts, speaking for himself and ninety-five other Latin American fathers, spoke to the benefits of a renewed diaconate.[58] While many functions (which he does not articulate) of the diaconate were already done by laypersons, there were still others that the deacon would carry out as an ordained member of the hierarchy. The restoration of the diaconate was not to lessen the role of the laity but to increase it, and that the lay apostolate, while most important, is not an end in itself.

It was at this point that Cardinal Suenens presented what is arguably the strongest and most coherent argument for the diaconate evident in the documents.[59] Before considering his intervention, however, one should first examine his original recommendation in support of a renewed permanent diaconate. During the antepreparatory phase, Suenens indicated his support in his letter of November 10, 1959. First alluding to the 1957 address by Pius XII in which the pope had observed that the question of restoring the diaconate was not yet ripe but was worthy of continued attention, Suenens wrote that the council would provide a most appropriate opportunity to highlight this question. He wrote that a diaconate distinct and separate from the priesthood, a state in which married men might also be admitted, would be part of a movement of overall renewal in the church. The diaconate was one of several ministries consistently and traditionally recognized in the life of the church. Suenens wrote that the church has a command from the Lord to proclaim the gospel to all peoples and to baptize all nations. Such a task is impossible without the coming together of all the faithful, especially those whose lives are devoted to the mission of evangelization. The deacon is presented as a minister of this evangelization who can be assigned to serve in different ways depending on the pastoral needs of the area in which he serves, including the proclamation of the gospel, catechesis, and other areas for the work of redemption. Cardinal Suenens would write later, "Undoubtedly, this decision [to renew the permanent diaconate] was made for pastoral reasons, but these were not the only factors operative. The restoration of a Permanent Diaconate finds its fundamental clarification and justification in the sacramental character of the diaconate itself."[60] During the conciliar debate, it would be Suenens himself who would attempt to articulate this "sacramental character of the diaconate."

We return now to Cardinal Suenens's intervention. He began by outlining the theological principles on which the diaconate is based. Citing the authority of scripture, the apostolic fathers, constant tradition, and the liturgical books of East and West, he spoke of the many charisms evident throughout the church, distinct from the priesthood, which were set up to provide direct assistance to the bishop in the care of the poor and the nurturing of the community. To say that these tasks can be given to laypersons does not mean that the diaconate is not needed. These tasks should be given only to persons (whether ordained or not) who have the necessary graces. The church has the right to the benefit of all the graces given to it by God, including the graces of the diaconate.

Suenens then turned to the situation in the contemporary world. He urged the fathers not to make a universal decision for or against the diaconate. Rather, they should decide if there was any area or situation that might benefit from it, and then phrase its decision in such a way as to enable it to take effect in those regions in which the bishops decided it was appropriate. In other words, the council should not close off universally any means by which the grace of God may flow into the church. Therefore (quoting from the draft), "where episcopal conferences judge the restoration of a permanent diaconate opportune, they should be free to introduce it."[61]

In reviewing the debate from this point on, the arguments in favor of the restoration take on a much more positive note, with fewer objections being raised. Suenens's intervention signaled a milestone in the debate, for his articulation of a theology of the diaconate helped focus for the fathers the essential elements of the issue, and not just the functional dimension of the diaconate. In addition, he added an important tactical element previously lacking in the argumentation; namely, that the council was not being asked to dictate a universal course of action for the church. Rather, their duty was to look for ways in which bishops (and conferences of bishops) could be enabled to use whatever means necessary and available to provide pastoral care for their people. One such means was the diaconate. Finally, this was a way of supporting the developing discussions the bishops were having concerning the nature and role of the episcopate itself. With the bishop seen as responsible for the ordering of ministry in his own diocese, in collaboration and discussion with fellow bishops in the region, the concepts of episcopal collegiality, subsidiarity, and collaboration were highlighted.

Following Cardinal Suenens's address, the discussion continued, but all subsequent interventions show the influence of his thought. Cardinal Paul-Marie Richaud spoke strongly in favor of the restoration (although he had originally opposed the proposal during the preparatory phase), especially with the option given to the conferences of bishops to decide whether or not to request its implementation.[62] Bishop Franjo Šeper cited three reasons why he favored the restoration: (1) the nature of the diaconate itself, (2) ecumenical reasons (between the Eastern and Western churches), and (3) pastoral reasons.[63] He disagreed with those who feared that ordaining married men to the diaconate would weaken the celibacy of priests. On the contrary, he stated that the service of married deacons would strengthen the church. He concluded by saying (like Suenens) that the council was not to say "Amen" to the status quo but to provide for the future needs of the church.[64] Bishop Frane Franič rejected the proposal, but for many of the same reasons cited previously: (1) it would be dangerous for vocations to the priesthood; (2) it would be dangerous for the law of celibacy; (3) it would be dangerous to have a married diaconate in many parts of the world; (4) that a permanent, married diaconate was unnecessary; (5) that it would be easier to install laymen into various ministries than to restore the diaconate; and (6) for economic reasons.

From this point on, the speakers emphasized points previously made, either for or against restoration. Vorgrimler reports that a total of forty-five bishops, speaking on behalf of 795 fathers, spoke in favor of restoration. Twenty-five speakers, representing only eighty-two fathers, rejected the idea. However, because the debate on the diaconate was part of the much larger debate on the episcopacy, and particularly on the notion of episcopal collegiality, a document consisting of five questions was drafted which sought "to learn the mind of the assembly as exactly as possible."[65] The first four questions concerned the sacramental nature of the episcopate and the relationship between papal primacy and episcopal collegiality. The fifth question pertained to the diaconate:

> Whether it pleases the Fathers to have the schema consider the opportuneness of restoring the diaconate as a distinct and permanent level of the sacred ministry, as necessary for the Church in various regions.[66]

Since the debate on the diaconate was so heated concerning the possibility of a married diaconate, the subject of the restoration of the permanent diaconate in theory (i.e., with no mention of celibacy or any other particular questions of ecclesiastical discipline) was added to the list of questions on the episcopate. The vote, taken on October 30, 1963, shows that of 2,120 votes cast, 1,588 were in favor of restoration and 525 were against it (seven were invalid).[67]

Armed with the opinions expressed during the debate and the vote of October 30, the text was revised one final time.

The Final Draft: **Lumen Gentium** *(1964)*

The third draft of *Lumen Gentium* was distributed at the Eightieth General Assembly on September 15, 1964. The text on the diaconate was now paragraph 29 of chapter 3.[68] The text was in two parts and greatly expanded over the previous draft. The first part deals with the office of deacon in general, and some of the functions of the deacon in particular. The second part deals with the rationale and procedures for the diaconate's restoration as a permanent order, one that is open to married men.

Part One

The diaconate is still described as in a "lower order of the hierarchy," an order in which he is installed through the imposition of hands. The diaconate is clearly a part of the sacrament of orders according to the text, since deacons are "strengthened by sacramental grace." The ancient threefold ministry of the deacon is stressed more strongly than in the second draft. Instead of the rather limited list of functions of the former draft, this one describes the deacon's ministry as "a service of liturgy, word and charity to the People of God," which he exercises in communion with the bishop and his presbyterate: one ministry, with the responsibilities shared among the three orders. The bishop has ultimate authority and responsibility, but his priests and deacons, who share in his ministry, assist him.

The ten functions listed are clearly illustrative and not meant to be exhaustive. They expand on the theme of *diakonia* in liturgy, the Word, and charity. Deacons administer baptism solemnly (as ordinary ministers, a change from the second draft), care for and distribute the Eucharist, assist at and bless marriages in the name of the church (not listed in the second draft), bring Viaticum to the dying (not listed in the second draft), proclaim sacred scripture to the faithful, instruct and exhort the people, preside at the worship and prayer of the faithful to minister sacramentals, and preside at funerals and burials. These and additional functions are summarized by saying that deacons are dedicated to works of charity and administration.

Part Two

Having outlined the *munera* of the diaconate, the draft declared them to be of the highest importance to the life of the church *(ad vitam Ecclesiae summopere necessaria)*. But the current discipline of the Latin church made it difficult for them to be provided in many areas. Therefore, in the future, the diaconate can be restored as a permanent level of the hierarchy. Regional conferences of bishops, with the approval of the pope, can decide whether these deacons should be appointed *pro cura animarum* and where. Finally, it would be reserved to the pope to decide whether the diaconate could be conferred on married men of mature age or on qualified young celibate or married men. A *nota explicativa* informed the fathers that this section would be handled by separate votes to allow a precise counting on the critical question of celibacy and the diaconate. The commission already knew, from the results of the voting on October 30 that the council wanted to restore the diaconate. It was still the sticky question of celibacy that was troublesome.

The Voting on Celibacy[69]

Lumen Gentium was divided into thirty-nine sections for voting, with a final vote on the entire document taken on October 30, 1964; five of these sections related directly to the diaconate. Specifically, paragraph 29 (on the diaconate) was divided into five sections (35–39), each with its own vote. On October 28, votes were taken on sections 35 and 36. These were fairly certain, since they pertained to the office of deacon in particular and the desirability to restore it as a permanent rank. The section on the *munus diaconi* (section 35) passed with a vote of 2,055 to 94; the voting on restoration (section 36) was 1,903 pro and 242 contra.

On October 29 the tougher questions were faced. Section 37 included the text that the conferences of bishops needed the consent of the pope to restore the diaconate in their regions. This was passed by 1,523 to 702. The diaconate could be conferred on mature married men (1,598 pro, 629 contra). But the clause allowing diaconate to be conferred on younger men without the law of celibacy was rejected by a vote of 1,364 to 839. (It is interesting to note, however, that over 800 bishops had no objection to ordaining younger men deacons *without* the obligation of celibacy.[70])

The Final Text

With the voting complete, the only change to the text that was necessary was the final sentence, which now read, "With the consent of the Roman pontiff it will be possible to confer this diaconate on married men of more mature age, and also on suitable young men for whom, however, the law of celibacy must remain in force."[71]

Conclusion

Many reasons led to the decision of the Second Vatican Council to renew the diaconate. But for many of the bishops, the sacramental diaconate became a way to recognize the lessons learned so tragically at Dachau: that the church itself was Christ's servant in and for the world, and that there was a need for a sacramental expression of that diaconal nature. At the very end of the council, Pope Paul VI reflected on the work of the council and what it meant to the church.

> We stress that the teaching of the Council is channeled in one direction, the service of humankind, of every con-

> dition, in every weakness and need. The Church has declared herself a servant of humanity at the very time when her teaching role and her pastoral government have, by reason of this Church solemnity, assumed greater splendor and vigor. However, the idea of service has been central.[72]

This vision of the church-as-servant finds a concrete sacramental expression in the renewed diaconate. Over the last forty years much has been done and learned about the diaconate throughout the world. Nonetheless, we have only begun to scratch the surface. Dachau—and one must now add all of the horrific and senseless acts of terror, violence, and horror that have taken place since—demands a new way of thinking about the diaconate. Keeping the radical roots of diaconate renewal in mind will be a constant inspiration and challenge as this renewed ordained ministry continues to develop and to respond to the needs of the contemporary church.

Part Two

TOWARD A THEOLOGY OF THE DIACONATE

God's love for us is fundamental for our lives, and it raises important questions about who God is and who we are. In considering this, we immediately find ourselves hampered by a problem of language.

—Benedict XVI, *Deus Caritas Est* 2

6

CHARTING A THEOLOGY OF DIACONATE: AN EXERCISE IN ECCLESIAL CARTOGRAPHY[1]

When Jesus speaks in his parables of the shepherd who goes after the lost sheep, of the woman who looks for the lost coin, of the father who goes to meet and embrace his prodigal son, these are no mere words: they constitute an explanation of his very being and activity. His death on the Cross is the culmination of that turning of God against himself in which he gives himself in order to raise man up and save him. This is love in its most radical form.
—Benedict XVI, *Deus Caritas Est* 12

Introduction: Theology and the Diaconate

The challenges faced when attempting to devise a coherent theology of the diaconate remind me of the famous Ph.D. comprehensive examination question that demands: "Describe the history of the papacy from its origins to the present day; concentrate especially but not exclusively on the social, political, economic, religious, and philosophical impact on Europe, Asia, the Americas, and Africa. Be brief, concise, and specific." Nonetheless, however difficult the task, the need to develop theologies of the diaconate remains no less necessary, even critical, at this point in time in the life of the church.

Perhaps the biggest challenge is the simple fact that comprehensive, systematic theological discourse on the diaconate has rarely, if ever, been done. Given the history of the diaconate and its potential as a renewed order, this is more than a little surprising. Consider the vision of one theologian on the eve of the Second Vatican Council, Dom Augustinus Kerkvoorde, OSB. Born in Belgium in 1913, he joined the Benedictines in 1932 and was ordained a priest in 1939. After earning a doctorate in Theology from Louvain in 1943, Kerkvoorde wrote extensively on sacramental theology and eucharistic spirituality. Like Karl Rahner and others, he became interested in the possibilities of a renewed diaconate shortly after the Second World War. In 1962, Karl Rahner invited Dom Augustinus to contribute to the major text he was editing on the diaconate, *Diaconia in Christo*.

In his article, Kerkvoorde observed that a theology of the diaconate had not been needed in the past since the diaconate had been for more than a millennium more of a "theoretical" function on the road to the priesthood, which, as such, did not "arouse a demand for a thoroughly elaborated dogma about the diaconate."[2] However, he forecast a change if the council renewed the diaconate:

> Once it becomes apparent that this rank may be revived in the near term, such theologies will undoubtedly spring up like mushrooms....There will be plenty of authors and publishers who will routinely pounce on this unexpected inheritance. If by that time theology has not succeeded in setting up some clear and simple principles for the restoration of the diaconate, and if its deepest meaning has not been made visible for both the learned and for the simple faithful, then this ancient and divinely established institution will easily soon be in danger of going down the same path as many other ecclesiastical institutions. The diaconate, which should take its normal place in the Church as an institution that will bring both balance and vitality, runs the risk of becoming a superfluous organ, smothered and frustrated—that is, if it is not first choked to death in the literature and in controversy before it can even be reborn.[3]

One might wish that Kerkvoorde's vision of significant theological activity on the diaconate would have been realized. Certainly there have been major contributions to diaconal theology,[4] but they have certainly not "sprung up like mushrooms," nor have many authors "pounced upon this unexpected inheritance"! Nonetheless, Kerkvoorde's caution was well founded that if the deepest meaning of a renewed diaconate were not made "visible" for "the learned and the simple," then the diaconate as a permanent order would soon become superfluous, smothered, and frustrated. His vision that the diaconate could be an order of "vitality and balance" seems even more appealing in today's world.

Nearly thirty-five years after Kerkvoorde's challenge, the Bishops' Committee on the Diaconate in 1996 released the results of a national study on the diaconate in which they identified seven "Issues for the Future."[5] The very first of these posed the following question, "How are the issues of the deacon's identity and acceptance to be resolved in light of the tendency of many to use the deacon to address the present shortage of priests?"[6] Another issue is closely related to the first: "What are the best means of response to the demonstrated need for a more focused effort on the national and diocesan levels to form and challenge deacons toward roles and ministries more clearly differentiated from the ministerial priesthood?"[7] The bishops conclude, "The challenge of the next decades will be to make these developments more theologically rich and thus to expand the deacon's sense of ministry, evangelization, and service continually, even beyond the parish."[8] While there is certainly much more than theology packed into these questions, theology is a necessary partner in the conversations demanded to address these and so many other related issues.

Plotting a Course: Ten Points of Reference

The 1998 *Basic Norms for the Formation of Permanent Deacon* (BNFPD) correctly asserts that "the effectiveness of the formation of permanent deacons depends to a great extent on the theological understanding of the diaconate that underlies it."[9] This theological understanding "offers the co-ordinates for establishing and guiding the formation process and, at the same time, lays down the end to be attained."[10] However, the document goes on to acknowledge that "the almost total disappearance of the permanent diaconate from the Church of the West for more than a millennium has certainly made it more difficult to understand the profound reality of this ministry."[11] It continues that there are nonetheless certain "authoritative points of reference" and proceeds to identify six of them,[12] acknowledging that these are not the only points of reference and that even these will need to be "developed and deepened."[13] Daring to go "where angels might fear to tread" (to quote Alexander Pope), I now propose ten points of reference that might contribute toward this development and deepening.

1. A proper theological understanding of the diaconate presumes a "new way of thinking" about the sacramental nature of the church and its ordering of ministry.

When I was a Commander in the Navy, one of the first things I learned is the necessary plotting of a course by selection of the right charts of the seas being sailed. Consider the various types of projections we use in our maps and charts: Mercator, Robinson, Polar, the Albers Equal Area, the Lambert Conformal Conic, the Mollweide, Orthographic, Gnomonic, and so many others. Why are so many needed? The reasons are simple and basic: to enhance accuracy and to avoid distortion. Those must also be the goals of the theologian: to enhance accuracy and avoid distortion.

Just as different map projections force us to look at the same piece of the earth or ocean in a new way, what is needed for a theology of ministry is a new way of thinking. Both Paul VI and John Paul II spoke of the *novus mentis habitus* ("new way of thinking") reflected in the discussions and documents of the Second Vatican Council. For example, during the preparation of the 1983 *Code of Canon Law*, Paul VI reminded the Code Commission that this new way of thinking provided by the council was to be reflected not only in the practical applications of the law but in the very structures and processes of the code itself. In promulgating the finished product, John Paul II reaffirmed that what is new in the new code is more than a few practical adjustments; it is the newness of Vatican II itself.[14]

As is well known, of course, critical components of the council's new way of thinking involved the way we describe the very nature and mission of the church itself. This is illustrated through any number of examples from the council and its documents. However, one particular event at the council seems to illustrate this vision quite powerfully and succinctly. On December 7, 1965, the day before the solemn closing of the Second Vatican Council in St. Peter's Square, Pope Paul VI offered his own reflection on the ultimate significance of the council's work in these words:

> We stress that the teaching of the Council is channeled in one direction, the service of humankind, of every condition, in every weakness and need. The Church has declared herself a servant of humanity at the very time when her teaching role and her pastoral government have, by reason of this Church solemnity, assumed greater splendor and vigor. However, the idea of service has been central.[15]

In short, the "new way of thinking" proposed by the council is reflected in a servant ecclesiology. This servant ecclesiology, then, becomes the proper "chart" on which to plot the course for a diaconal theology. It permits a new way of thinking about many things: about the meaning of sacramental initiation; about the resulting nature of ministry in general and ordained ministry in particular; about the multifaceted and multidimensional relationships that are involved in lives of Christian discipleship; about the nuances that exist in the sacrament of orders itself. Several contemporary theologians, including Richard Gaillardetz, have called for a renewed effort at finding new ways to relate commissioned, installed, appointed, and ordained ministries. This creative approach reflects the challenge of not putting new wine into old wineskins (Luke 5:37), and a similar new way of thinking will now inform each of the following points.

2. The diaconate is part of the mystery of the church as trinitarian communion in missionary tension.

Using a phrase first found in *Pastores Dabo Vobis*, the 1998 *Basic Norms for the Formation of Permanent Deacons* cites as an essential theological reference point the fact that "we must consider the diaconate, like every other Christian identity, from within the Church which is understood as a mystery of trinitarian communion in missionary tension." Pope John Paul II was fond of saying that the Trinitarian communion is "model," "reference," and "archetype" of ecclesial communion. One theologian has captured this relationship briefly but well when she writes:

> Our baptism into the paschal mystery of Jesus immerses us into a God who is not the poverty of aloneness, God as an isolated individual, but God as the richness of trinitarian communion. Nowhere else is there such absolute oneness and yet such utterly unique personhood. Nowhere else does the mystery of human persons called to both autonomy and communion find its source and goal than in the infinite uniqueness and communion of the persons who are God. And precisely in not running away from the price of our own personhood we begin to discover that the proclamations central to the Christian message are not simply doctrines to be believed, but reality that can be experienced, reality that can transform experience.[16]

Theologies of diaconate—as indeed *all* theologies of *ministry*—must begin with a full appreciation of the power, risk, and mystery of sacramental initiation into the Trinity. This provides a common sacramental identity while establishing the possibilities for creative, dynamic, Spirit-filled, and transformative mission. Categories of theological discourse that insist on excessive distinctions between "the baptized" over against "the ordained" will benefit from dialogue with trinitarian theology as the archetype of all ecclesial ministry. Furthermore, ongoing intensive research into the relationship of sacramental initiation on the varieties of commissioned, installed, instituted, and ordained ministries must be encouraged.

The profound implications of sacramental initiation and trinitarian communion on the categories of contemporary ministries, which of course includes the diaconate, need further development. The second phrase of this set of coordinates, much as longitude is to latitude—that this trinitarian communion is lived "in missionary tension"—gives communion a vector, a direction, a goal: in short, a mission. In many ways, the points that follow are all attempts at describing facets of this mission. But as part of our new way of thinking, perhaps we can take a powerful insight from Cardinal Roger Mahony of Los Angeles. In a recent address to the eucharistic congress held in the Diocese of El Paso, Texas, he shared his conviction that "it is not so much that the church has a mission; it is rather more that the mission has a church."

> What is this mission? It is none other than that of Jesus, Christ, the Word, and of the Holy Spirit, the gift of God's love dwelling in our hearts. Jesus' mission is to announce the time of God's favor, the coming of the reign of God. Jesus proclaimed the reign of God as the fulfillment of God's hope, desire and intention for the world now and to come. In God's reign, truth, holiness, justice, love and peace will hold sway forever. Jesus established the church to continue and further this mission....This mission is so central to the word and work of Jesus that the Second Vatican Council affirmed and emphasized that *mission* defines the church. The church in every dimension of its life and practice exists for mission: to proclaim in word and deed the reign of God to people in every culture, time and place.[17]

The mission of the church is shared by all in communion; the participation of one ordained into the order of deacons is collaborative and collegial, one that speaks the words of Christ in his name and in the name of the church. The deacon acts as a minister ordered in the Spirit by his bishop, an instrument of Christ and of the church Christ established to carry on his mission.

3. The christological dimension of diaconate is expressive of the kenōsis *of God.*

John Paul II wrote that "the prime commitment of theology is seen to be the understanding of God's *kenōsis*, a grand and mysterious truth for the human mind, which finds it inconceivable that suffering and death can express a love which gives itself and seeks nothing in return."[18] While much of the literature that has developed on the nature of the ordained ministry has focused on the priesthood, very little has been done to address the nature of an ordained ministry that is *not* sacerdotal. This means that existing categories of theological discourse must be carefully critiqued to determine their applicability to the diaconate.

While discussions of the sacerdotal orders often speak of their relationship to the priesthood of Christ, it seems to me that a possibility for a particularly diaconal language might be found in the notion of *kenōsis* itself, as found, for example, in the famous hymn in Philippians, in which we hear that Christ "emptied himself, taking the form of a slave, becoming as human beings are" and even accepting death on a cross (Phil 2:6–11 New Jerusalem Bible). It is this very act of self-emptying that results in Christ's exaltation; this counterintuitive path of emptying to exaltation becomes the very path for Christ's disciples to follow.[19]

Christ's own *kenōsis* is of course a part of each Christian's life, and of the life of the Christian community. Jean Corbon speaks of two *kenōses* when he writes:

> Having become the Church, we must live the Church's life as a *kenosis* of the Spirit. The gift to us of God's ever faithful love must be answered by an authentic life of charity which the Holy Spirit pours into our hearts. We too must give our gift fully; that is, we must divest ourselves of ourselves in that same *kenosis* of love.[20]

Ordination to any order celebrates a sacramental empowerment of the church. The church is empowered by the Spirit with the particular gifts of the ordinand now being placed at the permanent and public service of the church itself. Through ordination the deacon is likewise empowered, not with the *sacra potestas* often associated with the sacerdotal orders of bishops and presbyters but with a *kenotic power*, a power or strength to empty himself in service to the church through his participation in the apostolic ministry of the bishop.

The linkage between the apostles' exercise of authority and kenotic self-sacrifice in imitation of Christ is found in several places in the New Testament, as discussed previously in chapter 2. During his homily at the Mass of the Lord's Supper in 2004, Pope John Paul II pointed out that Jesus, in washing the feet of the apostles, performed an act "that normally would be done by a servant, thus wishing to impress on the minds of the Apostles the meaning of what would shortly happen. In fact, the passion and death are the fundamental service of love by which the Son of God freed humankind from sin."[21] The implication of this passage for the identity and ministry of the apostles is profound, since it links the kenotic self-sacrifice of Christ to the life of the disciple. "To 'have part with Jesus' through washing means to be part of the self-giving love that will bring Jesus' life to an end, symbolically anticipated by the foot washing."[22]

Furthermore, those who would be leaders in the community of disciples are to be identified by their own self-sacrificing love in imitation of the *kenōsis* of Christ. As seen in chapter 2, quoting Francis J. Moloney:

> The theme of death is behind the use of the word *hypodeigma* [v. 15]. This expression, found only here in the N[ew] T[estament]...is associated with exemplary death. Jesus' exhortation is not to moral performance but to imitation of his self-gift....Entrance into the Johannine community of disciples meant taking the risk of accepting the *hypodeigma* of Jesus, a commitment to love even if it led to death.[23]

The *Directory for the Ministry and Life of Permanent Deacons* concludes:

> The primary and most fundamental relationship [of the deacon] must be with Christ, who assumed the condition of a slave for love of the Father and mankind. In virtue of ordination the deacon is truly called to act in conformity with Christ the Servant. (#47)

Kenotic power is not the exclusive province of the deacon, but it is the deacon who serves as the sacramental focus for the *diakonia* of the entire community. That is why Patrick McCaslin and Michael G. Lawler can say, "A parish, which is a local incarnation of Church and of Jesus, is not sacramentally whole if it is without either priest or deacon."[24] Just as the presbyter shares in the sacred power of the priesthood with the bishop, so too does the deacon share in the kenotic power of the diaconate with the bishop.

The challenge for the contemporary diaconate is to realize the ramifications of this *kenōsis*, a totally self-sacrificial strength for service. In real terms this means that deacons must divorce themselves from any expressions, attitudes, and behaviors that smack of clericalism or the acquisition of power and authority for its own sake. This means that there should be something unique in the ways in which deacons serve that demonstrates this kenotic dimension. Excessive concern over the wearing of clerical attire or clerical forms of address, or an attitude that certain ministries may be "theirs" by right of ordination may be signs in opposition to the kenotic nature of the diaconate.

4. The "ad intra" and "ad extra" methodology of Vatican II can assist in the development of theologies of ministry.

At the suggestion of Cardinal Leon-Josef Suenens of Belgium, Pope John XXIII decided that the council's work would examine the church both *ad intra* and *ad extra*. This balanced approach helped the council fathers focus not only on the internal structures of the church but on the church's relationships and mission as well.

Applying this approach to the nature of the diaconate within the constellation of ministries would seem to be a necessary and helpful dimension of theological activity. Ultimately, the meaning of diaconal ordination is found not only within itself but most significantly in its relationship with others. As theologian Edward Kilmartin wrote: "Ministries of the Church must be consistent with the nature of the Church, or more precisely, derived from the nature of the Church. The way in which one conceives the nature of Church determines whether a particular form of ministry is acceptable."[25] Much of the decision to renew the diaconate as a permanent order of the hierarchy came from a recovery of an ancient notion by many of the bishops at the council that the church itself was diaconal. Such a renewed emphasis on the *diakonia* of the church supported the renewal of a permanent order that sacramentalizes that *diakonia*. The renewed diaconate, therefore, is "derived from the nature of the Church."

John Paul II, in his 1987 address to the diaconate community gathered in Detroit made the following observation:

> The service of the deacon is the Church's service sacramentalized. Yours is not just one ministry among others, but it is truly meant to be, as Paul VI described it, a "driving force" for the Church's *diakonia*. You are meant to be living signs of the servanthood of Christ's Church.[26]

The challenge for theology, of course, is to develop a theology of diaconate that is consistent with, and respectful of, the sacramental identity and legitimate ministries of all other persons. When theologians consider the sacramental meaning of the deacon's ordination, they must do so in concert with the sacramental meaning of initiation as well as the sacramental meaning of presbyteral and episcopal ordinations. Conversely, when theologians distinguish the sacramental meanings of lay ministry, lay ecclesial ministry, and the ordained ministries of priests and bishops, they must do so without ignoring, minimizing, or doing violence to the sacramental meaning of diaconal ordination.

5. The permanence of the diaconate is at the core of the deacon's identity.

Despite often facile statements to the contrary, the diaconate never disappeared from the ordained ministries of the church. From the earliest scriptural references to the diaconate in the letters of St. Paul through today, the church has had deacons. What has happened, of course, is that the *way* in which the diaconate has been exercised has changed over the centuries. When the Second Vatican Council spoke of the diaconate, it focused on its renewal, revival, and restoration as a *permanent* order, in contrast to the *transitional* order it had become. In other words, the emphasis by the council was less on the "renewal" than on the "permanence" of the order. Expressed differently, it might be said that what was "restored" was the *permanence* of the diaconate, *not* the diaconate itself.

This new-found permanence was in sharp and radical contrast to the practice of more than a millennium, in which all ordinations were transitional, leading inexorably to the "pinnacle" of presbyteral ordination. Many theologians, including Thomas Aquinas, saw no sacramental significance to a bishop's ordination, seeing the bishop primarily as a priest who had received greater administrative jurisdiction. In the 1917 Pio-Benedictine *Code of Canon Law*, for example, we read that "first tonsure and orders are to be conferred only on those who are proposed for ascending to the presbyterate and who seem correctly understood as, at some point in the future, being worthy priests." Vatican II deliberately reversed this practice, reclaiming the proper sacramental identity of the deacon's and the bishop's ordination and, in the case of the deacon at least, permitting this state of life to be exercised in a permanent way. The sacramental configuration of the deacon to Christ the servant is a permanent effect of ordination.

It is for this reason that the subject of retaining the transitional diaconate continues to be a matter of significance in theological discourse. The maintenance of a transitional order of ministry seems to be contradicted by the council's decisions concerning tonsure, the minor orders, the subdiaconate, and the restoration of the permanency of the diaconate. The only sacramental vestiges of the *cursus honorum* rest with those deacons who transition into the presbyterate, and those presbyters who transition into the episcopate. The use of one sacramental order as a necessary prerequisite to another is a pattern that, at a minimum, is no longer absolute and should be most closely examined. This is especially true if the sacramental potential of the renewed permanent diaconate is to be realized. The very permanence of the order of deacons lies at the theological core of the deacon's sacramental identity and ministry.

6. Theologies of diaconate must recognize the unique sacramental relationship between the deacon and the bishop.

Vatican II reminds us that the bishop is the head of the diocesan church. It is the bishop who by virtue of his ordination has the fullness of responsibility for the *diakonia* of word, sacrament, and charity in the church. The bishop is the chief teacher, the chief liturgist, as well as the "Father of the Poor." It is the bishop who, in the words of Susan Wood, Rick Gaillardetz, and others, "orders" ministry in the church. He appoints, installs, commissions, and ordains members of the diocesan church for service.

In a particular sacramental way, the deacon has his own unique relationship with the bishop. From the earliest scriptural references to the diaconate and throughout its "golden age," the deacon and his exercise of ministry have been linked to that of the bishop. This unique relationship continues to be stressed in contemporary magisterial documents. Liturgically it is expressed most significantly when, during the ordination of a deacon, *only* the bishop lays hands on the ordinand, contrasted with the ordination of presbyters and bishops, where *all* the members of those orders lay hands on the ordinands. The deacon, from the moment of ordination, is "ordered" to a participation in the bishop's own ministry. On certain occasions, some bishops continue to wear the deacon's dalmatic under their chasubles, again as a sign of their own diaconal responsibilities.

Helmut Hoping writes:

> The presbyter represents the bishop *in situ*, that is, in the parishes, where they have governance of the parishes to

> which they have been assigned, and where they are responsible for presiding at the Eucharist.…The deacon also has a share of the apostolic mission of the bishop. The deacon represents the bishop *in situ* in *diakonia*, which…is at the direct disposal of the bishop.[27]

One often rightly hears of the special sacramental and sacerdotal relationship that bonds the bishop with his body of priests. One should also hear of an analogous sacramental and diaconal relationship that bonds the bishop—the chief deacon of the diocese—with his body of deacons.

7. *The diaconate renewed by the Second Vatican Council is not simply a restoration of the ancient diaconate.*

The contemporary diaconate is a new expression of this ancient ministry in the church. It is important to examine how this particular ministry relates to other ministries in the church. This renewed incarnation of the diaconate has emerged in a century of extraordinary social, economic, and political upheaval, and during a time of rapid—and some would say explosive—growth in lay ministry, coupled with a drastic decline in the number of presbyters. In light of these factors, it is important to discern the proper areas of ministry for the diaconate, so that it does not develop into a kind of substitute for sacerdotal ministry, on the one hand, or a clericalized form of lay ministry, on the other. The *Directory for the Ministry and Life of Permanent Deacons* states:

> In every case it is important, however, that deacons fully exercise their ministry, in preaching, in the liturgy and in charity to the extent that circumstances permit. They should not be relegated to marginal duties, be made merely to act as substitutes, nor discharge duties normally entrusted to non-ordained members of the faithful. Only in this way will the true identity of permanent deacons as ministers of Christ become apparent and the

> impression avoided that deacons are simply lay people particularly involved in the life of the Church. (#40)

While a study of the scriptural and patristic evidence is important to an understanding of the diversity of function exercised by the ancient diaconate, it is critical to emphasize that the contemporary diaconate exists in a different set of cultural, geographical, political, and ecclesial realities. What history shows is an order flexible in its exercise and adaptable to a variety of pastoral situations; this makes the diaconate an order pregnant with potential in meeting contemporary needs. It would be unfortunate to attempt a rigid "restoration" of the ancient diaconate and thereby lose its inherent freedom for ministerial response. The contemporary diaconate is grounded on the balanced exercise of the threefold ministry; it is precisely in this balanced exercise that the deacon serves as a sacrament of unity, living through his ministry and life the marriage of witness to Christ, the praise of God, and the care of neighbor. Christian discipleship demands *martyria*, *leitourgia*, and *diakonia:* the deacon serves as a public and permanent sign of the unity binding these three dimensions together. His particular role is to remind the church of its own sacramentality, of its own *diakonia*, of the church's responsibility to be a "sign and instrument" and "leaven and soul" in creating a more just world (*Lumen Gentium* 1; *Gaudium et Spes* 40).

8. The renewal of the diaconate must be understood within the broader context of reform and renewal.

In chapter 5, we saw that the first stirrings of a renewed diaconate rippled through Germany in the nineteenth and early twentieth centuries. This was not an isolated movement for enhanced works of charity; rather, it was part of an overall movement of renewal as the church attempted to discover its relationship to the modern world. This contextualized proposal for the renewed diaconate was further developed following Dachau and the Second World War and may be seen in the discussions of Vatican II. In the ongoing development of the contemporary diaconate it is necessary to consider the diaconate in this broader context. In certain areas, the diaconate is perceived as a movement in opposition to reform and renewal, perpetuating an ancient, now-antiquated hierarchical order. As experience with the renewed diaconate continues, this context of reform and renewal will need to be developed: as the church continues to find creative ways to meet the needs of an increasingly complex world, the church will need all of its resources, and the diaconate is one of those instruments of renewal. The diaconate recognizes the heritage of the church's tradition in light of living faith and the constant presence and action of the Spirit.

9. The deacon's ministry of word, sacrament, and charity is a function of leadership across the full spectrum of the triple **munus** *of word, sacrament, and charity.*

The entire diaconal ministry revolves around pastoral leadership, not in terms of positional authority resulting from a participation in the bishop's own *episkopē* (e.g., offices such as diocesan bishop, vicar general, or pastor), but in the sense of leading, inspiring, enabling and modeling for other members of the church what servant-leadership can mean in living the demands of Christian discipleship in the contemporary world. The question of the relationship of the *episkopē* that characterizes the sacerdotal orders of bishop and presbyter to other forms of pastoral leadership demands critical examination that goes far beyond the scope of this presentation. Similarly, the question of how the deacon, who participates in a unique, nonsacerdotal way in the pastoral ministry of the bishop, might share in the bishop's *episkopē*, is also unresolved and in need of further explication. However, it may at least be said that the deacon is a leader in the community; the deacon, who receives no unique "power of order," is empowered to speak and act in the name of Christ and of the church. Leadership is a baptismal charism, to be exercised in some way by all; leadership affirmed by ordination is leadership recognized permanently and publicly for the good of the church. Nathan Mitchell has written:

> By restoring the diaconate as a permanent role with the church's ordained leadership, Paul VI implicitly broke

> the long-standing connection between ordination and "sacramental power."...Theirs is a ministry, rooted like all others in a recognition of baptismal charism, that places pastoral leadership before sacramental power. The diaconate represents, then, those New Testament qualities of ministry which Schillebeeckx has aptly described as "the apostolic building up of the community through preaching, admonition and leadership." The restoration of the diaconate is thus important not because it resurrects an ancient order that had all but faded in the West, but because it affirms the principle that *recognition of pastoral leadership is the fundamental basis for calling a Christian to ordained ministry.*[28]

Since the deacon's ministry is a participation in the bishop's own *diakonia* of word, sacrament, and charity, and with his public responsibility for the community, the deacon can make others aware of connection between faith and life. "In his ministry of the altar, he lays the needs of human beings on the eucharistic table, and naturally he also speaks of these needs when he preaches. He must make the parish aware of urgent situations of need, motivating them to share with one another and to give practical help."[29]

10. Theologies of the diaconate must explore the untapped potential of expanded diaconal ministry, while avoiding the dangers of functionalism, to which the diaconate is particularly susceptible.

In years past, the ordination of priests and bishops spoke of the communication of powers to be exercised by the newly ordained. For example, the ordination of the presbyter conferred the power to offer the sacrifice of the Mass, and the ordination of the bishop conferred the power to ordain. This led in some circles to the unfortunate tendency to understand ordination as simply the transference of unique powers to the ordinands.

This tendency to a functional approach to the diaconate is both a challenge and an opportunity. Since the deacon shares so many ordinary ministerial functions with presbyters, bishops, and laypersons, the challenge seems to be to find unique diaconal functions as if this will somehow justify the need for the diaconate in the first place. Some bishops, theologians, and parishioners have a sense that if there are no such unique diaconal functions, there is no need for the sacramental diaconate.

However, the shared functionality of the diaconate opens doors for an opportunity of a more profound understanding of sacramental ordination, an understanding that rightly focuses on the sacramental significance of the order as prior to its specific functions. Just as it is well accepted and understood that a proper sacramental understanding of the priesthood lies far beyond a simple listing of a priest's faculties, or that the sacramental understanding of matrimony extends far beyond the listing of a couple's daily activities, so too being a deacon is much more than a simple list of diaconal functions.

How might the deacon, as a sacramental sign of Christ's own *kenōsis*, and as an official minister of the church's *diakonia* on behalf of his bishop, function in a way that extends this sacramental identity in practical ways? Cardinal Walter Kasper has given us much food for thought in his own reflections on the diaconate. For example, he writes that the basic attitude of the deacon must "include a perceptive eye for those suffering distress, illness, or fear. The task is to bring a healing that sets free and empowers them to trust and so to serve and love others in their turn." Furthermore, he challenges deacons to go beyond the provision of simple menial service alone; rather, "the goal of diaconal activity is not simply help, but the empowering of life, so that those who lie prostrate may get to their feet....In some situations, the deacon can and must become the public advocate of the weak and powerless and of all those who have no other voice or lobby."[30]

Much of Kasper's work echoes the vision of the German researchers into the diaconate prior to Vatican II. Those researchers saw the deacon as the bishop's envoy to the most in need. Dedicated to building up the community in the name of the bishop, the deacon would have a very public identity as well as a commensurate responsibility for preaching in the midst of the assembly. This diaconal preaching was to stir up the fires of the community's own *diakonia*.

Kasper describes the deacon as the obvious and public "contact partner" for all those in need, to whom they know they can look confidently for help. As the official representative of the community "he is the obvious contact person" for regional Catholic charity organizations and health centers.

The parish-based ministry of the deacon is extremely important in Kasper's view. He echoes McCaslin and Lawler when he suggests that it would be a good idea to provide at least one deacon for every parish so that the sacramental nature of the parish might be complete. He writes:

> Each parish has to make sure that *diakonia* is realized. This means that faith and preaching, as well as the Eucharist and liturgy must be oriented to *diakonia*. Faith without *diakonia* is not a Christian faith. Preaching without *diakonia* is not Christian preaching. A non-diaconal parish celebrating the Eucharist may express its faith, but its faith remains dead; in the final analysis it cannot find God, as they miss the point that God reveals himself in the people, especially in the poor.[31]

One of Kasper's other ideas is already finding increasing support here in the United States. While the deacon may most frequently be assigned to parish ministry, Kasper writes that deacons should also be considered for assignments with an even broader scope, of city, deanery, and region. In the last national study on the diaconate, alluded to earlier, one of the principal findings was that while deacons have been well-received in parish-based ministry, one of the primary challenges for the future would be "to broaden its ministries in order to be model, animator and facilitator of charity and justice" within the diocesan church.[32] To this end, many bishops now give their deacons a dual assignment: one to a parish and another to a diocesan or regional institution for service.

Kasper writes:

> I am thinking here of hospitals, homes for the elderly, spiritual care in places of work, in prisons, in refugee shelters, etc. I also include co-operation in the leadership

> of a diocese in those regions, where the main question is that of diaconal leadership. In this context, I would like to point out that for the bishop the community of deacons of a diocese can be a welcome panel of advisors. The deacons can act as the eyes and ears of the bishop in identifying areas of need and can help him in his task of being father to the poor.[33]

Such a vision restores some of the ancient responsibilities of the deacon, and the challenges it embodies would be profound, especially in the formation of deacons. Increasingly, ministries involving health care, prisons, and other areas of social concern, are becoming more specialized, with stringent professional standards for their practitioners. Deacons assuming leadership roles in such areas not only will need the personal gifts and talents to serve in these areas, but will often need diocesan support to attain the appropriate professional credentials to enable their participation in them.

Finally, at the even broader level of more regional, national, and international ministries, one may turn again to the *Directory for the Ministry and Life of Permanent Deacons*.

> A deeply felt need in the decision to re-establish the permanent diaconate was and is that of greater and more direct presence of Church ministers in the various spheres of the family, work, school, etc., in addition to existing pastoral structures.[34]

Deacons can and should exercise leadership in community-based service initiatives. Such service can take many forms, defined by the deacon's own skills and qualifications, the sociopolitical structures of the society in which he lives, and the needs to be met.

Furthermore, in terms of canon law, the deacon is the *only* cleric who may participate in various offices of public life, always with the permission of his bishop. While canon 285 §3 prohibits clerics from assuming "public offices which entail a participation in the exercise of civil power," canon 288 exempts permanent deacons from this and other canons. While this does not exhaust the possibilities of community-based ministry, it remains largely unexamined.

While precise data are unavailable, some deacons are serving as judges in civil and criminal courts, elected members of local governments, and even serving in positions of military authority. Such participation by deacons in offices of public life is unexplored territory for many reasons. Certainly there is concern that some forms of public life may be inappropriate for an ordained minister. Still another factor is the risk that the level of public scrutiny on the lives of its officials may be detrimental to the deacon and his role in the church. For these and similar reasons, the participation of a deacon in offices of public life is often an extraordinary, *ad hoc* matter between the deacon and his bishop. Nonetheless,

> It must not be forgotten that the object of Christ's *diakonia* is mankind. Every human being carries the traces of sin but is called to communion with God. "God so loved the world that He gave His only Son, so that all who believe in Him might not die but have eternal life" (John 3:16). It was for this plan of love that Christ became a slave and took human flesh. The Church continues to be the sign and instrument of that *diakonia* in history.... Growth in imitation of Christ's love for mankind—which surpasses all ideologies—is thus an essential component of the spiritual life of every deacon. (*DMLPD* #49)

How the deacon, as a minister of the church in the world and as a leader in the church's *diakonia*, may best carry out these responsibilities in community-based ministries, is an area that needs much greater examination. Opportunities for such service ought to be the subject of intense and intentional scrutiny by bishops, deacons, and those responsible for the formation of deacons.

Conclusion

This chapter has been a modest introduction into some of the issues to be dealt with in considering a theology of the contemporary diaconate. In the remaining chapters, several of these themes will be developed further.

7

FOUNDATIONAL THEOLOGICAL THEMES AND THE DIACONATE: *KENŌSIS* AND *THEŌSIS*

The prime commitment of theology is seen to be the understanding of God's kenosis, *a grand and mysterious truth for the human mind, which finds it inconceivable that suffering and death can express a love which gives itself and seeks nothing in return.*
—John Paul II, *Fides et Ratio* 93

Introduction

At a recent clergy convocation, I overhead one attendee say to a friend, "I don't know what the big deal about the diaconate is. After all, it's not a *real* vocation like priesthood or religious life." Many reasons might be offered for this misperception, but chief among them is the failure of theologians to construct an adequate theology of the diaconate that captures the imagination of the church, recognizes its shared sacramentality with the sacerdotal orders of bishop and presbyter, while respecting its uniquely diaconal, nonsacerdotal character. To do this, I believe we must ground such a theology in the most foundational theological themes available to us.

The themes developed in this chapter are not unique or exclusive to the diaconate; however, while applicable to all disciples, they find a particular sacramental expression in the order of deacons. As has been asserted from the beginning of this study, the diaconate flows out of the very nature of the church; a theology of the diaconate begins at the heart of what it means to be a disciple of Christ. To that end, this chapter will concentrate on the implications of two of the most ancient and fundamental theological themes: *kenōsis* and *theōsis*.

In 1998, Pope John Paul II authored *Fides et Ratio*, an encyclical letter addressed "To the Bishops of the Catholic Church on the Relationship of Faith and Reason." In identifying contemporary tasks for theology, he offered a challenge to all who pursue theology at this time in the life of the church, writing that "the prime commitment of theology is seen to be the understanding of God's *kenōsis*, a grand and mysterious truth for the human mind, which finds it inconceivable that suffering and death can express a love which gives itself and seeks nothing in return."[1] The second theme, *theōsis*, is perhaps even less well known in the Western tradition. *Theōsis* has a particularly rich heritage in the Eastern traditions of the church and is most commonly translated in English as "divinization."

This examination proceeds in three sections: *kenōsis* and *theōsis* and their foundational character in the tradition; their impact on the nature of the church and ministry, and finally, how they might contribute to a deepening understanding of the nature of the renewed diaconate and its potential in the diverse ministries of the contemporary church.

Kenōsis and *Theōsis*: Vectors of Discipleship

Windows into the Divine

In 1990 the Congregation for the Doctrine of the Faith provided this summary of God's saving plan:

> Out of His infinite love, God desired to draw near to man, as he seeks his own proper identity, and walk with him (cf. Lk 24:15). He also wanted to free him from the

> snares of the "father of lies" (cf. Jn 8:44) and to open the way to intimacy with Himself so that man could find there, superabundantly, full truth and authentic freedom.[2]

This summary offers an interesting starting point. Out of love, God wishes to "draw near" and journey with humanity, with the objective of opening "the way to intimacy" with God. In theological terms, one might say that God's movement toward humanity is reflected in *kenōsis;* the movement toward intimacy with God is reflected in *theōsis.* Both movements begin and end, if you will, in God. Before turning to their meaning for humanity, one must first consider what they reveal about God.

Referring to *kenōsis,* Lucien Richard has written:

> Who is God in light of the kenosis? What is needed is a reevaluation in our understanding of God so that kenōsis will appear not as a process of de-divination but rather as an attribute of God's love disclosed in the compassionate existence of Jesus....In a kenotic Christology, God is considered as absolute letting-be, as self giving, as self-spending. Kenōsis is understood as the way God relates to the world; creation is a work of love, of self-giving.[3]

John's Gospel reminds us that God is love, and this love is so total and absolute that we may say that God is by nature kenotic, with creation itself the great letting-be. God's nature is revealed in a particular, unique way in Christ.

Turning now to the *kenōsis* of Christ, using the classic text from Philippians, it is possible to see in Christ's kenotic action the revelation of the divine nature itself, along with God's longing to restore human intimacy with God:

> Who, though he was in the form of God,
> Did not regard equality with God
> As something to be exploited,
> But emptied himself,
> Taking the form of a slave,
> Being born in human likeness.

And being found in human form,
He humbled himself
And became obedient to the point of death
Even death on a cross.

Therefore God also highly exalted him
And gave him the name
That is above every name,
So that at the name of Jesus
Every knee should bend,
In heaven and on earth and under the earth,
And every tongue should confess
That Jesus Christ is Lord,
To the glory of God the Father. (Phil 2:6–11)

This self-emptying, then, is not about Christ surrendering or forsaking his divine nature (Richard's "de-divination"), but expressing the divine nature most fully. Richard writes that the Philippian hymn "presents Jesus as recognizing that being equal with God means most profoundly to be 'not grasping.' The self-emptying of Jesus unto death—and death on the cross—is the revelation that to be God is to be unselfishness itself."[4] Richard continues by citing Hans Urs von Balthasar, "It is precisely in the *kenosis* of Christ (and nowhere else) that the inner majesty of God's love appears, of God who 'is love' (1 John 4:8) and a 'trinity.'"[5] Johannes Baptist Metz has observed,

> God "became human" and took on our flesh. We say this all too casually, because inadvertently we are accustomed to consider only the biological event, the external process. But the assumption of a human's type of Being is primarily a spiritual venture pulsing through the free activity of our heart.[6]

In a powerful reflection on the temptations of Christ, Metz continues,

> To become human means to become "poor," to have nothing that one might brag about before God....Satan

> wants to make Jesus strong, for what the devil really fears is the powerlessness of God in the humanity that Jesus has assumed. Satan fears the Trojan horse of an open human heart that will remain true to its native poverty, suffer the misery and abandonment that is humanity's, and thus save humankind. Satan's temptation is an assault on God's self-renunciation, an enticement to strength, security and spiritual abundance; for these things will obstruct God's saving approach to humanity in the dark robes of frailty and weakness.[7]

As seen above, the reason for God's *kenōsis* is *theōsis*, the restoration of intimate communion with God. In the Philippian hymn, one might say that the "exaltation" of Christ in v. 9 suggests this intimacy, which is Christ's by nature but which is opened to humanity through grace. Consider the opening verses of the Second Letter of Peter:

> Simeon Peter, a servant and apostle of Jesus Christ,
>
> To those who have received a faith as previous as ours through the righteousness of our God and Savior Jesus Christ:
>
> May grace and peace be yours in abundance in the knowledge of God and of Jesus our Lord.
>
> His divine power has given us everything needed for life and godliness, through the knowledge of him who called us by his own glory and goodness. Thus he has given us, through these things, his precious and very great promises, so that through them you may escape from the corruption that is in the world because of lust, and may become participants in the divine nature. (2 Pet 1:1–4)

Peter reminds his readers that the power of Christ has been given to all the faithful, who have been called to Christ's own "exaltation" in "glory and excellence" so that all may become "partakers of the divine nature." This scripture has inspired considerable theological, spiritual, and mystical reflection throughout the tradition on what it might mean to become "partakers of the divine nature."[8] This is especially true in the Eastern heritage of the church.

For example, the deacon Ephrem of Edessa, the great third-century Syrian doctor of the church wrote extensively on the meaning of the incarnation of Christ and how it fits into God's plan of salvation. Seely Beggiani has identified two great themes to be found in the writings of Ephrem: that God is Mystery, and that God has called all to become like God.[9] Beggiani writes, "Adam and all humans were created not only in the image of God but in the image of the future Christ....Christ, by his incarnation, restores the divine image and completes the work of divinization."[10] Two passages from Ephrem highlight these themes:

> God had seen that we worshipped creatures.
> He put on a created body to catch us by our habit.
> Behold by this fashioned one our Fashioner healed us,
> And by this creature our Creator revived us.[11]

In another meditation, Ephrem is even more succinct:

> The Deity imprinted Itself on humanity,
> So that humanity might also be cut into the seal of the Deity.[12]

The profound nature of these insights finds continuing expression throughout the history of the tradition. During a 1998 audience, John Paul II presented a reflection entitled "The Spirit Enables Us to Share in Divine Nature." After reviewing a number of scriptural and patristic sources, he turned to Thomas Aquinas:

> These assertions are repeated by St. Thomas: "The Only-begotten Son of God, wanting us to be partakers of his divinity, assumed our human nature so that, having become man, he might make men gods" (Opusc. 57 in festo Corp. Christi, 1), that is, partakers through grace of the divine nature.[13]

Lex Orandi, Lex Credendi

It has long been part of the tradition of the church, captured well in the famous expression of Prosper of Aquitaine in the fifth century, *ut legem credendi lex statuat supplicandi:* that the way of praying *(lex supplicandi)* determines the way of believing *(lex credendi)*.[14] Often shortened to *lex orandi, lex credendi*, this principle suggests that our beliefs find living, sacramental expression in and through the symbolic discourse of worship. The concepts of *kenōsis* and *theōsis* are found in many ways in the liturgies of the universal church. In a striking parallel between East and West, one may compare the "preparation of the gifts" in the Mass of the Latin church with the rite of intinction in the Maronite divine liturgy. During the preparation of the gifts, the deacon adds a small amount of water to the wine, saying, "By the mystery of this water and wine may we come to share in the divinity of Christ, who humbled himself to share in our humanity." In the "prayer of intinction" that accompanies the action of the priest placing a piece of the consecrated bread into the consecrated wine, the priest prays: "You have united, O Lord, your divinity with our humanity and our humanity with your divinity; Your life with our mortality and our mortality with Your life. You have assumed what is ours and you have given us what is yours for the life and salvation of our souls. To you be glory forever."

Citing another example, Beggiani reports that the same theme is found in the Maronite baptismal liturgy: "By sharing our human nature, weakened through Adam's sin, you enabled us to share in your divinity, and to receive the gift of life."[15] Not only are these examples powerful reflections and celebrations of the centrality and fundamental character of *kenōsis* and *theōsis*; the fact that these themes connect the Eucharist and baptism strikes me as quite significant. The implications of *kenōsis* and *theōsis* lie at the very core of discipleship, for they describe the heart of the relationship of divine with the human.

Through sacramental initiation (baptism, chrismation/confirmation, and Eucharist) disciples are immersed in the life of the Trinity. As has been seen, however, this trinitarian life is no static reality. If it is in the nature of God to be "absolute letting-be, as self-giving, as self-spending,"[16] then so too must be those who share in this life through grace. It is in and through the disciple's own kenotic self-donation, in sacramental "imitation of Christ," that the disciple finds the door open to the divine. In recalling the *kenōsis* of Christ, the disciple recognizes God's self-emptying into Christ, who images this kenotic divinity in a perfect and unique way. In other words, Christ does not empty himself at the incarnation simply to reclaim his divinity upon the *consummatum est* on the cross. Rather, what is being suggested here is that Christ is most divine at Christ's most human; he is most powerful at his weakest. On the one hand, *kenōsis* in itself reveals something about God and, likewise, about ourselves. *Theōsis*, on the other hand, gives *kenōsis* purpose and direction. One cannot seek God without emptying oneself; one empties oneself to find God.

The Kenotic and Theotic Leadership of Deacons

> For the nurturing and constant growth of the People of God, Christ the Lord instituted in His Church a variety of ministries, which work for the good of the whole body. For those ministers, who are endowed with sacred power, serve their brethren, so that all who are of the People of God, and therefore enjoy a true Christian dignity, working toward a common goal freely and in an orderly way, may arrive at salvation. (*Lumen Gentium* 18)

Chapter 3 (paragraphs 18–29) of *Lumen Gentium* situates the apostolic ministry of the ordained in the context of the whole people of God. Through their service bishops "with their helpers, the priests and deacons" (20) sacramentalize Christ's mission. Already immersed in the life of the Trinity through the sacraments of initiation, the ordained are further configured to Christ.

This configuration to Christ is expressed in various ways in church documents. Canon law, for example, states that the ordained "are consecrated and designated, each according to his grade, to nourish the people of God fulfilling in the person of Christ the Head the functions of teaching, sanctifying and governing."[17] The *Catechism of the Catholic Church* states that ordination "configures [deacons] to Christ, who made himself the 'deacon' or servant of all."[18] John Paul II, in a 1995 address to a joint *plenarium* of the Congregations for the Clergy and Catholic Education, stated that "the deacon receives a particular configuration to Christ, the head and shepherd of the church, who for love of the Father made himself the least and the servant of all."[19] Eventually these two congregations issued jointly two documents on the diaconate. The Congregation for Catholic Education's *Basic Norms for the Formation of Permanent Deacons* states that through ordination, a deacon "is constituted a living icon of Christ the servant within the Church."[20] The Congregation for the Clergy likewise speaks of the deacon's configuration to Christ, "who made himself the 'deacon' or servant of all," and that through ordination the deacon is configured to "Christ's consecration and mission."[21] The document also points out that the deacon has "a distinct identity and integrity in the Church that marks him as neither a lay person nor a priest."[22]

Describing this distinct identity of the deacon lies at the core of the challenge in developing adequate theologies of the renewed diaconate. As stated throughout this work, the renewal of the diaconate as a permanent order marks the first time in more than a millennium that one could be ordained to a clerical order (in other words, distinct from the laity) that is *not sacerdotal* (in other words, distinct from the priesthood). It is precisely at this point of distinction that the largest lacunae exist: in the popular mind, in scholarly research, and in official church teaching.[23]

In chapter 6, we saw that Nathan Mitchell asserts that the distinctiveness of the renewed permanent diaconate lies in "pastoral leadership":

> By restoring the diaconate as a permanent role with the church's ordained leadership, Paul VI implicitly broke the long-standing connection between ordination and "sacramental power."...The restoration of the diaconate is thus important not because it resurrects an ancient order that had all but faded in the West, but because it

> affirms the principle that *recognition of pastoral leadership is the fundamental basis for calling a Christian to ordained ministry.*[24]

The concept of pastoral leadership, however, is a broad and indistinct category; such leadership is exercised by many in the church. Perhaps the foundational concepts of *kenōsis* and *theōsis* may refine notions of pastoral leadership. While "servant-leadership" has become a popular theme since introduced by Robert Greenleaf in the 1970s, a truly "keno-theotic" leadership adds a particular spiritual and theological specificity to leadership. Such an understanding may serve as a nexus of leadership theory and a theology of the diaconate. Some brief observations on contemporary leadership theory will be made in the next section of this chapter.

Apostolic ministry, fully expressed sacramentally in the episcopal order, is to be characterized by an emptying of self for others. This is a ministry, like Christ's, of total self-sacrifice on behalf of others. Those who have a share in the apostolic ministry freely accept this aspect of Christ's identity as part of their own. Apostolic ministry is centered on the Eucharist: it flows from the minister's participation in Christ's own sacrifice of himself, celebrated in the form of a sacred memorial meal. The *diakonia* of apostolic ministry is eucharistic, a breaking and sharing of one's life for the building up of the body in memory of Christ.

Notions of leadership, as frequently understood, may at first seem at odds with such sacrificial behavior. Two brief anecdotes reflect this apparent dichotomy. Following a presentation for deacons and their wives at which the ministry of deacons was described in terms of leadership, at least one deacon was heard to observe that he "was a servant, not a leader." Such an understanding cannot see leadership as a function of service, or servanthood as an inherent part of leadership. Our second example occurred during a meeting discussing the traits to be sought in applicants for diaconate formation, in which "leadership" was suggested as one of those necessary traits. The consultant directing the meeting took exception, however, when she stated quite forcefully that "good deacons are never leaders, and leaders should never become deacons." The irony was that this observation was made during a national gathering of directors of diocesan diaconate offices, most of whom were themselves deacons exercising significant leadership roles on behalf of their bishops. If the consultant was correct, then the hundreds of deacon-directors assembled were either bad leaders or bad deacons![25]

In a more academic vein, Edmund Hill has related the nature of authority as found in the New Testament with the language of power. He describes the nature of "ministerial authority" as described by Jesus as an "absurd paradox."

> Authority ordinarily means the power to give commands and to enforce them; to lay down the law with little expectation of being gainsaid; to wield influence, to control, to rule, to guide effectively. Ministry, if we stick to the real meaning of the word, which is perhaps still more evident in the Greek equivalent *diakonia*, means simply to serve. In fact it means the opposite of authority; it means carrying out commands, accepting law as laid down by others, being ruled, controlled, influenced, or at most being an instrument through which the possessor of authority exercises influence, control and rule.
>
> So, "ministerial authority" looks like a contradiction in terms. If it is not to be that, then it has to involve either a radical, revolutionary recasting of the idea of authority, or an evaporation of the idea of ministry, of service. There can be no doubt which of the two is involved when Jesus combines the two terms, not only in the gospel texts but in his own person. There we see that the notion of authority is radically recast, while the idea of service is rigorously maintained in all its crude literalness. The authority of Christ himself, and therefore of all who share in it, is an authority *only* for the sake of service; an authority to wash the feet of the disciples; an authority to care for others, to consider their interests; an authority to give his life as a ransom for many.[26]

God is the source of all power, and in the Christian tradition "the sources of power derived from God are manifested historically through Jesus Christ and through the Holy Spirit."[27] This means that the church, in developing its own application and exercise of the ongoing presence and action of God's power, must do so in light of Christ's leadership and example. Given Christ's command to lead in a new way, a way that is radically countercultural, those who would presume to lead must do so in a way that serves the greater good of the community. James Coriden puts it quite succinctly, "Power in the Church is power to serve."[28] I suggest that one way that might be used to describe the deacon's unique participation in the apostolic ministry as iconically kenotic.

This kenotic power reflects the model of *diakonia*, Christ, as found in the Philippian hymn. Through sacramental ordination, the deacon celebrates a new sacramental relationship with the Christ who came to serve and not be served. "A deacon is a member of the Church who, in response to God's perceived election and call, reaches out to be of service in the Church, and, in this way, incarnates the presence of Jesus, who is the deacon of the presence of God."[29]

Kenotic power is not the exclusive province of the deacon, but it is the deacon who serves as the sacramental focus for the *diakonia* of the entire community. That is why Patrick McCaslin and Michael Lawler can say, "A parish, which is a local incarnation of Church and of Jesus, is not sacramentally whole if it is without either priest or deacon."[30] Just as the presbyter shares in the sacred power of the priesthood with the bishop, so too the deacon shares in the kenotic power of the diaconate with the bishop. In other words, I am suggesting that *sacra potestas* may be reflected in two ways: *sacerdotal* and *kenotic*. In the same way that *Lumen Gentium* 10 orders the common priesthood of the baptized to the ministerial priesthood, it may be said that the common *diakonia* of the baptized is ordered to the ministerial diaconate. The ministerial diaconate sacramentalizes the self-emptying love of Christ on behalf of others to which the entire community of disciples is called. It does not supplant, it does not replace, it does not subsume; through the "sacramental grace" received at ordination (see *Lumen Gentium* 29), the deacon receives the strength to empty himself in the service of others through official ministry in word, sacrament, and charity.

Describing *kenotic power* in terms of a polarity between *power* and *kenōsis* helps describe the sacramentality of *diakonia*, both within the church itself and in those who share in apostolic ministry. The tension between power and powerlessness reflects a continuum from power-full-ness to power-less-ness. As Christ demonstrated in his own life and through his teaching about leadership to his disciples, the one who would be a leader in Christ's image must first surrender power and take the position of a servant, one without power. What is critical in this understanding is the fact that a kenotic empowerment represents a dynamic reality that may be a source of creative energy, a real strengthening, a true force for service. *Kenōsis* moves beyond simply giving up power. *It is an active emptying, not simply the acceptance of powerlessness.*

This idea of kenotic empowerment returns us to Karl Rahner, who wrote:

> By willing itself, power wills what is other than itself. The transition to the other, to allowing the will of others, to unconditional consent to the generosity of the divine will, demands of the finite will, which is not the source of its own power, a self-abandonment, self-sacrifice, self-mediation through weakness, by questioning its own power....The redemption of power is the cross....The cross of power involves for the Christian not only readiness for self-sacrifice, but willingness to accept power in its vulnerable earthly conditions. But even then it will only be accepted with detachment and will be valid only because it comes from God.[31]

Rahner's observation opens the way again to speak of the theotic dimension of *kenōsis*. The paschal mystery of Christ draws us from incarnation through the cross to resurrection and ascension. One pours oneself out, not to lose oneself but to find oneself in God. In ministerial terms, one might say that kenotic power is exercised not as a simple expression of social justice or social service, but as a way to draw others more fully into the paschal mystery of Christ and to guide others to salvation. Walter Kasper remarks, "This diaconal ministry of the deacon is not a one-sided social or charitable task: deacons are not ordained social workers!"[32] He then cites Ignatius of Antioch, who describes them as "deacons of the mysteries of Jesus Christ."[33] In short, theological understandings of the diaconate that attempt to identify diaconal ministry with social ministry alone are inadequate. With remarkable clarity, the *Catechism of the Catholic Church* links two sacraments in their "outward" orientation toward others: matrimony and orders. These sacraments "are directed towards the salvation of others; if they contribute as well to personal salvation, it is through service to others that they do so. They confer a particular mission in the Church and serve to build up the People of God" (#1534).[34]

How might these foundational themes find practical application in the contemporary church? The next section seeks insights from contemporary leadership theory.

Suggested Pastoral Applications

Max De Pree and Leadership Theory

Max De Pree is chairman emeritus of office furniture manufacturer Herman Miller, Inc. He is recognized as a pioneer in the use of profit sharing, work teams, and other participatory leadership practices. He is a member of *Fortune* magazine's Business Hall of Fame and a best-selling author. Shortly after being honored nationally with a Lifetime Achievement Award by the President of the United States and the Business Enterprise Trust, the De Pree Leadership Institute was established at Fuller Theological Seminary.

In a 2002 article, "Servant-Leadership: Three Things Necessary,"[35] De Pree's "three things necessary" for servant-leadership are (1) an understanding of the fiduciary nature of leadership; (2) a broadened definition of leadership competence; and (3) the enlightenment afforded leaders by a moral purpose. Each will be reviewed in turn.

The Fiduciary Nature of Leadership

Fiduciary, of course, refers to the notion of trust. A leader who understands the fiduciary dimensions of leadership is one who sees herself as responsible for holding "many things in trust for their followers."[36] De Pree cites five "paths" of fiduciary leadership:

> 1. *Leadership is not a position.* Noting that "a promotion has never made anyone a leader," De Pree continues by observing that "fiduciary leaders design, build, and then serve inclusive communities by liberating human spirit and potential, not by relying only on their own abilities or experience or judgment."[37] Consider this path in light of pastoral leadership in the church. Fiduciary leadership is not restricted to those who are ordained, and certainly not to those assigned to the responsibilities of a particular ecclesiastical office. Rather, fiduciary leadership can be exercised by many within the parish. Notice the reliance on real collaboration by a fiduciary leader, a person who sees the wisdom and, indeed, the necessity of seeking others' "abilities, experiences, and judgment."
>
> 2. *Organizations should become centers of learning and collaboration.* De Pree builds upon this notion of collaboration and adds the dimension of learning. "By making it possible for people to grow and to work together, fiduciary leaders try to invest and enlarge the knowledge and talent that they hold in trust for individuals."[38] It is not a considerable stretch to see this path as necessary in a parish at all levels. Any number of official church documents, including papal encyclicals and documents from national conferences of bishops, remind parishioners that evangelization is the mission of the church and that catechesis is the responsibility of all. Adult faith formation, in fact, is to be the norm against which all other forms of catechesis are to be judged. More than simple intellectual knowledge, an evangelizing catechesis (to borrow a phrase used often by Catherine Dooley) is an essential component of parish life. The "fiduciary leaders" of such a parish will recognize the necessity for the parish to be a "center of learning" and collaboration. In fact, the fiduciary leader includes himself or herself in the community as one who

is just as much in need of this ongoing learning, development, and call to collaboration.

3. *Fiduciary leaders balance the related ideas of individual opportunity and a concept of community.* "In this balance, they insist on disciplined accountability to and for others."[39] It is significant to highlight the fact that this "disciplined accountability" is not restricted to an accountability to the leader's superiors in a chain of authority, but I believe it includes a disciplined accountability to those served as well. If a leader holds "many things in trust" for those served, the leader should be eager to show how this trust has been fulfilled. Furthermore, one may begin to see in this pathway a sense of the *communio* of Christ's disciples. The community being served is not called into existence by the force of the leader's will, or by ecclesiastical fiat; rather it is called into existence by God. In a community of disciples, the individual responsibility and opportunity of each disciple find their ultimate expression. This is the balance that the fiduciary leader seeks to maintain and nurture.

4. *Fiduciary leaders work to build trust.* In short, trust is the "coin of the realm" as it were, the means through which collaboration, learning, and *communio* are developed. De Pree refers to a note he once received from an employee that read, "Your trust is the grace that enables me to be creative." "Trust is clearly the basis for covenantal relationships, which are far more productive than contractual ones."[40] Kasper echoes this insight when he applies it to the diaconate: "The task [for the deacon] is to bring a healing that sets people free and empowers them to trust and so to serve and love others in their turn."[41] It should be clear by now why De Pree has a leadership institute named for him at a theological seminary. His stress on the importance of covenantal relationships in a text on leadership theory may seem strange to those used to reading such terms in theological literature. However, it is the recognition that concepts such as these are not,

and should not, be restricted to ecclesiastical venues alone that makes his insights all the more attractive and helpful.

5. *Fiduciary leaders leave legacies.* De Pree explains this path by giving two examples. The first is a quotation from *Gaudium et Spes:* "The future is in the hands of those who can give tomorrow's generations reasons to live and hope."[42] The second is a Native American saying that "the world does not belong to us; we merely borrow it from our grandchildren."[43]

When one has accepted this fiduciary nature of leadership, according to De Pree, one also must accept his next two points: broadening a definition of leadership competence and finding a clear moral purpose.

Broadened Definition of Leadership Competence

De Pree grounds his expanded view of leadership competence in a succinct statement that the usual indicators of assessing tangible leadership competence must be balanced with a concern with "how well leaders handle relationships."[44] He then offers five areas for building such competence.

1. *The leader perceives, defines, and expresses reality.* De Pree observes that "defining and expressing reality for an organization is important because it ends the numbing isolation that is so prevalent and so deadly today."[45] It falls to those who minister as leaders in the church also to perceive, define, and express reality. It is no coincidence that it has been the role of the deacon since patristic times to serve as the "eyes, ears, heart, and soul" of the bishop, as well as a minister of the word within the assembly and to the world.

2. *The future lies in the selection, nurture, and assignment of key people.* Not only is this an important leadership principle, but it finds specific application for the deacon, who

is often the coordinator of volunteers and other members of the pastoral staff in caring for the needs of the parish. Similar to the earlier discussion of collaboration, this insight likewise stresses the fiduciary responsibility of the deacon-leader to promote others' gifts, talents, and experience specifically for leadership.

3. *A competent leader bears personal responsibility for knowing, understanding, and enabling the creative people in an organization.* Notice that this area ends not with an acceptance of personal responsibility but with taking that responsibility for the identification and nurture of others' talents. The competent leader is not defensive or coercive about her or his own creative abilities, but seeks out and encourages those abilities in others. Once again, the focus of the competent leader is always on others and the relationship that is to be enjoyed between leaders and followers in common. Not only that, it is the leader's "personal responsibility" for promoting that relationship, and she is to be held accountable for it.

4. *Competent leaders are transforming leaders.* Citing Charles Handy, De Pree observes that "the total pragmatist cannot be a transforming leader." "Competent leaders guide their organizations, and the people in them to new levels of learning and performance, transforming the present into a reaching toward potential.... Transforming leadership is a process of learning and risking and changing lives."[46] It can be quite easy in the day-to-day exercise of pastoral ministry to get caught up in the myriad details of life "as it is" and lose sight of a responsibility to be prophetic, to call the community into life "as it ought to be" in light of the gospel. In a sense there needs to be an "eschatological arc" to ministry, a constant transformation into what we are called to be.

5. *Competent leaders discover, unleash, and polish diverse gifts.* "If we as individuals remain stifled, our organizations will die."[47] Who in our parishes "remains stifled"? What ways exist, what challenges present themselves, for

> transforming fiduciary leaders to find ways to unleash *all* of these gifts?

Finding Clear Moral Purpose

"Without moral purpose, competence has no measure, and trust has no goal."[48] De Pree, himself a Christian, sees moral purpose "as a sign of God's presence in our leadership. It's up to leaders to keep the signs of moral purpose alive and visible in organizations."[49] Following his established pattern, he offers five signs of moral purpose.

His first sign of God's presence is *a wholehearted acceptance of human authenticity*. This authenticity is found in one fact, and one fact only: that all members of an organization are creatures of God, made in God's image. "Authenticity needs to dominate our relationships and our understanding of justice. The implications of this belief are enormous for leaders."[50] One of the implications of authenticity leads to De Pree's second sign for moral purpose: that *all are thereby entitled to certain rights*, which he enumerates as the right to belong; the right to ownership; the right to opportunity; the right to a covenantal relationship; the right to inclusive organizations. Even more important, perhaps, "leaders with a clear moral purpose work to make these rights real."[51]

De Pree's third sign is the most simple yet most profound: *truth*. Not a concept often associated with the business world, truth for De Pree is critical to all present and future relationships. Without truthfulness, relationships—and organizations—are doomed. "To assume blithely that untruthfulness has no consequence for our world is mighty risky."[52] Truth and truthfulness point the way to the fourth sign, *vulnerability*, which De Pree describes as "a gift of all true leaders to their followers."[53] His comments here deserve to be presented in full:

> Moral purpose enables leaders to be vulnerable because it changes the rules of measurement. A clear moral purpose removes the ego from the game. It means that leaders no longer need to succeed on the terms that make some leaders intolerant, inaccessible, and insufferable.

> Vulnerable leaders are open to diversity of gifts from followers. They seek contrary opinion. They take every person seriously. They are strong enough to abandon themselves to the strengths of others.[54]

Finally, the last sign of a leader with a clear moral purpose is found in the leader's willingness to *share the results* of the organization's mission. All who share in the mission of the organization have every right to share in its fruits. De Pree cites 1 Cor 9:7: "Who plants a vineyard without eating its produce? Or who shepherds a flock without using some of the milk from the flock?"

In gleaning these insights from De Pree, one is immediately struck by their spiritual depth and maturity, with application to any kind of communal relationship, including ecclesial structures and relationships. Consider the number of times in which fiduciary leadership is described in *kenotic* terms: that leadership itself is not the exclusive province of one who holds an official position of leadership, that the fiduciary leader is one who focuses on relationships, putting others ahead of self, and of making oneself vulnerable for the sake of the larger community. Given De Pree's own spiritual heritage, one may even point to *theotic* dimensions: that the end of leadership is not simply tangible results dealing with the "bottom line" of financial profit and loss, but the nurturing of gifts and relationship based on each person's authenticity as a creature of a loving God. The implications of these insights for the specific "fiduciary leadership" of the deacon are profound.

The Leadership Potential of the Diaconate

This section suggests additional leadership initiatives that might be undertaken by deacons in several venues in the contemporary church: parish-based ministry, regional ministry, and community ministry.

Paul Philibert has written that the priest today is probably best described as "a generative mentoring pastor—one whose responsibility is to maintain harmony while bringing into cooperation the rich and diverse gifts of all the members of the community."[55] Such a description may be made of the deacon, so often referred to as the "animator" (Paul VI, John Paul II) of the church's *diakonia*. Interestingly, Philibert picks up on this connection between generativity and "animator" when he writes, "The role of pastor and animator of the local church's varied charisms is far more demanding than the role of liturgical presider alone."[56] The same could be said, with only minor revision, of the deacon. Therefore, what follows is a suggestion of what might be done by deacons as "generative animators" of the diocesan church.

Parish-based Ministry

The Second Vatican Council referred to the parish as being "like a cell" *(velut cellula)* of the diocese, a basic community which "gathers into a unity all the human diversities that are found there and inserts them into the universality of the Church."

> Participants in the function of Christ, priest, prophet and king, the laity have an active part of their own in the life and action of the Church....The laity should develop the habit of working in the parish in close union with their priests, of bringing before the ecclesial community their own problems, world problems, and questions regarding human salvation, to examine them together and solve them by general discussion. According to their abilities the laity ought to cooperate in all the apostolic and missionary enterprises of their ecclesial family. (*Apostolicam Actuositatem* 10)

The challenging words of the council have yet to be realized in many parish communities. Faced with shifting population centers—creating rapid growth in some parishes and an exodus from others—many parishes are simply striving to survive. Coupled with this situation, the growing shortage of presbyters in many areas creates even more intense stress on some communities. As many dioceses develop strategies for closing, merging, and clustering parishes, some parishioners wonder if their parish will continue to exist in any form. This leads many to think about parish-as-church in a minimalist mode: what is absolutely necessary (contrasted with what be "nice to have") if they are to survive as a Catholic parish? The answers quite naturally focus on the Eucharist and the community's ability to have someone present who can preside at the Eucharist. In such a view, having deacons or lay ecclesial ministers, who cannot "say Mass" or "hear confessions," seems far less critical. The result of this popular perspective is that the ordained ministry of the deacon (and even the bishop) is perceived as of much less significance in the life of the parish. The value of a deacon is often characterized merely by those functions in which he is perceived as being able "to help Father" in the performance of certain "priest"-like ways.

In addition, the church's social-justice ministry at the parish level, even if a deacon is involved, is usually not seen as the responsibility of the entire parish. Rather, involvement in social-justice ministries is more often than not the province of a handful of volunteers who take them on as personal ministries.

It is at this point that the ministry of the deacon could be critical, and yet it remains largely unrealized. As the church's sacramental icon of *diakonia*, the deacon should have as a primary duty the building up of diaconal parishes, communities that realize and live their own diaconal responsibilities. Walter Kasper writes:

> Each parish has to make sure that *diakonia* is realized. This means that faith and preaching, as well as the Eucharist and liturgy must be oriented to *diakonia*. Faith without *diakonia* is not a Christian faith. Preaching without *diakonia* is not Christian preaching. A non-diaconal parish celebrating the Eucharist may express its faith, but its faith remains dead; in the final analysis it cannot find God, as they miss the point that God reveals himself in the people, especially in the poor.
>
> The Church lives wherever the corporal works of mercy are practiced: feeding the hungry, giving drink to the thirsty, clothing the naked, giving shelter to strangers, liberating prisoners, visiting the sick and burying the dead. The Church also lives wherever the spiritual works of mercy are practiced; correcting sinners, teaching the ignorant, giving counsel to the doubters, comforting the

> distressed, enduring the troublesome, forgiving those who offend us, praying for the living and the dead.[57]

The deacon as community builder can inspire, motivate, encourage, and assist the parish in its pastoral planning efforts. Many deacons bring a variety of community-building and planning skills to ministry from their professional and family life. The deacon can also exercise leadership through sacramentalizing the link between word, sacrament, and charity *(martyria, leitourgia, diakonia)*, which are the constitutive elements of church life. In these and similar ways, the deacon fulfills duties of administration that have been associated with the diaconate since the patristic era. The deacon also serves again as a visible link between the love and worship of God and the love and care of neighbor, which was so prevalent in the patristic heritage.

Specifically, the deacon can provide apostolic leadership in addressing the great needs of the contemporary world. The "issues of special urgency" identified by *Gaudium et Spes* may serve as an agenda of opportunities for diaconal leadership. The deacon, most often operating in the context of family and work, brings special sensitivity to such issues as the dignity of marriage and the family, the proper development of culture, economic and social life, the political community, and the fostering of peace and the establishment of a community of nations. The first venue of leadership in these issues is—or ought to be—the parish.

The deacon is suited for such leadership not only in virtue of life experience but through sacramental ordination as well. The deacon stands empowered as a sign of Christ's own *kenōsis*, a sign that human life is not about seeking material wealth, possessions, and positions of power and domination. Rather, the communion of disciples is called to empty themselves in addressing the needs of others.

Regional-Diocesan Ministry

While most deacons exercise ministry in parish settings, they remain ministers in service to the entire diocese. Through ordination and incardination deacons are responsible for building up the community, often through diocesan structures. Given the impact of current demographics and other factors on parish life, many dioceses are approaching pastoral planning and ministry from a regional or even diocesan-wide basis. Unfortunately, as documented in the most recent national survey on the diaconate, too often deacons are perceived as parish-based ministers. The central finding of the study was the following:

> The restored Order of the Diaconate, largely parish-based, has been successful and increasingly important for the life of the Church. The primary challenges of the diaconate for the future are to broaden its ministries beyond its largely successful and increasingly indispensable adaptation to parish life and to emphasize more strongly that deacons, through ordination, are called to be model, animator, and facilitator of ministries of charity and justice within the local church.[58]

Qualified deacons may be given assignments to coordinate outreach ministries throughout the deaneries or diocese, strategic planning efforts, or other diocesan or interdiocesan initiatives. Such a vision restores some of the ancient responsibilities of the deacon, and the challenges it embodies would be profound, especially in the formation of deacons. Increasingly, ministries involving health care, prisons, and other areas of social concern are becoming more specialized, with stringent professional standards for their practitioners. Deacons assuming leadership roles in such areas will not only need the personal gifts and talents to serve in these areas, but will often need diocesan support to attain the appropriate professional credentials to enable their participation in them.

Community-based Ministry

> A deeply felt need in the decision to re-establish the permanent diaconate was and is that of greater and more direct presence of Church ministers in the various spheres of the family, work, school, etc., in addition to existing pastoral structures.[59]

Deacons can and should exercise leadership in community-based service initiatives. Conformed in a special way to Christ "the Head and Servant" (in the words of John Paul II), the deacon imitates Christ in reaching out beyond the limits of the church. Such service can take many forms, defined by the deacon's own skills and qualifications, the sociopolitical structures of the society in which he lives, and the needs to be met. Nonetheless,

> It must not be forgotten that the object of Christ's *diakonia* is mankind. Every human being carries the traces of sin but is called to communion with God. God so loved the world that He gave His only Son, so that all who believe in Him might not die but have eternal life" (John 3:16). It was for this plan of love that Christ became a slave and took human flesh. The Church continues to be the sign and instrument of that *diakonia* in history.... Growth in imitation of Christ's love for mankind—which surpasses all ideologies—is thus an essential component of the spiritual life of every deacon. (*DMLPD* #49)

How the deacon, as a minister of the church in the world and as a leader in the church's *diakonia* may best carry out these responsibilities in community-based ministries, is an area that needs much greater examination. Opportunities for such service ought to be the subject of intense and intentional scrutiny by bishops, deacons, and those responsible for the formation of deacons.

Conclusion: Ministers of the Chalice

The challenge for the contemporary diaconate is to realize the ramifications of *kenotic* power exercised in a *theotic* purpose, a power that is given to be given away, a totally self-sacrificial strength for leadership through service. In real terms this means that deacons divorce themselves from any expressions, attitudes, and behaviors that smack of clericalism or the acquisition of power and authority for its own sake. This means that there should be something unique in the ways in which deacons lead in and through service that demonstrates this kenotic dimension. The deacon should always bring a uniquely diaconal and kenotic quality to any assignment: his sacramental extension of and participation in the ministry of the bishop, his witness and dedication to the church's inherent *diakonia*, and his commitment to the entire diocesan church and the community in which he lives and serves, leading all to salvation.

Deacons are often referred to as "ministers of the chalice," normally referring to his ministry at the altar. During the preparation of the gifts in the Latin church, it is the deacon who takes up the empty chalice and fills it with wine and adds a few drops of water with the words we considered before, "By the mystery of this water and wine, may we come to share in the divinity of Christ who humbled himself to share in our humanity." At the end of the Eucharistic Prayer, it is the deacon who elevates the chalice now filled with the Precious Blood of Christ. At communion, it is the deacon who often ministers the chalice to the assembly. After communion, the deacon is again handed the empty cup for purification and readiness for the next sacrifice. Given the deacon's identity as the minister of the chalice, it seems appropriate to end with the Prayer of the Chalice, which appears on the next page.

Prayer of the Chalice

Father, to Thee I raise my whole being,
a vessel emptied of self. Accept Lord,
this my emptiness, and so fill me
with Thyself—Thy Light, Thy Love,
Thy Life—that these precious gifts
may radiate through me and over-
flow the chalice of my heart
into the hearts of all with
whom I come in contact this
day, revealing unto them
the beauty of
Thy Joy
and
Wholeness
and
the
Serenity
of Thy Peace
which nothing can destroy

8

THE MEANING OF DIACONAL ORDINATION: A CONVERSATION WITH SUSAN K. WOOD

By the imposition of the bishop's hands and the specific prayer of consecration, the deacon receives a particular configuration to Christ, the Head and Shepherd of the Church, who for love of the Father made himself the least and the servant of all.

—John Paul II, *The Deacon's Ordination* 3

Sacramental Catechesis and the Rite of Ordination

This chapter is an exercise in sacramental catechesis. Long before Prosper of Aquitaine's famous *lex orandi, lex credendi*,[1] the church connected faith and worship. The liturgy itself is an indispensable source for theology. Through the symbolic discourse of sacramental celebration, the church is re-created, and we come to a deeper understanding of God's presence and action in the life of the church. Indeed, through the liturgy, we connect the paschal mystery of Christ with our own experience of life, and what it means to be part of the people of God. Through a study of the liturgy, then, we may discern a matrix of meaning. What is the church doing and saying about its own nature when it celebrates the sacraments of initiation, and what does this mean to the people involved and to the larger community? What is the church doing and saying about its own nature when it reconciles, and what does this mean to the people involved and to the larger community? What is the church doing and saying about its own nature when it witnesses and blesses the creation of a covenant relationship between a bride and groom, and what does this mean to the people involved and to the larger community? What is the church doing and saying about its own nature when it calls and ordains members for service to the body of Christ, and what does this mean to the people involved and to the larger community? It is through the actual celebration of the sacraments themselves that we may come to discern, however dimly, the nature and meaning of various aspects of the church's own nature and life.

The purpose of this chapter, then, is to examine the rite of diaconal ordination to gain insights about what this might teach us about the nature of the church, the nature and role of its deacons, and what all of this means in the church and world today. Through the symbolic discourse of the ordination rite, what is the church attempting to say and to do and to be? This is on the positive side of the ledger.

We must also, however, consider the negative aspects of what we find. Our liturgical celebrations, of course, are not holy writ, and they develop and evolve as finite human creatures struggle to find ever more meaningful terms of symbolic discourse. The celebration of ordination, including diaconal ordination, certainly evidences this kind of growth and development. What are we to make of the rite when it seems to contradict or inadequately capture the sense of other theological sources, or when the rite seems to conflict with the experience the people of God bring to the celebration? David Power has written, "One norm for the interpretation of symbols is stated in the axiom: symbols articulate and transform experience. It demands attention to the interaction between experience and symbol."[2]

I have subtitled this chapter, "A Conversation with Susan K. Wood." Professor Wood is one of only a handful of contemporary theologians who has attempted to examine the diaconate through the lens of diaconal ordination and then to suggest theological responses to that examination. Particularly helpful is the fact that she does this work within the larger framework of the other ordained and lay ministries of the church.[3] I hope merely to extend the conversation that she has so ably initiated and to pursue further the matter of a contextual theology of the diaconate.

This chapter is divided into two major sections. First is a historical outline of the development of diaconal ordination, surveying three medieval sacramentaries (the Leonine, the Veronese, and a later edition of the Gregorianum). Second, I examine the current rite of diaconal ordination.

Historical Overview: The Ordination of Deacons

> Now during those days, when the disciples were increasing in number, the Hellenists complained against the Hebrews because their widows were being neglected in the daily distribution of food. And the twelve called together the whole community of the disciples and said, "It is not right that we should neglect the word of God in order to wait at tables. Therefore, friends, select from among yourselves seven men of good standing, full of the Spirit and of wisdom, whom we may appoint to this task, while we, for our part, will devote ourselves to prayer and to serving the word." What they said pleased the whole community, and they chose Stephen, a man full of faith and the Holy Spirit, together with Philip, Prochorus, Nicanor, Timon, Parmenas, and Nicolaus, a proselyte of Antioch. They had these men stand before the apostles, who prayed and laid their hands on them. (Acts 6:1–6)

With the simple words of this well-known passage, St. Luke describes the origins of the diaconate in the church. In fact, while this account from the Acts of the Apostles is still held by some to mark the beginning of the diaconate, "more careful scholarship, however, has brought into question such an identification of the seven chosen to minister to the Hellenistic Christians with those otherwise called 'deacons.'"[4] These seven are *never* referred to as deacons, and the functions performed by Stephen and Philip are "more like that of presbyters or even apostles."[5] Nonetheless, this passage is particularly significant for anyone interested in the ministries of the early Christian churches, for in this hazy description we may discern certain trends in the way the early church sought to identify the pastoral needs of the communion of disciples, to select persons to meet those needs, and to install these ministers in a public and prayerful (i.e., liturgical) way. So, whether the Seven were actually "deacons" in a modern sense or not, this passage serves as the ground for any study of diaconal ordination.

Focusing on the liturgical features in this passage, we may identify three major elements: the role and responsibility of the community to choose the appropriate ministers for itself ("full of the Spirit and of wisdom"), the prayer of the apostles, and the imposition of the apostles' hands. In varying degrees, these three elements have remained (at least within the official text) in subsequent rites of ordination.

Terms Associated with Ordination in the Patristic Period

Pierre Jounel writes, "In approaching the study of the liturgy of ordinations...it is important to know in advance what precise meaning the patristic period gave to the words *ordo*, *ordinatio*, and *ordinare* and their Greek equivalents."[6] Jounel stresses that the original meanings of these terms as used by the early church must be kept in mind as we examine the development of the rite.

Ordo, meaning "corps" or "order," was a common term in the civil and social life of the community, referring to any distinct subgroup within the larger community that performed some specific function at the service of the community. Roman senators, for example, were referred to corporately as *ordo clarissimus*, a group distinct *(clarus)* from the community they governed. Jounel and Herman A. J. Wegman both point out that this distinction is further verified by the common use of the expression *ordo populusque* ("the order and the people") to identify the entire community, composed of those governed and the corps of those who govern.[7]

Ordo, after its adoption by the Christian community, soon developed a less collective denotation. Rather than the entire corps of clerics, the term came to apply to the various ranks within the clergy, such as the *ordo episcoporum* ("the order of bishops") and the *ordo presbyterorum* ("the order of presbyters"). It was only in the twentieth century that the more collective use of *ordo* returning to the church:

> After falling into practical disuse among theologians and canonists, *ordo* in the collective sense was brought back into use by Pius XII in several of the Apostolic Constitutions whereby he established the Catholic hierarchy in mission countries and, even more so, by the Second Vatican Council in its Dogmatic Constitution *Lumen gentium* on the Church (no. 22).[8]

Ordinatio, also borrowed from civil practice, described the public appointment of a person to an *ordo*. It communicated the person's new relationships within the community's social structure as a whole and identified the person as a member of a specific order. This need not be understood exclusively as simply dividing the community into "lay" and "ordained" categories. Orthodox theologian and now Metropolitan of Pergamon John D. Zizioulas has observed that the theological significance of the link between the Eucharist and baptism/chrismation lies in the fact that

> it reveals the nature of baptism and confirmation as being essentially an ordination, while it helps us understand better what ordination itself means....The immediate and inevitable result of baptism and confirmation was that the newly baptized would take his particular "place" in the eucharistic assembly, i.e., that he would become a layman.[9]

In other words, the neophyte Christian had become a member of a particular *ordo* in the eucharistic assembly. This is an important theological distinction to keep in mind, although our focus will be on the later Christian usage of this language in the specific context of ordination to particular orders of official ministry within the church.

With regard to the Greek terminology associated with early ordinations, the importance of the gesture of laying on of hands is stressed. Jounel writes:

> In secular Greek an official was said to be "instituted" or "established" in his office *(kathistatai)*; he could also be said to be "designated" *(cheirotoneitai)*. Hippolytus applies both terms to ecclesiastical offices, but limits the use of the second to ordinations in the strict sense, that is, to offices that make the chosen person a member of one of the three levels in the hierarchic structure and for which a consecration is required. The ritual gesture used in this consecration was the imposition of hands *(cheirothetein)*; it was of Jewish origin and is attested in the Acts of the Apostles. Hippolytus' intention in his choice of words is to bring out the fact that an ordination *(cheirotonia, cheirotonein)* necessarily implies an imposition of hands.[10]

Although the *Didache* makes reference to the election of bishops and deacons by each community of disciples, no specific details of an ordination rite are offered. The first extant ordination ritual for deacons is found in the *Apostolic Tradition*, often attributed to Hippolytus of Rome (ca. 215).[11] As seen in chapter 3 above, a deacon is to be ordained after he is selected "after the fashion of those things said above,"[12] referring back to the instructions concerning the ordination of the bishop, who is chosen by all the people. The pattern described is strikingly similar to *Acts:* the deacon (like bishop and presbyter) must be chosen by the people. He is then brought to the bishop, who alone imposes hands on him and offers a prayer of consecration:

> When the deacon is ordained, this is the reason why the bishop alone shall lay his hands upon him: his is not ordained to the priesthood but to serve the bishop and to carry out the bishop's commands. He does not take part

> in the council of the clergy; he is to attend to his own duties and to make known to the bishop such things as are needful. He does not receive that Spirit that is possessed by the presbytery, in which the presbyters share; he receives only what is confided in him under the bishop's authority.[13]

The significance of the bishop's solo action, rather than a communal action involving bishop and presbyterate, cannot be overstated. As we saw in great detail in chapter 3, the deacon has from the earliest recorded evidence, been associated intimately and uniquely with the bishop in service to the bishop and to the community the bishop heads. Thus, the essential elements of a deacon's ordination emerge as ritual expressions of a community–deacon–bishop relationship grounded in the Spirit. The election by the community identifies to the bishop its choice of a person to serve the community; by the laying on of hands, the bishop accepts the deacon as the community's servant; through the prayer of consecration, the bishop grounds the entire action in the Spirit which vivifies the community. Jounel writes, "All ordination rituals that have been used in the [Roman] Church flow from that given by Hippolytus…the Roman liturgy has always prescribed the rites to which the *Apostolic Tradition* assigns normative value."[14]

Early Roman Rituals

The ancient prayers associated with ordinations in the rituals from the fifth to the eighth centuries are contained in the Leonine Sacramentary (ca. 500, a codex from the Verona collection of liturgical manuscripts), the Verona Sacramentary (ca. 560), and the Gregorian Sacramentary (ca. 610). These prayers have remained essentially the same to the present day, except for the prayer for the consecration of a bishop, which was replaced in 1968 by the prayer given in the *Apostolic Tradition*.[15]

Group XXVIII of the Leonine Sacramentary refers to the *consecratio episcopi* ("consecration of a bishop"), *benedictio super diaconos* ("blessing over deacons"), *consecratio presbyteri* ("consecration of a presbyter"). Note the obvious distinction in the titles of the prayers themselves: while the bishop and priest are "consecrated," the deacon is "blessed." However, the sequence of these actions is also significant: the blessing of deacons follows closely the consecration of bishops. In other words, the diaconate is bound to the episcopate, and while it is presented as a separate and distinct order, it is subordinate to and dependent on the bishop. The actual prayer for the ordination of a deacon follows the same pattern as that used in the prayers for a bishop and priest. First the bishop refers to the hierarchy as a gift from God to the church. Second, the bishop invokes the Spirit on the ordinand. Lastly, the bishop prays that the new minister be given the strength to carry out his new responsibilities. While the title ascribed to the action varies, the substantive content of the prayers is quite similar.

The same pattern is consistent with the later manuscript from the same collection known as the Verona Sacramentary. Again the blessing over the deacon is placed between the consecration of a bishop and that of a priest, and the prayers again describe the hierarchy as a gift of God to the church, given for the service of the church and the needs of the people. The deacon is designated a special assistant to the bishop, who alone possesses the fullness of the ministry.

In the Gregorian Sacramentary, more of the rite emerges. For example, the dialogue between the bishop and a representative of the people concerning the worthiness of the candidate for ordination is specified. Following the rite of election, the candidates for ordination and the people pray together before the bishop (alone, in the case of the ordination of a deacon) imposes hands on the head of the ordinand.

In the specific formulae for diaconal ordination, it may also be observed that the diaconate is becoming more and more associated with liturgical service only. "The great Fathers of the fourth and fifth centuries referred to deacons, but it is clear from their writings that the permanent diaconate was declining."[16] The emergence of the *cursus honorum*, discussed in detail in chapter 3, is also finding its way into the rites of ordination. This trend is clearly evident in the prayers associated with ordination examined here. At the end of each consecratory prayer (including the one used for deacons), the Spirit is called down upon the newly ordained so that they may perform their duties well, and ultimately advance to a higher degree *(dignisque successibus de inferiori gradu per gratiam tuam caperre potiora mereantur)*.[17] The increasing emphasis on liturgical service may also account for references to the ancient order of Levites who served in the Jewish Temple. References to presbyters as the successors of the Aaronic priesthood and deacons as the Levites of the new covenant may still be found in today's ritual.

The rites of diaconal ordination in these sources are not surprisingly more mature than that described in the *Apostolic Tradition*. The first act during the ordination was the ratification of the ordinand by the community. This was followed by a prayer of petition by the entire assembly; the imposition of hands by the bishop on the ordinand (in silence); the prayer of consecration; the kiss of peace given by the bishop and exchanged by the newly ordained deacon with the fellow members of the diaconal order; and the newly ordained's first participation in the Eucharist as deacon.

Franco-German Influence

The period from the sixth to the tenth centuries has been called "the center of gravity in the western liturgy."[18] As will be seen, the blending of Roman ritual with Franco-German influence will create rites of ordination that were codified by the Council of Trent and retained almost unchanged until the revisions of 1968.

"Romano-Frankish usage replaced a liturgy that combined simplicity and depth with a set of rites whose purpose was to show what effects grace and sacramental power have on those who receive them."[19] Therefore this revised liturgy is more graphic and, in a sense, more theatrical: prayers are interrupted to insert other rituals to act out the meaning of the prayer. In the ordination of a deacon, this liturgy emphasizes the investiture of the new deacon in his liturgical garb, and the presentation of the Book of the Gospels. These innovations parallel similar additions to the rituals of episcopal and presbyteral ordinations, which now included anointings, presentation of insignia of office, and investiture. In a later edition of the Gregorianum, for example, mention is made of the Litany of Saints being prayed before the ordination itself, and an additional prayer is provided for use when the deacon is invested with the stole.

Similar accretions to the rite would continue over the succeeding centuries. As Susan Wood points out, the rites of ordination used until the revisions of 1968, which had been promulgated by Pope Clement VIII in 1595, were little more than "a compilation of texts and ceremonies from several earlier sources, reflecting doctrinal and cultural influences from the fifth to the end of the thirteenth century. Essential rites, such as the laying on of hands, were buried under secondary rites."[20] With this in mind as historical context, we turn to the reform of the ordination rites in the twentieth century.

The Postconciliar Rites of Ordination (1968 and 1990)

Significant liturgical reform in the ordination rites began with Pius XII. In 1947, he declared the essential elements of ordination to the episcopate, presbyterate, and diaconate to be the imposition of hands and the prayer of consecration, but no changes to the rite were made at that time.[21] Following the various decisions of the Second Vatican Council, however, such revisions had become absolutely critical. Not only were the existing rites themselves problematic even under pre–Vatican II understandings of ordained ministry, but the council's renewal of the episcopal and diaconal orders demanded immediate attention. The 1968 text, therefore, was "the first book of the post–Vatican II liturgical reform project for the Roman Rite."[22] What was gained by having a rapid development of a usable ordination rite, however, suffered by the haste with which it had been prepared. Wood provides a useful summary of the developments between the 1968 text and the revised text of 1990.[23]

The following table contrasts the two rites and will serve as an outline for the comments that follow.

Table 5. Comparison of 1968 and 1990 Rites of Diaconal Ordination

Source: For the section contrasting the 1968 *Prayer of Consecration* and the 1990 *Prayer of Ordination*, including footnotes for that section, Susan K. Wood, *Sacramental Orders*, 157–58. Further adapted, revised, and expanded by William T. Ditewig.

1968	1990
Calling, Presentation, and Election	*Calling, Presentation, and Election*
The rite calls for a deacon to call the ordinand forward, and for a "priest designated by the bishop" to present him to the bishop and to testify as to his worthiness. The 1968 translation has the priest asking the bishop to ordain the candidate "for service as deacon." The bishop then asks, "Do you judge them worthy?" and the priest responds, "After inquiry among the people of Christ and upon recommendation of those concerned with his training, I testify that he has been found worthy."	While the basic pattern remains the same, the translation is altered. Now the priest asks the bishop to ordain the candidate "to the responsibility of the diaconate." In responding to the bishop's question about worthiness, the priest now responds, "After inquiry among the Christian people and upon the recommendation of those responsible, I testify..."
Homily	*Homily*
The rubric introducing the homily notes that the bishop will speak to the assembly and the candidate about the office of deacon and the meaning and importance of celibacy in the church.	The rubric now omits the reference to celibacy in itself, and instead reminds the bishop to "take into consideration whether those to be ordained are both married and unmarried, or only unmarried, or only married. The suggested homily now includes separate sections to be used for each of these eventualities.
Commitment to Celibacy	*Promise of the Elect*
In the rite, the promise of celibacy is treated as a distinct element, immediately following the homily	Now the promise of celibacy, for those who are unmarried, takes place within the examination of

Continued

Table 5 Continued

and before the examination of the candidate begins.	the candidate. This part of the rite is now referred to as the "Promise of the Elect" rather than the "Examination of the Candidate." The focus is on the full range of promises made by the candidate, which may include celibacy. Where the 1968 translation asked if the candidate was prepared to "assist the bishop and the priests"; the translation now refers to "the Priestly order."
Examination of the Candidate	
Promise of Obedience	*Promise of Obedience*
Litany of Saints	*Litany of Supplication*
Laying on of Hands	*Laying on of Hands*
Prayer of Consecration[24]	*Prayer of Ordination*
"Almighty God, giver of honors, distributor of orders, and apportioner of offices"	"you bestow every grace, you apportion every order and assign every office." This eliminates reference to honor with its corresponding interpretation of office as status elevation.[25]
"You enrich it with every kind of grace and perfect it with a diversity of members to serve the whole body in a wonderful pattern of unity." This translation, however, fails to translate the fact that this unity is ascribed to "the law": *Cuius corpus, Ecclesiam tuam, caelestium gratiarum varietate distinctam suorumque conexam distinctione membrorum, per legem totius mirabilem compagis unitatem...* (emphasis added)	"You enable your Church, Christ's body, to grow to full stature as a new temple, adorned with every kind of heavenly grace, united in the diversity of its members and formed into a wonderful pattern of unity by the Holy Spirit." Here the unity of the church is ascribed to the Holy Spirit.

Table 5 Continued

"You established a threefold ministry of worship and service for the glory of your name. As ministers of your tabernacle you chose the sons of Levi and gave them your blessing as their everlasting inheritance." This translation eliminates the military language of the original: *nomini tuo militare constituens:* "performing as a soldier."	"As once you chose the sons of Levi to minister in the former tabernacle, so by gifts of grace you established the threefold rank of ministers to serve your name" *(nomini tuo servire constituens)*. This form eliminates the military references as well as mention of the reward promised to the sons of Levi. The emphasis is clearly on service.
"May his conduct exemplify your commands and lead your people to imitate his purity of life" *(In moribus eorum praecepta tua fulgeant, ut suae castitatis exemplo imitationem sanctae plebis acquirant)*. The literal Latin text prayed that deacons might lead God's people to holiness through the example of their "chastity."	"May your commandments shine forth in their conduct so that by the example of their way of life they may become a model for your holy people" *(In moribus eius praecepta tua fulgeant, ut suae conversationis exemplo imitationem sanctae plebis acquirant)*. The literal Latin text prays that deacons might lead God's people to holiness through the example of their conversion of life. The change from "by the example of his chastity" to "by the example of his conversion of life" adapts the prayer of ordination to the ordination of married deacons at the same time that it broadens the concept of virtue that must characterize a deacon's life.
Investiture with Stole and Dalmatic	*Investiture with Stole and Dalmatic*
Presentation of the Book of the Gospels	*Handing On of the Book of the Gospels*
Kiss of Peace	*Kiss of Peace*

The Introduction to the Rite of Ordination of Deacons

As mentioned above, there were serious flaws in the 1968 rite of ordination. These include, for example, "the theologically questionable listing of orders in its title, its lack of a 'General Introduction' *[praenotanda]*, the infelicity of the consecratory ordination prayer for presbyters, and the absence of a rite for assuming celibacy associated with ordination to the diaconate."[26] For an introduction, we may look to the Apostolic Constitution *Pontificalis Romani Recognitio*, published in 1968, which approved the new rites of ordination to the diaconate, presbyterate, and episcopate (note the restoration of the term *ordination* rather than *consecration* for a bishop). It likewise states that in the ordination of deacons, "hands are laid not for the priesthood, but for the ministry.[27]...[T]hey serve the people of God in the *diaconia* of liturgy, word, and charity, in communion with the bishop and his presbyterium."[28] (This distinction that deacons are ordained not for priesthood but for ministry is significant. Nathan Mitchell observes that this highlights the fact that deacons are not merely "subordinate" members of the hierarchy; they are *different*.[29] The relationship between the ranks of the clergy is no longer bishop–priest–deacon; rather, it is now, after the renewal of the diaconate as a permanent order, bishop–priest and bishop–deacon.) Paul VI in this Apostolic Constitution recalls the Apostolic Constitution *Sacramentum Ordinis* of Pius XII, in which Pius declared that "the sole matter of the sacred orders of diaconate and presbyterate is the laying on of hands; likewise the sole form is the words determining the application of this matter."[30] Paul VI then continues to supply the new consecratory prayer.

Wood points out that the 1990 General Introduction "is divided into four sections: the importance of the ordination, the duties and ministries of the participants in the ordination, instructions for the ordination, and the requisites for the celebration."[31] She goes on to point out a significant shortcoming in the listing of various functions of the deacon; specifically, that the listing is largely liturgical, leaving out additional and essential functions of word and service. This will be discussed in greater detail as we consider the words and actions of the rite itself.

The Ordination Rite

Call, Election, Consent

The ordination rite occurs in the context of the Mass, following the proclamation of the Gospel. In both the 1968 and 1990 rites, the initial elements of diaconal ordination are the calling of the candidate, his presentation to the bishop, the election by the bishop, and the consent of the people. There are several interesting points within this part of the rite. In both rites, the candidate is called forward by name by a deacon. Then a priest presents the candidate to the bishop, asking that the candidate be ordained a deacon. In a dialogue with the priest-presenter, the bishop asks if the candidate is worthy. After the priest testifies that the candidate is worthy, the bishop "elects" the candidate for ordination and the assembly is invited to show their approval; in the United States that is usually by applause.

In pastoral practice it is not unusual for the same deacon who calls the candidates to present them to the bishop and to testify as to their readiness, especially when that deacon is the director of the diocesan diaconate office or of the formation program itself. If a presbyter is involved, he should be someone with a particular connection to the formation process: he could be the vocation director for the diocese, the director of the diaconate, or perhaps the diocesan vicar for clergy. An interesting change between the 1968 and 1990 rites comes in the testimonial made as to the candidate's worthiness. In 1968, consultation has been made with the people of God and with those concerned with the candidate's formation; in 1990, consultation has been made with the people of God and "those responsible." It is possible, of course, to read this change as meaning precisely the same thing as the 1968 rite; on the other hand, it is possible that this is an attempt to suggest a broader consultation. Regardless of this interpretation, the pastoral reality here is that, in many dioceses, the community is not truly consulted in any substantive way. There are evaluations from faculty and staff, and there are usually required assessments by the candidate's pastor and from a diocesan selection board, but it is rare that the community in which the deacon will serve is consulted about their acceptance and support of the deacon. The applause that normally concludes this part of the rite is actually congratulatory in nature, recognizing the bishop's action in accepting the candidate. Contrast this with the practice in many Eastern Catholic churches, in which the bishop asks the people to indicate their approval *prior* to the election, and the assembly responds, "*Axios!*," "He is worthy!"

The Homily

At first glance, the 1990 suggested homily appears significantly altered from the 1968 text, especially with its separate sections for married and unmarried elect. Before looking directly at the homily, however, it is important to note the methodological concern raised by Joncas; namely, that the homily is merely a suggested text, not a "fixed ritual text."[32] Thus, although it is possible that these texts are used verbatim by some bishops, that is exceptionally rare in practice. I agree with Joncas that, while the suggested text is illuminating, it should not "be given the same 'weight' as fixed texts intended for public proclamation."[33] Nonetheless, assuming that the suggested homily text is used by the bishop as a source in the preparation of his own homily, it is important to consider it in that light.

The first thing observable in the 1968 text is that the homily is initially addressed to the entire assembly; while this is good as far as it goes, it is significant that the bishop begins by referring to the ordinand as their "relative and friend." Surely many of the assembly are, in fact, relatives and friends of the ordinand, but the larger issue is that the sacraments are not simple family affairs. The sacramental role of the assembly is far more significant and extensive; the assembly gathered is, and represents, the local church. Unfortunately, the 1968 text is echoed in the 1990: "since these our sons who are your relatives and friends...." It is hoped that bishops will avoid such a restrictive notion of the assembly when preparing the actual homily used at the ordination and that future revisions of the rite will take this into account.

The 1968 text refers to the ordinand being "raised" to the order of deacon, and that he is "to be promoted." Mary Collins has referred to this as "status elevation" language, and, as seen in the table above, Joncas and Wood suggest that this language has been mitigated in the 1990 text of the Prayer of Ordination.[34] However, in the suggested homily text at least, the English translation still speaks of the "advancement" *(ad Ordinem diaconorum sint provehendi)* of the candidates and about the order "to which they are about to be raised" *(ad qualem ministerii gradum sint ascensuri)*. During the homily, the bishop shifts his attention and speaks directly to the candidates. The translations of the 1968 and the 1990 texts are almost identical, and the status elevation language remains. In 1968: "My son, you are being raised to the order of deacons. The Lord has set an example for you to follow"; in 1990: "Now, dear sons, you are to be raised to the Order of the Diaconate. The Lord has set an example, that just as he himself has done, you also should do" *(Vobis authem, filii dilectissimi, ad Ordinem diaconii provehendi, Dominus dedit exemplum, ut, quemadmodum ipse fecit, ita et vos faciatis)*.

The homily does a good job of integrating the three dimensions of the deacon's ministry. It "emphasizes the service of deacons and connects the service they perform to their service at the altar."[35]

The structure of the 1990 proposed homily includes three options for the bishop: one for use if both married and unmarried candidates are to be ordained, one for use if only unmarried candidates are present, and a final one if only married candidates are present. In 1968, the homily was followed immediately by having the unmarried elect stand in front of the bishop and make their promise of celibacy. Much of the material in the 1990 section of the homily directed to the unmarried elect is drawn directly from the 1968 charge by the bishop to those about to promise celibacy. In the 1968 text, the bishop says, "By this consecration you will adhere more easily to Christ with an undivided heart; you will be more freely at the service of God and mankind, and you will be more untrammeled in the ministry of Christian conversion and rebirth." In the 1990 homily section, the bishop says, "Compelled by the sincere love of Christ the Lord and embracing this state with total dedication, you will cling to Christ more easily with an undivided heart. You will free yourselves more completely for the service of God and man, and minister more effectively in the ministry of spiritual rebirth." While the language of having an "undivided heart" remains, the reference to being "untrammeled" has been removed. Speaking as one who is married, I find this language troubling theologically and personally. The text implies that married persons are themselves incapable of clinging to Christ with an undivided heart (which all disciples are called to do), or that (in the language of the 1968 text) married persons are somehow "trammeled" in their capability to serve others. The problems are not restricted to matrimony, however; the text also seems to reduce the charism of celibacy to notions of "availability" to serve (to "be more freely at the service of God and mankind" and to "minister more effectively"). There is nothing in the text to call the entire assembly to a greater appreciation of the far more theologically significant eschatological witness of the celibate state.

The section addressed to married elect is no less problematic, and in fact may be even more so. First, it has been drawn completely from the original 1968 text,[36] with absolutely no mention of the state of marriage whatsoever! Even in the "combined text" which may be used when both married and unmarried elect are present, the introductory clause says only, "Whether or not you have been called to holy celibacy."[37] Wood observes that the longstanding experience of the church with only transitional (and celibate) deacons is still emphasized in the current text, while it fails "to contextualize the rite according to the experience and responsibilities of married candidates."[38]

In conclusion, this section of the homily is most unfortunate, pointing to a lacuna to be noted later in the rite: while celibate elect are asked to affirm and promise their commitment to the celibate state of life, married elect are never asked to affirm and renew their commitment to *their* state of life, a state of life that is in itself a sacrament of the church (unlike celibacy). Finally, just as the true significance of the celibate state lies in its eschatological witness, so too the sacramental state of matrimony offers its own eschatological witness to the whole church. Therefore, these sections of the rite represent, in my opinion, a most egregious oversight, one that we can only hope bishops correct in their own homilies, and that will be corrected in future revisions of the rite itself.

Promise of the Elect

Susan Wood offers a succinct summary of the five (or six) promises now made by the elect.[39] In the 1968 rite, the promise of celibacy was made immediately following the bishop's homily and distinct from the rest of the promises. In the 1990 text, however, the promise of celibacy is now integrated into the other promises. Wood correctly observes that missing from the list of promises is anything related to works of charity, which one might assume would be an important part of the rite. Joncas makes this same point. He goes on to ask, if celibate candidates are asked to profess publicly their commitment to serve within the celibate state, "should not the married candidates be asked to publicly commit themselves to the same things in the modality of the sacrament of marriage? This raises the further question of what ritual acknowledgment should be given to the spouses and families of married deacon-candidates."[40] Jounel notes that in the 1968 French ritual, a married ordinand's wife is asked to give her acceptance publicly of "what this ordination will entail for her conjugal and familial life."[41]

The Promise of Obedience

The elect now approaches the bishop, places his hands in the bishop's, and promises respect and obedience to the bishop and his successors. Wood and others have questioned the suitability of the feudal liturgical gesture itself, although the implications of the promise of obedience itself are unquestioned. Wood states:

> The promise of obedience originated at the time of the lay investiture controversy when clerics were subject to lay authority and considered as serfs subject to a feudal landlord. The promise to the bishop opposed lay investiture by emphasizing that the priest is subject to the bishop and him alone.
>
> The General Introduction, no. 11c, allows national conferences of bishops to specify the form by which the elect for the diaconate and the presbyterate are to promise respect and obedience. In this day and age, a gesture

> less linked to a feudal relationship would be more appropriate.[42]

Ordination is about relationships. There is the relationship of the ordinand to Christ, to the ordaining bishop, to the rest of the order into which the ordinand is being incorporated, and to the entire people of God. The rite of obedience speaks directly to the relationship of ordinand and bishop. Let me suggest that what Wood says about the presbyter's promise of obedience applies as well to deacons:

> The presbyter's [deacon's] promise of obedience to the bishop also connects him to the local church. In committing himself to serve the bishop obediently, he thereby commits himself to serve the people of that diocese, to make the objectives of the diocesan church his own, and to commit himself to furthering its mission....The relationship between presbyter [deacon] and bishop is more than jurisdictional regulation, but is also personal representation. The presbyter [deacon] represents the bishop who represents the local church. There is no genuine priestly [diaconal] ministry except in communion with the supreme pontiff and the episcopal college, especially with one's own diocesan bishop.[43]

Now consider the observation of German theologian Helmut Hoping:

> The presbyter represents the bishop *in situ*, that is, in the parishes, where they have governance of the parishes to which they have been assigned, and where they are responsible for presiding at the Eucharist. The deacon also has a share of the apostolic mission of the bishop. The deacon represents the bishop *in situ* in *diakonia*, which—as has become clear—is at the direct disposal of the bishop. As a function of the Church's governance, the diaconate highlights the *diakonia* of every single Christian.[44]

Canon 266 specifies that "through the reception of the diaconate, a person becomes a cleric and is incardinated in the particular church or personal prelature for whose service he has been advanced." Canon law regarding incardination reflects the sacramental relationships established through ordination. While the canonical effect of incardination takes place upon the celebration of diaconal ordination, the rite of obedience is witness to these relationships as well. I join with Wood in hoping that an alternative liturgical form may be found to replace the excessively feudal gesture now in place, so that the full significance of the rite itself may be discerned in a more contemporary way.

The Prayer of Ordination

Following the Prayer of Supplication, the elect kneels before the bishop for the laying on of hands, which takes place in silence. Then follows the Prayer of Ordination. Wood provides an excellent summary of the structure and content of the prayer.[45] In a fine summary, she writes:

> The prayer of ordination for deacons spells out the holiness of life expected of them in much more detail than do the ordination prayers for presbyters or bishops, both of which focus more on the specific tasks of ministry. This indicates that people minister more by who they are than by what they do, also indicating that diaconal ministry is more about presence than task, about who a deacon is than what he does....However, the absence of mention of specific tasks of ministry may also be a sign that the rite developed prior to significant experience of the diaconate in the life of the Church or an indication that diaconal ministry is not as easily specified as presbyteral or episcopal ministry.[46]

Table 5 above outlines specific developments between the 1968 and 1990 editions of the rite; the section of the table concerning the Prayer of Ordination is taken directly from Wood. Joncas summarizes, "In every case the modifications of the diaconal consecratory ordination prayer downplay status-elevation and hierarchical ranking language and play up Spirit-empowered service in the lives of deacons."[47]

Investiture with Stole and Dalmatic

Now that the ordination is complete, a series of explanatory rites take place, the first being the vesting of the new deacon in the liturgical vestments of the order. The stole is a sign of ordination for each of the three orders. Prior to the reforms of Vatican II, the way one wore the stole denoted one's order: deacons, by wearing the stole over the left shoulder and caught up at the right hip; priests, by wearing the stole over both shoulders and crossed diagonally across the chest; the bishop, by wearing the stole over both shoulders with the ends hanging straight down in front. Since Vatican II, bishops and priests wear the stole in an identical manner, hanging straight down, while the deacon continues to wear his as before. The dalmatic was originally a papal vestment, but it was soon conferred by the emperor Constantine on all bishops. Eventually, by the eleventh century, it was required for both bishops and deacons. Bishops, on occasion, continue to wear the dalmatic under the chasuble; it is the normal outer vestment for deacons. Given this history, the dalmatic can be a powerful sign of the relationship that should exist between the bishop and his deacons; unfortunately, most people are unaware of this connection.

Presentation of the Book of the Gospels

Now properly vested, the new deacon returns to the bishop and is presented with the Book of the Gospels, along with the bishop's charge: "Receive the Gospel of Christ, whose herald you have become. Believe what you read, teach what you believe, and practice what you teach." Wood observes that "service to the gospel represents one of the three services to which a deacon is ordained, the other being service in the liturgy and service in charity." In fact, it is interesting that the other two services are not explicitly highlighted in the rite. While it may be argued that the clothing of the new deacon in his liturgical vestments signifies his liturgical role, there are no accompanying explanatory texts or actions to contextualize the vesting. Perhaps even more significantly, however, there is no liturgical celebration of the deacon's charitable mission. Future revisions of *De Ordinatione* would benefit from consideration of an expansion of the explanatory rites to provide a more balanced approach to their structure.

Wood raises an interesting question concerning liturgical preaching by deacons. She observes that "the Roman Catholic Church *in the United States* currently authorizes deacons to preach" (emphasis added) at the services and sacraments at which they preside. She writes, "In a Eucharistic Liturgy, the homilist should ordinarily be the presiding bishop or presbyter."[48] In response, it should be clarified that diaconal preaching, especially at the liturgical services and sacraments at which deacons preside is not simply the practice in the United States; it is a universal practice. In fact, as we saw in chapter 5, it was part of the vision of the bishops and priests who desired the renewal of a permanent diaconate in the nineteenth and twentieth centuries, that preaching by deacons was one of major reasons for the renewal of the order in the first place. This has not been the perception in the United States, however, where the discussion about the diaconate and the perception of deacons in the late 1960s had not reached the maturity attained by many European theologians over the previous century. In the United States, deacons were perceived primarily as ordained social workers, with little responsibility for liturgical ministry or for catechesis. In Europe, by contrast, deacons were seen primarily as *official teachers* and preachers who extended the ministry of the church into projects of social and community transformation.

Wood finds James M. Barnett's conclusion convincing; he concludes that "preaching was not a diaconal function in the early Church and that it should not be today."[49] I respectfully suggest that the patristic and canonical evidence on the practice of diaconal preaching in the ancient church is not as univocal as once supposed, and I would cite the work of Joseph Pokusa in this regard.[50] In just one example, Pokusa describes the canonical evidence of deacons leading communities in the absence of a bishop or presbyter. It may be assumed with some confidence that deacons in such situations preached at community prayer, and the writings of St. Augustine in support of the catechetical responsibilities of deacons, suggesting that they also would be involved in public preaching and teaching.

However, whether diaconal preaching was a specific or ordinary function of the deacon in the ancient church seems less determinative than the needs of the contemporary church. Why should the development of the contemporary diaconate be restricted only to its patristic antecedents? For example, the roles of the contemporary presbyter are not restricted only to his patristic functions; for that matter, the same could be said of a contemporary bishop. Why, then, should such restrictions be placed on the contemporary diaconate? The question ultimately is whether the church has a need for diaconal preaching. Here the historical evidence outlined in chapter 5 would suggest that the early pioneers of a renewed diaconate in Germany and France, as well as the bishops at Vatican II, saw preaching as something they wanted contemporary deacons to do. In short, preaching by deacons would seem to be a natural development in the evolution of the diaconate.

The Kiss of Peace

The rite of ordination concludes with the deacon's receiving the kiss of peace from the bishop, and then sharing the kiss of peace with the other deacons present. This parallels the practice of presbyteral and episcopal ordinations, although Wood correctly observes that there is no mention in *Lumen Gentium* 29 of a "diaconal college" analogous to that of the presbyteral or episcopal college. Still, the more ancient sacramental term, as we saw at the beginning of this chapter is that of ordo. The kiss of peace shared among the deacons during the ordination ritual is an expression of the diaconal *ordo*, which is ancient in its roots.

Conclusion

Throughout the chapter, I have highlighted several areas that may be clarified in future revisions of the rite. In summary, they include the role of the assembly and the local church in the ordination of its ministers, the continuing use of status elevation language, which, though greatly reduced, persists; the inadequate integration of the reality that most deacons exercise their ministry in the context of sacramental married life; and, finally, the lack of specificity in identifying the *full* nature of the "service" to which the deacon is being ordained.

With regard to the role of the assembly, Joncas offers his own conclusion, that "critical attention seems to be shifting to the perceived exclusion of the laity from active participation in the ordination liturgy and the process by which ordination rites are generated."[51] He cites the September 1992 newsletter of the Bishops' Committee on the Liturgy, which says in part, "Greater attention needs to be given to the legitimate and active presence and participation of the laity at ordinations."[52] and continues to provide a number of concrete and beneficial suggestions.

Language of status elevation, while greatly reduced in the 1990 rite, is still found, particularly in the suggested homily; future revisions will need to take this into account. It would appear that perhaps the revisions of the 1968 rite focused particularly on the Prayer of Ordination and with perhaps slightly less attention to detail in other parts of the rite; this has led to a certain inconsistency in this regard.

Another matter that fails to reflect the lived experience of the community and the ministers being called from that community in service to it is that of the married state of life of the vast majority of deacons. As seen above, Wood observed that the experience of the church, prior to the Second Vatican Council was with a transitional and celibate diaconate. The experience of the church has now largely gone in the opposite direction, with the majority of deacons serving permanently and within the married, not celibate, state. The rite needs significant revision if the church is more accurately and adequately to reflect these changes. The answer to the question posed by Joncas, whether married candidates should be asked to affirm their own state of life just as celibate candidates do theirs, is a resounding affirmative. Furthermore, future revisions should also make more explicit the eschatological dimensions of both matrimony and celibacy.

Finally, we come to one of the most fundamental challenges in the rite: the specific nature of the deacon's "service." Wood echoes the views of many when she convincingly concludes that the rite of ordination

> certainly highlights the service which is characteristic of this order and which brings to visibility the service which is characteristic of the nature of the Church....As noted, however, it does not precisely specify the forms this service may assume with the Church other than naming a threefold ministry to the liturgy, the gospel, and works of charity, thus allowing a flexibility to the exercise and development of this order in the life of the Church.[53]

David Power is not so generous to the rite, or to this inability to specify the nature of "service" and the ministry of the deacon. He has written:

> The effort to express new meaning for the diaconate in recent revisions of the ordinal is unsuccessful for the simple reason that there is no clear ministry or office actually exercised to provide the experiential component of symbolic transformation. The experience is either that of a supernumerary in a parish or of a person who could better meet the needs of the people as an ordained presbyter.[54]

This ambiguity about the specific nature and function of the deacon's "service" is going to plague the renewal of the diaconate until it is addressed directly and concretely. We have already made reference to the invaluable word studies of John Collins, in which he most accurately expands the very concept of *diakonia* beyond the previously accepted categories of menial social service. The rite of ordination will remain deficient in this regard until the church has gained far more practical experience with the servant-leadership of the deacon. Perhaps as some of the ideas presented in the previous chapter, inspired by the work of Walter Kasper and others, take root in the lived experience of the church, suitable revisions may be made to the rite of ordination itself. Further suggestions in this regard will be examined in the next chapter.

9

THE EMERGING CHALLENGES: ISSUES FOR REFLECTION AND ACTION

Introduction

The purpose of this book has not been to offer simply a historical account of the ancient diaconate or the renewal of the order at the Second Vatican Council; nor has it been intended as a kind of a *ferverino* or *apologia* for the diaconate, which, as Owen Cummings has written, should not be needed in any case.[1] Frankly, as important as diaconate history is, and as interesting and challenging as the current state of the diaconate can be, neither of these can match the challenges that lie ahead. Therefore, as we draw to a close, we turn our attention to several critical issues that need to be faced now and into the future, and these are not simply matters of concern to the diaconate itself.

When one approaches the question of the diaconate, one usually hears, "What are deacons *for*? What do they *do* and *why* are they needed?" Of course, the appropriate answer to these questions, which has become a commonplace, is, "It's not about *what* deacons do but about *who* they are." True enough, perhaps, but this response has become nearly jingoistic and, even as correct as it is, ultimately inadequate and unsatisfying. Upon closer examination, we see that the problem is that *all* such questions and answers presuppose something that is not self-evident or all that certain; namely, that we have a solid grasp of who we *all* are as church and what we are *all* called to be and to do *as* church. This is why the emphasis in our examination has been on the context of deacons *within* a diaconal church. The only way an ordained diaconate makes any sense whatsoever is within that broader context of a diaconal church, and living out the implications of what that means is the most fundamental challenge of all.

The Nature and Mission of the Church-as-Servant

One of the great insights of the Second Vatican Council was its identification of the church-as-servant. This servant ecclesiology is evident throughout the conciliar documents: from the opening words of *Lumen Gentium (LG)* describing the church as being "a kind of sacrament, a sign and an instrument of communion with God and of unity among all" (*LG* 1), through the powerful call in *Gaudium et Spes (GS)* that the church "exists as the leaven and, as it were, the soul of human society in its renewal by Christ and transformation into the family of God" (*GS* 40). The church is to carry on the work of Christ, who came into the world "to bear witness to the truth, to save and not to judge, to serve and not to be served" (*GS* 3).[2] The church does this by being able "in a way adapted to each and every generation, to respond to the perennial questions which people ask about the meaning of life, both present and to come, and how one is related to the other" (*GS* 4). Under the guidance of the Holy Spirit, "all of the People of God [*Totius Populi Dei*], and particularly all pastors and theologians, are to listen to, discern, and interpret the various voices of our times in the light of the divine Word, so that revealed Truth may be more deeply penetrated, better understood and more effectively presented" (*GS* 44).

All members of the church, initiated into Christ, share in Christ's ministry of service across the threefold *munus* of teaching, sanctifying, and ruling. All members act, as a result of their sacramental initiation, *in persona Christi.*[3] The council teaches in its Decree on the Apostolate of Lay People *(Apostolicam Actuositatem [AA])*: "As participants in the function of Christ the Priest, Prophet, and King, the laity have their own active roles in the life and activity of the Church" (*AA* 10).[4]

This universal commission to service based on sacramental initiation into the dynamic life of the Trinity sustains a conclusion that "no member of the Church ought to be purely passive, simply the recipient of someone else's ministrations. Everyone is to serve and to be served."[5]

Repeated reference has been made throughout this text to the several conciliar and postconciliar papal statements of the church's diaconal nature from Paul VI through Benedict XVI, statements that reflect a broad-based ecclesial understanding being expressed by other bishops and theologians. This being said, however, what has this meant in practical, pastoral terms? Is the gospel being preached more effectively? Is the church recognized in its servantness? Do we consistently, as the people of God, engage the world as its servant of conversion, as "the leaven and soul" of human society?

As a reflective exercise, perhaps we may turn to the second part of the capstone document of the Second Vatican Council, the Pastoral Constitution on the Church in the Modern World, *Gaudium et Spes*. Although the entire document is foundational in nature, Part Two takes the theological vision of Part One and focuses intently on "Problems of Special Urgency." This was originally intended as an appendix to the main document, but the council fathers decided instead that the issues being highlighted were of such critical importance that they should not be relegated to an appendix, but were part of the very fabric of the constitution itself. In the introduction to its presentation of "Certain More Urgent Problems," the council fathers had this to say:

> Having set forth the dignity of the human person, and the function *[munus]* to which they are called, both individually and collectively, throughout the entire world, the Council now directs the attention of all people, in the light of the Gospel and of human experience, to certain particularly urgent contemporary problems which are most deeply affecting the human race.
>
> Of the many subjects arousing universal concern today, it may be helpful to concentrate especially on these: marriage and the family, human culture, economic, social and political life, the bond between the family of peoples, and

> peace. On each of these problems, the principles and light of Christ shines, by which Christians may be led and all people may be enlightened as they search for solutions to these problems and their implications. (*GS* 46)

I propose that we now reflect on these problems, which remain as urgent today as they were in 1965, and perhaps even more so. In each area, we can build a list of people and organizations dedicated to addressing the problem; that is not my point. Examine carefully the language of the council: these are problems to be addressed not merely by official agencies of the church, by national or international organizations, or even by special committees of the parish pastoral council. They are to be the mission and concern of *each* and *every* Catholic in one way or another; being a Christian, a follower of the kenotic Christ, means that we cannot delegate these responsibilities to others. Discipleship demands our own personal attention.

Marriage and the Family

As an initiated member into a servant church, what is our personal responsibility for the problems affecting marriage and family life today? It is not enough simply to watch the news on TV or the Internet and decry the situation: what am *I* doing about it? If we are married, how do we model a Christian response to the challenges of contemporary marriage and family life, and do we extol its many blessings to others? It is easy to slip into the kind of watercooler banter that makes light of such things (mother-in-law jokes, perhaps, or jokes about the "ball-and-chain"), but how often has humor been taken to extreme? When looking at our own family life, how attractive is it to others? In other words, if we hold that marriage and family life are good things, blessed by God as a sacramental state, does our own living of that reality attract others to want to share in that same blessing? Or do people see us and say, "Well, if *that's* what married life is supposed to be, I think I'll pass."

What steps are being taken in your parish and community to support and assist married people in their many responsibilities? Regardless of one's politics, Hillary Clinton's observation that "it takes a village to raise a child" is worthy of note. Are there ways, *precisely because we are servant Christians and value such things*, that we can form a group to help with child care so single parents can work, or any number of other such initiatives? Moving beyond neighborhood and parish, what opportunities are provided by local civic governments that can be used, supported, or adapted by servant Christians? What is offered or coordinated through your diocese? Do you know the persons on the diocesan staff who may serve in this area, who can be additional resources and support?

In short, if people were walking by your parish church some evening, or by your home, would they immediately say, "Oh, those folks are always so giving and supportive, and they go out of their way to help"?

Proper Development of Culture

We've all done it: seen a trailer for a new movie, or a billboard about some new product or fashion, and remarked how low things have gone in terms of cultural expression; one friend of mine refers to this (perhaps somewhat vaguely) as the "NASCARization of America." But, precisely as servant Christians, what can we do about it? I have found the following quotation from *Gaudium et Spes* to be particularly affirming, yet challenging at the same time: "There is a growing number of men and women in every nation and culture who are conscious that they themselves are the craftsmen and molders of their community's culture" (*GS* 55). *Gaudium et Spes* continues to outline a variety of ways in which we can make a difference in the culture around us. Recall the charge to be the leaven and soul of society; it is by being "craftsmen and molders" of culture that servant Christians can help in the transformation and conversion of culture. So how do we do that?

Again we turn to the personal: is the proper development of culture something that marks me as a human being? Do I demonstrate in my own life respect for others by my choice of language, by my acts of respect for others, by my own refusal to be drawn into behaviors and attitudes which demean, cheapen, or ridicule others? This is where the transformation of culture begins. Does this extend outward into our family life and into the parish and broader community? Are there efforts at parish and community levels with which I can become associated? If not, might I be able to start something? Again, I am not talking about anything particularly onerous here, or some kind of "campaign against Hollywood." Rather, I am suggesting small, simple things that might be undertaken in a neighborhood or a parish: getting a group together to clean up graffiti, pick up trash along the roads, or some other form of quiet yet powerful witness. The point is to transform quietly, as a servant, from within.

Economic and Social Life

The Second Vatican Council teaches: "In economic and social life, too, the dignity and entire vocation of the human person as well as the good of society as a whole have to be respected and fostered; for the human person is the source, the focus and the end of all economic and social life" (*GS* 63).

The bishops of the council were particularly concerned that while a few people had almost unlimited economic possibilities, the vast majority of people have nothing. "Luxury and misery exist side by side" (*GS* 63) is a powerful summary of much of the council's thought in this area. However, God has given gifts to be shared by all creation, not by only a few. So what is the servant Christian to do? "Don't we have agencies for this? And, after all, we have a committee at the parish that is focused on social concerns; they take care of that for us. Besides, I don't have much anyway; I can't afford to worry about everyone else: I have enough to do just trying to provide for myself and my family."

The servant Christian realizes that she or he must get involved in some way. As with the previous questions, are there already neighborhood, parish, or community groups that could use support of some kind? In particular, what steps can be taken locally to address the causes of some of the economic inequities that exist in your community? It is important to perform the corporal works of mercy: to feed the hungry, to clothe the naked, to shelter the homeless and so on; but what are the conditions that led their hunger, their nakedness, and their homelessness? The servant Christian quietly finds ways not only to offer immediate help and support but to begin addressing the social, political, and economic causes of the need.

Are the Catholics of your community known by others as an entire community of servant Christians? I spent twenty-two years as a Navy officer, and my family and I moved many times from duty station to duty station around the world. At one point, we were able to buy a home of our own, instead of renting or living in government housing. Our new community was blessed with five Catholic parishes and numerous Protestant churches. Within a week of moving into our home, we received perhaps two dozen letters and packets from the local Protestant churches, warmly welcoming us to the area, introducing the key ministers and contact persons for their churches, and inviting us to join with them in community and in praising God. Not a single note, letter, or packet arrived from any of the Catholic parishes, and yet if they had wished, they could have had access to the same housing-market information the Protestant churches had received. If we were not committed Catholics, such a lack of outreach to the newcomer might have turned out much differently since, as strangers, we might have turned to a community whose welcome was warm and inviting.

Again, I stress that what I am suggesting here is *not* that "the Catholic Church" is not already involved corporately with many of these issues; rather, I wonder how, on the local level, we are perceived as individual Catholics and as a Catholic community: are we seen as servant Christians always looking for ways to serve and to respond to need, or are we seen as aloof and insulated from those outside our own group?

> Christians engaged actively in modern economic and social progress and in the struggle for justice and charity must be convinced that they have much to contribute to the prosperity of mankind and to world peace. In these activities, both as individuals and as group members, may they give a shining example to others. (*GS* 72)

The Political Community

Flowing rather naturally from the previous "need of special urgency" is the council's concern over the active participation of *all*

Catholics in the political life of a community. This has become increasingly noteworthy in recent years in the United States, as politicians take positions at odds with Catholic teaching. This is exacerbated when Catholic politicians themselves struggle to balance personal integrity, religious conviction, and political realities. The words of the bishops at Vatican II ring as true today as they ever did:

> In our times profound transformations are to be noticed in the structure and institutions of peoples; they are the accompaniment of cultural, economic, and social development. These transformations exercise a deep influence on political life, particularly as regards the rights and duties of the individual in the exercise of civil liberty and in the achievement of the common good.... (*GS* 73)

From the outset of their treatment on political life, the council fathers reminded their readers that political structures are established *by* individuals, families, and "the various groups which make up the civil community" because they are aware of their own inability to achieve a "truly human life" by their own unaided efforts. The goal is for the common good of each individual within the community. In other words, political systems are supposed to be at the behest of the community, not the other way around. Furthermore, every individual has an obligation to participate in this process: "All citizens ought to be mindful of their right and duty to promote the common good by using their vote" (*GS* 75).

Here again the concern is not that the official, institutional church should be involved in political issues; rather, the focus throughout the document is on the rights and obligations of *every individual Christian* in the process. As servant Christians, giving of ourselves for the common good, what specific ways are open to us to be "a shining example by their sense of responsibility and their dedication to the common good; they should show in practice how authority can be reconciled with freedom, personal initiative and with the solidarity and the needs of the whole social framework, and the advantages of unity with profitable diversity" (*GS* 75).

Notice that every Christian is called to this obligation, not merely groups that we empower to act in our name. As servants, we

Christians are called always to work for the *common good* of all, not simply for a particular political agenda; as servants, we let go of ourselves and our own desires and seek to act for the larger good of others.

Fostering of Peace and the Establishment of a Community of Nations

The last of the urgent needs mentioned by the council fathers is no surprise. Although written after two World Wars and at the height of the cold war, its message is no less urgent today. The teaching can be summed up well in this brief passage:

> The Council proposes to outline the true and noble nature of peace, to condemn the savagery of war, and earnestly to exhort Christians to cooperate with all in securing a peace based on justice and charity and in promoting the means necessary to attain it, under the help of Christ, author of peace. (*GS* 77)

Taking their lead from (now Blessed) Pope John XXIII's then recently released encyclical *Pacem in Terris* ("Peace on Earth"), the bishops speak of peace as more than the mere absence of war; rather, true peace can be enjoyed only when human affairs are ordered rightly according to the mind and plan of God. In many ways, true peace can *only* be attained when all of the concerns already addressed in the previous paragraphs are met: true respect for the nature and vocation of the human person; the importance of the family, economic justice, and the common good sought through the political process.

The bishops acknowledge that the process leading to peace will find perfection only with the coming of Christ—but that each person has an obligation to work toward that goal. Again, this is not the place for an in-depth discussion of *Gaudium et Spes* or even this section of it; rather, we are concerned with how the church-as-servant in the world works to meet the goals set for it by the council and, indeed, by Christ. As with many national and international issues, the temptation is to believe that they are too big to be solved by one lone individual watching events unfold on a television set every night. As servant Christians, there is a responsibility *for the sake of others* to sacrifice oneself for the promotion of true justice and peace in the world.

This means searching out ways in which to do this within the spheres in which we live. Not only might we become involved in issues pertaining to a particular war, but we might also take a look at what is contributing to violence within our own neighborhoods and communities. If the causes of that violence can be addressed, if even some patterns of violence can be broken, the benefits will be felt outside the immediate region. True peace is achievable only through seeking the right ordering of biblical justice, and each of us can serve to "order" things in our immediate vicinities as much as we can.

Concluding Reflection on the Church-as-Servant

As I explained at the beginning of this part of the chapter, I see the most fundamental challenge facing the church that continues to emerge from Second Vatican Council in the third millennium as the full realization and acceptance of the church's own identity, both as individual servant Christians and as a universal servant communion, as Servant in the image of Christ. I have used Part Two of *Gaudium et Spes* as a kind of checklist of areas in which the servant-leadership of all Christians is demanded, expected, and necessary. I have attempted to stress in particular the need for us to be, and to be perceived by others as, true *servants*. This second dimension is not a reflection of a merely human desire to be admired; it is necessary because of the very sacramental nature of the church itself. If we are truly a "sign and instrument" of communion, then being *visible* is an essential, constitutive character of our servant nature. Realizing this servant sacramentality of the entire people of God is a foundational challenge that also serves as a hermeneutic for understanding the next level of challenges to follow.

Particular Challenges for the Diaconate

Out of this matrix of a sacramental servant church we move into a consideration of the specific challenges to be met with regard to church's own servants, the deacons. David Power has observed:

> The restoration of the permanent diaconate is of vital importance to the organic ordering of the church's ministry and to what is represented by the sacrament of order. There is much hesitation and lack of clarity on this score in church teaching, in theology, and in practice.[6]

Addressing the following challenges may assist in developing the greater clarity needed. Obviously, the church faces many more challenges than these with regard to the diaconate, but addressing these will be a start.

Challenge 1: Elimination of the Vestiges of the Cursus Honorum

A proper understanding of the diaconate presumes a "new way of thinking" about the sacramental nature of the church and its ordering of ministry. This new way of thinking restores a more organic approach to hierarchical ministry that is not dependent on the *cursus honorum*. The diaconate is a "full and equal" order, related to but independent of the presbyterate. When the church operated under a presbytero-centric model of ordained ministry, seeing the minor orders and lesser major orders of subdeacon and deacon as ordered to eventual ordination to the presbyterate, a transitional diaconate developed. But the contemporary diaconate is not about providing "on-the-job" training to future priests; the goals and demands of each order are unique to each other. It seems not only unnecessary but undesirable to continue to ordain to the diaconate seminarians in formation for the presbyterate.

Other vestiges of the *cursus honorum* remain. Bishops continue to be ordained from the order of presbyters, and contemporary law requires that candidates for ordination to the diaconate and presbyterate first be installed by the bishop in the lay ministries of lector and acolyte. These formally instituted ministries were adapted from the former minor orders by Pope Paul VI in *Ministeria Quaedam* (1972). Unfortunately, perhaps because of their origins in the minor orders, Paul restricted these new "lay" ministries to males only. Since these ministries have not been deemed pastorally necessary by the vast majority of bishops, only candidates for ordination are generally installed in them. The result is that they are now experienced by many as a continuation of the former minor orders: stages through which one passes on the way to an eventual ordination. Ironically, examining the pattern now experienced especially by candidates for the presbyterate, seminarians follow a path not unlike the former *cursus honorum.* One is accepted into formal candidacy (the successor rite to tonsure); then one is installed as a lector, followed by installation as an acolyte. Finally comes ordination as a deacon. Deacon seminarians are then ordained presbyters, and some of them will be ordained bishops.

The fact is that one of the implications of Vatican II's decision to renew the diaconate as a permanent order of ministry was the end of the *cursus honorum.* For the first time in well over a millennium, a person could be ordained to a major order of ministry without the expectation of subsequent ordination as a presbyter. With the council-directed suppression of the minor orders and the major order of the subdiaconate, it was clear that the *cursus honorum* was supposed to be over.

The ancient practice of the church did not require that presbyters be drawn from the order of deacons, and bishops were not always presbyters. There is no doctrinal necessity for one order to lead inexorably to the next. Furthermore, our current understanding of the sacrament of holy orders, based on the teaching of Vatican II, is that the bishop is the *prime* minister, with two derivative orders, presbyters and deacons, who assist him in sacerdotal and diaconal ways. In short, rather than an *ascending* progression that makes a "higher" order dependent upon receiving a "lesser" order, it is the other way around: the bishop with the fullness of orders is responsible for sharing his ministry with two assisting orders.

Susan Wood argues convincingly that there is no longer a need "to ordain to the 'lower' orders before ordaining to the 'higher' orders,"[7] and correctly concludes that "the permanent diaconate is normative for our understanding of the theology of the diaconate....[Normativity depends] on which experience gives us our most complete understanding of the meaning of the sacrament."[8] As we saw in chapter 3, James M. Barnett believes, and the evidence supports this conclusion, that "the decline of the diaconate springs more from the development of the idea of *cursus honorum* than from any other single factor."[9] Therefore, it is reasonable to postulate that it will be only with the overcoming of the remaining vestiges of the medieval *cursus honorum* that the normative, permanent diaconate will continue its proper development.

Finally, this "new way of thinking" about the diaconate suggests that Patrick McCaslin and Michael G. Lawler were correct to observe that (as stated earlier) "[a] parish, which is a local incarnation of Church and of Jesus, is not sacramentally whole if it is without either priest or deacon."[10] Church teaching on the sacramental nature of the church and the sacramental identity of the deacon are consistent in identifying *diakonia* as a constitutive element of the church. If that statement is true—and that certainly has been the major premise of this book— then every diocese, and indeed every parish, is entitled to the sacramental presence of the deacon. Leaving the diaconate as an option available only if desired by the presbyterate and bishop, which is often the case, seems as misplaced as suggesting that a parish can exist without the presbyterate.

Challenge 2: Recognition of the Unique Character of Diaconal Ordination

Another challenge for the contemporary diaconate is to realize the ramifications of *kenōsis* on the nature and role of the deacon, who receives a sacramental grace that is described in the *Catechism of the Catholic Church* as a "special strength," a totally self-sacrificial strength for service. In real terms this means that deacons must divorce themselves from any expressions, attitudes, or behaviors that smack of clericalism or the acquisition of power and authority for its own sake. There should be something unique in the ways in which deacons serve that demonstrates this kenotic dimension. In a particular exercise of governance, that flowing from canon 517

§2, which we will explore shortly, such an assignment is not a "right" flowing from ordination. Ordination in itself is not sufficient to qualify a person for pastoral office; other qualities of personality and professional competence are necessary.

The pressure underlying this challenge is increasing for a variety of reasons. The pattern of ordained ministry in the church has been so predominantly "priestly" over the last millennium that it is easy to apply "priestly" understandings even to an order that is not, in itself, priestly. Given the relative youth of the renewed diaconate, deacons often encounter one of two initial reactions in the community they serve: they are either treated as laypersons (since "ordination" is mistakenly seen as applying only to priests) or as some kind of junior priest ("After all, last year we had a seminarian here who was a deacon; he's gone back to the seminary to get ready to be ordained [meaning to the priesthood]. When will *you* be ordained [meaning to the priesthood]?" Here we see part of the problem associated with our first challenge.

Second, with the shortage of presbyters, there is increasing pressure on deacons to assume increasing responsibilities usually given to priests; deacons are often expected to fill the void. Great care needs to be exercised in this regard. As we have seen repeatedly, deacons were not "renewed" to supply for a shortage of priests. Bishops and pastors need to keep this firmly in mind, especially when working out details of a deacon's ministerial assignment. When the church experiences a shortage of presbyters, it must do what is necessary to identify more presbyters, while not permitting other forms of ordained and lay ministry to be distorted or distracted from their own proper nature and purpose. Perhaps one of the most challenging statements of the entire 1998 *Directory for the Ministry and Life of Permanent Deacons* from the Congregation for Clergy is the following: "In every case it is important, however, that deacons fully exercise their ministry, in preaching, in the liturgy and in charity to the extent that circumstances permit. They should not be relegated to marginal duties, be made merely to act as substitutes, nor discharge duties normally entrusted to non-ordained members of the faithful" (*DMLPD* #40).

The fact that the diaconate is not a sacerdotal order reinforces the conclusion reached above that the ordination to the diaconate of seminarians in formation for the priesthood. It also means that the criteria for ordination to the diaconate need not—and indeed, *ought* not—be linked to or judged by, the priesthood. Rather, those selected for the diaconate should be those who have a vocation to serve as deacon. Wood writes, "If the Church chooses to ordain those persons who show evidence of a diaconal vocation, and who are already doing diaconal ministry, the requirements for diaconal ordination with respect to age, marital status and gender may have to be changed."[11] In particular, the question of the possibility of ordaining women to the diaconate should be given the proper scrutiny it deserves. The work of theologians such as Phyllis Zagano and canonists in work such as the analysis offered by the Canon Law Society of America, and even the recent document from the International Theological Commission point out that the institutional church has never spoken definitively on this question.[12] Furthermore, the challenge here is for the church to develop an organic and creative set of criteria for the diaconate that are based on the diaconate itself—*not* on criteria used for other ministries, even that of the priesthood. The questions to be asked are whether a person, *any* person, is called to act in the person of Christ *the Servant* and in the name of the church, capable of acting competently and capably in that service, and whether that person has demonstrated such Christlike service in life. This is not a question of "rights," since no one has a right to ordination; nor is it necessarily a matter of justice. It is not a question of someone feeling that they "need" ordination to serve; it is a question of the sacramental signs that the church itself needs. It is a question of affirming in the church a vocation to the diaconate already bestowed by God, and this discernment is distinct from that used for the priesthood.

Challenge 3: Deacons and Canon 517 §2

This canon is particularly significant in the contemporary church, providing as it does for the pastoral care of parishes when insufficient numbers of presbyters are available. For that reason, it is necessary to examine the development of this canon closely. The provisions of canon 517 §2 are new in the 1983 *Code* and it has no parallel in the Eastern code. It reads:

> If the diocesan bishop should decide that due to a dearth of priests a participation in the exercise of the pastoral care of a parish is to be entrusted to a deacon or to some other person who is not a priest or to a community of persons, he is to appoint some priest endowed with the powers and faculties of a pastor to supervise the pastoral care.

On the one hand, examining the role of the deacon under this canon may seem to place undue emphasis on an extraordinary circumstance, rather than an ordinary diaconal function. However, as discussed below, deacons are given a definite precedence under the law and in recent Vatican documents for this ministry; our purpose is to investigate why this is the case.

The goal of the canon is to ensure that full pastoral care is provided through the assignment of pastors to every parish, even when those parishes may not have the presence of a resident pastor. The history of the development of this canon is illustrative.[13] The context of the canon is the need for some person to provide for the *cura animarum* in each parish. Since only a priest can supply *full* care, provisions must be made to provide some priest with that responsibility, even if that priest is not resident in the parish. Furthermore, if the priest is not resident, someone else must coordinate day-to-day pastoral life. Consequently, the canon is found in the chapter dealing with pastors, parishes, and parochial vicars. From the beginning of the code revision process the possibility was considered that there might be insufficient numbers of presbyters to pastor every parish, which led to the drafting of the following text, discussed by the Pontifical Commission for the Revision of the Code of Canon Law, February 15–20, 1971.

> If, in unusual circumstances, according to the norm of law, a participation in the exercise of the pastoral care of a parish is entrusted to a person not signed with the sacerdotal character *(personae sacerdotali charactere non insignitae)*, or to a community of persons, a priest is to be designated to oversee *(moderetur)* the pastoral care, as would the proper pastor of the parish.[14]

The purpose of the canon is to provide the parish with a priest to oversee the pastoral care of a parish. It is only in the subordinate clause of the canon that the provision of on-scene pastoral leadership by someone other than a priest is found. During the discussion, the text was amended to clarify the proper authority to make such an assignment, and the approved text now begins:

> If, because of a lack of priests, a diocesan bishop has determined that participation in the exercise of the pastoral care of a parish is to be entrusted to some person....[15]

At the next session, discussions focused on the juridical status of the priest moderator, suggesting that he be assigned "with all the rights and obligations of a pastor *(cum omnibus parochi obligationibus et iuribus)*."[16] However, the commission concluded that, while certainly the moderator would have the rights of a pastor, he would not have all of the obligations; the revision ultimately approved at this session reads:

> [The diocesan bishop] is to designate a priest who, with the rights of a proper pastor, shall oversee *(moderetur)* the pastoral care....[17]

This canon was not considered again for five years. In March 1976, two amendments were accepted. First, the verb "designate" *(designat)* was changed to "appoint" *(constituat)*, and "with the rights of a proper pastor" was changed to "having the power of a pastor" *(potestate parochi gaudens)*. The approved text read: "The diocesan bishop is to appoint a priest who, having the power of a pastor...."[18] Again, the principal concern was the nature and responsibilities of the priest moderator, not the daily administrator.

Deacons were first mentioned in connection with the canon in May 1980. "If, because of a lack of priests, the diocesan bishop has determined that participation in the exercise of the pastoral care of a parish is to be entrusted to some deacon or even *(etiam)* to a lay member of the Christian faithful or to a group of them, he is to appoint...."[19] John J. McCarthy captures the significance: "This revised text is significant because it not only mentions explicitly the possibility of a deacon functioning as the on-site assistant but, by inclusion of the word 'even' *(etiam)*, seems to suggest that a deacon would be preferable in that role to a lay person or group of persons."[20] For reasons left undocumented, however, many of the revisions of this session do not appear in the resulting schema, including the reference to deacons.

In response to the 1980 schema, a *relatio* was prepared that addressed this proposed canon.[21] Bishop Falcao requested that the text be modified to address the fact that the person appointed to provide on-scene pastoral care does so "in an extraordinary and temporary manner *(modo extraordinario et temporario)*."[22] Furthermore, the bishop stated that "pastoral ministries can be entrusted to lay persons only in this way *(ministeria pastoralia hoc modo tantum laicis concredi possunt)*."[23] The significance of this observation is clear: the exercise of such a ministry by laypersons is always an *extraordinary and temporary* situation, implying that a cleric would do so in an *ordinary and permanent* manner. The next recommendation came from then-Bishop Joseph Bernardin, who suggested that the words "to a deacon" be added (one could say, "restored," since mention of the deacon had previously been suggested, then deleted from the schema). The response of the commission to Bishop Bernardin's suggestion, especially in light of the previous recommendation about the *extraordinary and temporary* nature of a layperson's appointment to this task, is illuminating. The commission responded that a specific inclusion of deacons was *not* necessary:

> Because it is clear: deacons always have, in a certain ordinary and permanent way *[modo quidem ordinario et permanenti]*, "participation in the exercise of the pastoral care of a parish." The norm of this § concerns only a participation entrusted to other members of the Christian faithful who have received no grade of the ministerial priesthood *[qui nullum gradum sacerdotii ministerialis receperunt]*.[24]

The focus of this response as it pertains to the on-scene provider of pastoral care is on the concession of an extraordinary participation in governance to laypersons in such situations. Deacons need no such concession, since they already enjoy, by virtue of diaconal ordination, an ordinary and permanent participation in this exercise of governance.

Nonetheless, for no documented reason, when the final text of the canon was prepared, the specific reference to deacons remained. However, whereas the text of the previous draft that referred to deacons implied a distinction between deacons and laity who might be entrusted with pastoral care ("the diocesan bishop [may entrust] the pastoral care of a parish to some deacon or *even [etiam]* to some member of the Christian faithful"), the final text does *not* include this distinction. It reads simply that pastoral care may be entrusted "to a deacon, to another person, or to a community of persons." Again, no explanation is provided. McCarthy concludes reasonably that "it could well be...that the omission stems from the response given in the *Relatio complectens synthesim:* deacons have priority as a consequence of ordination,"[25] an ordination that gives deacons a certain ordinary and permanent responsibility for pastoral care.

Recent Vatican documents reach the same conclusion. The 1997 interdicasterial instruction *Ecclesiae de mysterio* addresses the provisions of canon 517 §2 in part as follows:

> The right understanding and application of this canon...requires that this exceptional provision be used only with strict adherence to conditions contained in it. These are:
>
> a) *a shortage of priests* [emphasis in text] and not for reasons of convenience or ambiguous "advancement of the laity," etc.;
>
> b) this is *a share in the exercise of the pastoral care* [emphasis in text] and not de facto directing, coordinating, moderating or governing the parish; these competencies, according to the canon, are the competencies of a presbyter alone.
>
> Because these are exceptional cases, before employing them, other possibilities should be considered, e.g., using the services of retired presbyters still capable of

> such service, or entrusting several parishes to one priest or to "several priests jointly."
>
> *In any event, the preference which this canon gives to deacons cannot be overlooked* [emphasis added].[26]

In 1998, the Congregation for the Clergy was even more emphatic. In dealing with this canon, the congregation asserted:

> Where permanent deacons participate in the pastoral care of parishes which do not, because of a shortage, have the immediate benefit of a parish priest, they always have precedence over the nonordained faithful....When deacons are available, participation in the pastoral care of the faithful may not be entrusted to a lay person or to a community of lay persons (*DMLPD* #41).

Throughout this process, then, there is an underlying presupposition that deacons exercise some *ordinary* responsibility for the care of souls that goes beyond the responsibility of the baptized faithful. This opens up an important question for reflection: *What is the vision of diaconate that might support such a claim?* While the law is silent on the issue, one possibility suggests itself.

The deacon's exercise of governance is limited to offices and functions not requiring "the priestly character" such as pastor or parochial vicar. And yet, the deacon is given a certain canonical precedence over the laity when pastoral leadership is required in the absence of a presbyter. The nature of this preference demands attention. Could it be that in this canon the diaconate is still perceived as a participation in the ministerial priesthood as it was for so many centuries prior to Vatican II? For example, canon 453 of the 1917 *Code* required (as does canon 521 in the 1983 *Code*) that only a presbyter could validly "assume a parish."[27] Furthermore, canon 154 of the 1917 *Code* stated that "offices that encompass the care of souls either in the external forum or the internal cannot be validly conferred on clerics who are not initiated into priesthood."[28] This was an innovation of the 1917 *Code*, since "the former Canon Law did not insist on the priesthood at the time of appointment, but ruled that within a certain time after the appointment the cleric had to receive the priesthood."[29] This meant that prior to 1917, deacons (and other clerics, as that term was understood at the time) could validly assume the office of pastor of a parish—as long as they were eventually ordained presbyters.

It seems possible to speculate that such an understanding might still exert a certain subtle yet pervasive influence on the current law: the deacon as a participant—albeit a limited one—in the ministerial priesthood. If that is the case, it is cause for concern. In its 1984 *Permanent Deacons in the United States: Guidelines for the Formation and Ministry*, the National Conference of Catholic Bishops referred to the deacon's "leadership role" with regard to canon 517 §2, but the *Guidelines* caution that such ministry "is not central to or typical of the diaconal ministry," and that the deacon "is not to be conceived of as being a 'substitute priest....'"[30] This concern continues to deepen as a growing shortage of presbyters in many regions increases pressure on the diaconate to assume greater degrees of parochial leadership "in the absence of priests."

Challenge 4: Ongoing Development of Theologies of the Diaconate

As seen earlier, there was no need for a theology of the diaconate when the normative form of the diaconate was that of a *transitory phase* leading to the presbyterate; the operative theology was of the presbyterate, not the diaconate. Now, however, there is such a need. Further, there is a great need for specific work to develop adequate theologies that address the particular states of life in which diaconate is experienced. In particular, with more than 93 percent of permanent deacons serving as married men with families, a theology that considers the mutuality and interdependence of matrimony and orders is needed. A theology of celibate diaconate that is distinct from a celibate presbyterate is also needed. Many celibate permanent deacons are increasingly concerned that, since most people in the church experience the diaconate as "the married order" their own service is often marginalized. As the renewed diaconate continues to expand and mature, it must be the subject of commensurate theological and canonical examination so that its full potential may be realized.

Challenge 5: The renewal of the diaconate must be understood within the broader context of reform and renewal.

In the nineteenth century the first stirrings of a renewed diaconate rippled through Germany. This was not an isolated movement for enhanced works of charity; rather, it was part of an overall movement of renewal as the church attempted to discover its relationship to the modern world. This contextualized proposal for the renewed diaconate was further developed following Dachau and the Second World War and may be seen in the discussions of Vatican II. In the ongoing development of the contemporary diaconate it is necessary to consider the diaconate within this broader context. In certain areas, the diaconate is perceived as a movement in opposition to reform and renewal, perpetuating an ancient, now-antiquated hierarchical order. As experience with the renewed diaconate continues, this context of reform and renewal will need to be developed: as the church-as-servant continues to find creative ways to meet the needs of an increasingly complex world, it will need *all* of its resources, and the diaconate is one of those instruments of renewal.

This challenge also means that the deacons need to seek every opportunity to integrate themselves and their ministry into existing structures of service. Because the renewed diaconate is still in an early stage of its contemporary development, there are struggles to determine how best it "fits in." The danger is that the diaconate may become isolated or inward-looking as it seeks its own identity. On the contrary, the diaconate's identity is to be found precisely in a mature integration with other ministers and ministries.

Conclusion

The Second Vatican Council did not take place in a vacuum. It emerged out of a half century of World Wars, worldwide economic collapse, the rise of totalitarian regimes, the *Shoah*, and the beginning of the nuclear age. The event itself took place at the height of the cold war, with the Cuban missile crisis occurring during its first session. The bishops from around the world, many of whom had experienced firsthand the horrors of the previous years, came to Rome with a wide variety of concerns, ideas, and goals. Pope John had invited them to Rome, as he said during his opening address, precisely because they were pastors and brought the needs of their people with them. The bishops had submitted nearly nine thousand items for discussion, ranging from questions related to the church's moral teaching to its liturgical and sacramental life. For them, these were not theoretical issues and questions but matters of significant pastoral concern.

It was in this context that they took up the question of their own ministry as bishops, and the very nature of the church itself. In particular, they were concerned with the relationships of the church to the world in which it lived. How could the church be a more effective witness to the Gospel, serving to transform the world and prevent the tragedies of earlier decades from happening again? As the bishops discussed and debated the issues and constructed their strategies for the future, the question of a renewed diaconate emerged as part of the overall matrix of renewal.

The diaconate emerging today is part of the larger reality of an emerging church. The challenges facing the diaconate are challenges facing the entire church: How can we be more effective witnesses to Christ to a world so desperately in need of good news? How can a diaconate newly renewed be fully integrated into the church's own image of itself and its identity? This mission of evangelization and service is at the core of our identity, and all of us have an active role to play in it. Deacons, through their lives and ministry, serve the rest of the church in carrying out the mission.

Nothing captures the imagination of the emerging diaconate better than the bishop's charge given to the newly ordained deacon, and it is with these words that we close.

Receive the Gospel of Christ, whose Herald you have Become.
Believe what you read,
Teach what you believe,
And practice what you teach.

NOTES

Introduction

1. John Paul II, Apostolic Letter *Tertio Millennio Adveniente*, November 10, 1994 (Vatican City: Libreria Editrice Vaticana, 1994), #20.

2. "Catholic Freedom v. Authority" in *Time*, November 22, 1968.

3. Carl Sandburg, "Fog," in *Chicago Poems* (New York: Henry Holt, 1916).

4. Prior to 1972, the system of holy orders included a rite known as tonsure, by which a man became a cleric and thereby capable of being ordained; four so-called minor orders (porter, lector, exorcist, and acolyte; and three major orders (subdeacon, deacon, and priest). At the recommendation of the Second Vatican Council, Pope Paul VI revised this system, suppressing (in the Latin church) the tradition of tonsure and the four minor orders and the major order of subdeacon with the promulgation of *Ministeria quaedam* in 1972 (*Acta Apostolicae Sedis* 64 [1972]: 529–34).

5. William T. Ditewig, "The Once and Future Diaconate: Notes from Past, Possibilities for the Future," *Church* 20, no. 2 (Summer 2004): 51.

6. Paul VI, *Hodie concilium*, *Acta Apostolicae Sedis* 58 (1966): 57–64.

7. Paul VI, Apostolic Letter *Ad Pascendum* (August 15, 1972), citing Mt 20:28, *Acta Apostolicae Sedis* 64 (1972): 534–40.

8. John Paul II, "The Heart of the Diaconate—Servants of the Mysteries of Christ and Servants of Your Brothers and Sisters," Allocution to the Permanent Deacons and Their Wives, Given at Detroit, Michigan, on September 19, 1987, *Origins* 17 (1987): 327–29.

9. Benedict XVI, *Deus Caritas Est* (Vatican City: Libreria Editrice Vaticana, 2006), #1.

10. Ibid., #20.

11. I have placed "deacons" in quotation marks because, although since the time of St. Irenaeus this passage has been popularly associated with the "establishment" of the diaconate, contemporary scholarship no longer makes such an absolute association; this will be examined in more detail in

chapter 2. Nonetheless, the selection of the seven marks a turning point in the ministry of the church.

12. Benedict XVI, *Deus Caritas Est*, #21.

13. Ibid.

14. Ibid., #25.

15. United States Conference of Catholic Bishops, *National Directory for the Formation, Ministry, and Life of Permanent Deacons in the United States* (Washington, DC: United States Conference of Catholic Bishops, 2004) [hereafter *National Directory*], #39 (emphasis added).

16. Edward J. Kilmartin, SJ, "Lay Participation in the Apostolate of the Hierarchy," in *Official Ministry in a New Age*, ed. James H. Provost (Washington, DC: Canon Law Society of America, 1981), 94.

17. In general in this book, the words *priest* and *priesthood* include *both* presbyters *and* bishops. The word *presbyter* will be used when *only* that order is intended.

18. James H. Provost, "Permanent Deacons in the 1983 Code," *Canon Law Society of America Proceedings* 46 (1984): 175.

19. United States Conference of Catholic Bishops, *National Directory*, #50 (emphasis added).

20. *Lumen Gentium* (hereafter LG) 29, in *Decrees of the Ecumenical Councils*, ed. Norman P. Tanner, 2 vols. (Washington, DC: Georgetown University Press, 1990), 2:874; translation mine.

21. *Codex Iuris Canonici*, canon 337 §1: "Prima tonsura et ordinis illis tantum conferendi sunt, qui propositum habeant ascendendi ad presbyteratum et quos merito coniicere liceat aliquando dignos futuros esse presbyteros." English translation from Edward N. Peters, curator, *The 1917 Pio-Benedictine Code of Canon Law* (San Francisco: Ignatius, 2001), 337.

22. James M. Barnett, *The Diaconate: A Full and Equal Order*, rev. ed. (Valley Forge, PA: Trinity Press International, 1995), xiv.

23. This may be seen in recent statements from the Holy See, such as the multidicasterial "Instruction on Certain Questions Regarding the Collaboration of the Non-Ordained Faithful in the Sacred Ministry of the Priest" (Vatican City: Libreria Editrice Vaticana, 1997). Notice that even in the title, the laity are not referred to according to their baptismal status but rather according to what they are *not*.

24. Over forty years since the council, the diaconate has experienced remarkable growth not only in sheer numbers but also in terms of theology and praxis. The year 1998 was of particular significance in the history of the diaconate. In February of that year, the Congregation for Catholic Education and the Congregation for the Clergy jointly issued documents on the formation, ministry, and life of deacons. In identifying the purpose

of the documents in a Joint Introduction, referring to the experience gained through the "experiments conducted up till now" the documents signal a new phase in the maturing of the church in its official understanding of the diaconate. In the United States, these documents influenced the promulgation in 2004 of the *National Directory for the Formation, Ministry and Life of Permanent Deacons in the United States*. Accompanying this normative text was a comprehensive set of "Basic Standards of Readiness" establishing competencies for use throughout all phases of pre- and post-ordination formation. See Congregation for Catholic Education, *Basic Norms for the Formation of Permanent Deacons* [hereafter BNFPD] and Congregation for the Clergy, *Directory for the Ministry and Life of Permanent Deacons* [hereafter DMLPD] (Vatican City: Libreria Editrice Vaticana, 1998), and *National Directory.*

1. The Diaconate Today

1. CARA, "The Permanent Diaconate Today" (Washington, DC: CARA, 2000) [hereafter, CARA 2000].

2. CARA, "Profile of the Diaconate in the United States: A Report of Findings from CARA's Deacon Poll," CARA Working Paper Series 6 (Washington, DC: CARA, 2004) [hereafter, CARA 2004].

3. CARA, "Catholic Ministry Formation Directory Statistical Summary: 2005–2006" (Washington, DC: CARA, April 2006) [hereafter, CARA Formation 2006].

4. CARA, "Diaconate Post-Ordination Survey" (Washington, DC: CARA, May 2007) [hereafter, CARA Post-Ordination 2007].

5. United States Catholic Conference [now renamed the United States Conference of Catholic Bishops], *A National Study on the Permanent Diaconate of the Catholic Church in the United States, 1994–1995* (Washington, DC: United States Catholic Conference, 1996) [hereafter USCCB Study 1996].

6. CARA 2000.

7. CARA Annual Statistical Report.

8. See Congregation for Catholic Education, *Basic Norms for the Formation of Permanent Deacons* (Vatican City: Libreria Editrice Vaticana, 1998) and the *National Directory.*

9. CARA 2004, 14.

10. Ibid.

11. USCCB Study 1996, 2.

12. Ibid.

13. *National Directory*, #77, citing Congregation for the Clergy, DMLPD, #5.

14. USCCB Study 1996, 4.

15. Ibid., 13.

16. Ibid., 16.

17. CARA 2004, 25–26.

18. CARA Special Report, "Understanding the Ministry and Experience: Parish Life Coordinators in the United States" (September 2005).

19. USCCB Study 1996, 16.

20. Congregation for the Clergy, DMLPD, #40.

21. One may point to the *General Directory for Catechesis* as an example. Only twice are deacons mentioned: "In the Diocese catechesis is a unique service performed jointly by priests, deacons, religious and laity, in communion with the Bishop....Even if priests, deacons, religious and laity exercise catechesis in common, they do so in different ways, each according to his particular condition in the Church *(sacred ministers, consecrated persons and the Christian faithful)*" (#219). While the document proceeds to develop specific catechetical responsibilities for the Bishop, priests, religious and laity, it is silent about deacons. Furthermore, in its section on "Priests, pastors and educators of the Christian community" (#224–25), the role of presbyters is described as flowing "from the sacrament of Holy Orders which they have received." There is *no* complementary presentation on the role of deacons who, nonetheless, are charged at their own ordination: "Receive the Gospel of Christ, whose herald you now are. Believe what you read, teach what you believe, and practice what you teach."

2. Scriptural Roots

1. Pope Paul VI, *Evangelii Nuntiandi*, December 8, 1975, #11.

2. Paul VI, *Hodie concilium*, *Acta Apostolicae Sedis* 58 (1966): 57–64.

3. Lawrence Boadt, CSP, *Reading the Old Testament: An Introduction* (New York/Mahwah, NJ: Paulist, 1984), 543.

4. Ibid., 544.

5. Ibid., 545.

6. See, e.g., John Macquarrie, *Principles of Christian Theology*, 2nd ed. (New York: Charles Scribner's Sons, 1977; 1st ed. 1966), 113–15. Also Owen F. Cummings, *John Macquarrie: A Master of Theology* (Mahwah, NJ: Paulist, 2002).

7. Ignatius, *Trallians* 3:1, in *Early Christian Fathers*, ed. Cyril C. Richardson (New York: Collier Books, Macmillan, 1970), 99.

8. Boadt, *Reading the Old Testament*, 546.

9. Ibid.

10. Ibid.

11. Norbert Brockman, SM, *Ordained to Service: A Theology of the Permanent Diaconate* (Hicksville, NY: Exposition Press, 1976), 4.

12. Boadt, *Reading the Old Testament*, 547.

13. Ibid.

14. Ibid.

15. Ibid.

16. Ibid., 548–49.

17. Ibid.

18. Ibid., 551.

19. See, e.g., Jean-Paul Audet, *Structures of Christian Priesthood: A Study of Home, Marriage, and Celibacy in the Pastoral Service of the Church*, trans. Rosemary Sheed (New York: Macmillan, 1967); Bernard Cooke, *Ministry to Word and Sacraments: History and Theology* (Philadelphia: Fortress, 1976); Kenan B. Osborne, OFM, *Priesthood: A History of the Ordained Ministry in the Roman Catholic Church* (New York/Mahwah, NJ: Paulist, 1988); idem, *The Diaconate in the Christian Church: Its History and Theology* (Chicago: National Association of Diaconate Directors, 1996); Nathan Mitchell, OSB, *Mission and Ministry: History and Theology in the Sacrament of Order* (Wilmington, DE: Michael Glazier, 1982); James M. Barnett, *The Diaconate: A Full and Equal Order*, rev. ed. (Valley Forge, PA: Trinity Press International, 1995).

20. Edward P. Echlin, SJ, *The Deacon in the Church: Past and Future* (Staten Island, NY: Alba House, 1971), 3.

21. Jean Colson, *La fonction diaconale aux origines de l'Église* (Paris: Desclée de Brouwer, 1960). See also his "Les diacres à la lumière de l'histoire," *La vie spirituelle*, no. 116 (1967) : 442–67.

22. Brockman, *Ordained to Service*, 3–4.

23. John N. Collins, *Diakonia: Re-interpreting the Ancient Sources* (New York/Oxford: Oxford University Press, 1990), 3–4.

24. Osborne, *Diaconate in the Christian Church*, 13.

25. Ibid., 7.

26. Ibid., 8.

27. Ibid.

28. Peter F. Ellis, *The Genius of John: A Composition-Critical Commentary on the Fourth Gospel* (Collegeville, MN: Liturgical Press, 1984), 213.

29. Raymond E. Brown, *The Gospel According to John: Introduction, Translation, and Notes*, Anchor Bible 29, 29A (New York: Doubleday, 1966, 1970), 2:562.

30. Francis J. Moloney, SDB, *The Gospel of John* (Collegeville, MN: Liturgical Press, 1998), 375.

31. Ibid., 376.

32. Norman Perrin and Dennis C. Duling, *The New Testament: An Introduction*, 2nd ed. (San Diego: Harcourt, Brace, Jovanovich, 1982), 371–72.

33. George A. Denzler, "The Pastoral Letters," in *The Jerome Biblical Commentary*, ed. Raymond E. Brown, Joseph A. Fitzmyer, and Roland E. Murphy (Englewood Cliffs, NJ: Prentice-Hall, 1968), 354.

34. Robert A. Wild, SJ, "The Pastoral Letters," in *The New Jerome Biblical Commentary*, ed. Raymond E. Brown, Joseph A. Fitzmyer, and Roland E. Murphy (Englewood Cliffs, NJ: Prentice- Hall, 1990), 897.

35. Brown, *The Gospel According to John*, 574 n. 36.

36. Cooke, *Ministry to Word and Sacraments*, 347; see also Brockman, *Ordained to Service*, 11; Echlin, *Deacon in the Church*, 7.

37. Echlin, *Deacon in the Church*, 7.

38. Brown, *The Gospel According to John*, 294.

3. The Rise and Fall of the Ancient Diaconate

1. Robert Nowell, *The Ministry of Service: Deacons in the Contemporary Church* (New York: Herder & Herder, 1968), 40–41. Also cited in Edward P. Echlin, *The Deacon in the Church: Past and Future* (Staten Island, NY: Alba House, 1971), 3.

2. An earlier version of this section appeared in "The Kenotic Leadership of Deacons," in *The Deacon Reader*, ed. James Keating (Mahwah, NJ: Paulist, 2005), 248–77.

3. See, e.g., Echlin, *Deacon in the Church*, 19.

4. Graydon F. Snyder, "Ignatius of Antioch," in *Encyclopedia of Early Christianity*, ed. Everett Ferguson, 2nd ed. (New York: Garland, 1998), 559; see also F. R. Prostmeier, "Ignatius of Antioch," in *Dictionary of Early Christian Literature*, ed. Siegmar Döpp and Wilhelm Geerlings (New York: Crossroad, 2000), 297.

5. Ignatius, *Trallians* 3:1, in *Early Christian Fathers*, ed. Cyril C. Richardson (New York: Collier Books, Macmillan, 1970), 99.

6. Ignatius, *Magnesians* 6:1, in Richardson, *Early Christian Fathers*, 95.

7. Ignatius, *Smyrneans* 8, in Richardson, *Early Christian Fathers*, 115.

8. James M. Barnett, *The Diaconate: A Full and Equal Order*, rev. ed. (Valley Forge, PA: Trinity Press International, 1995), 52.

9. Ignatius, *Philadelphians* 10, in *The Fathers of the Church*, vol. 51, ed. Ludwig Schopp, trans. Gerald G. Walsh (New York: CIMA, 1947), 117.

10. Johannes Quasten, *Patrology*, 4 vols. (Westminster, MD: Newman, 1950), 1:80.

11. Polycarp, *Letter of Polycarp to the Philippians* 5:2, in Richardson, *Early Christian Fathers*, 133.

12. See Kenan B. Osborne, OFM, *Priesthood: A History of the Ordained Ministry in the Roman Catholic Church* (New York/Mahwah, NJ: Paulist, 1988), 103.

13. See Barnett, *Diaconate*, 53; Kenan B. Osborne, OFM, *The Diaconate in the Christian Church: Its History and Theology* (Chicago: National Association of Diaconate Directors, 1996), 30.

14. See B. Steimer, "*Didascalia*," in Döpp and Geerlings, *Dictionary of Early Christian Literature*, 171–72.

15. R. Hugh Connolly, *Didascalia Apostolorum: The Syriac Version* (Oxford: Clarendon, 1929), 109.

16. Ibid., 148.

17. Ibid., 111.

18. Ibid.

19. Ibid., 88.

20. Ibid., 150.

21. See B. Steimer, "*Apostolic Constitutions*," in Döpp and Geerlings, *Dictionary of Early Christian Literature*, 44, for date.

22. See ibid., for date and location.

23. Adolf Harnack, *Sources of the Apostolic Canons*, trans. John Owen (London: F. Norgate, 1895), 17.

24. Ibid., 39.

25. Quasten, *Patrology*, 1:93. See also David E. Aune, "Hermas," in Ferguson, *Encyclopedia of Early Christianity*, 521; and N. Brox, "Hermas," in Döpp and Geerlings, *Dictionary of Early Christian Literature*, 277–88.

26. Hermas, *Shepherd*, Vision 3.5.1, in Edgar J. Goodspeed, *The Apostolic Fathers: An American Translation* (New York: Harper and Brothers, 1950), 112.

27. Ibid., Parable 9.26.2, in Goodspeed, *The Apostolic Fathers*, 193.

28. Everett Ferguson, "Hippolytus," in Ferguson, *Encyclopedia of Early Christianity*, 531–32; B. R. Suchla, "Hippolytus," in Döpp and Geerlings, *Dictionary of Early Christian Literature*, 287–89.

29. Burton Scott Easton, trans. and ed., *The Apostolic Tradition of Hippolytus: Translated into English with Introduction and Notes* (Cambridge/New York: Cambridge University Press, 1934), 38–39.

30. Ibid.

31. Gregory Dix, *The Treatise on the Apostolic Tradition of St. Hippolytus of Rome* (London: SPCK, 1968), 57.

32. Ibid., 60.

33. Easton, *Apostolic Tradition*, 102.

34. Barnett, *Diaconate*, 65.

35. See, e.g., ibid., 65–66.

36. Cyprian, *Epistle XII*, in *The Ante-Nicene Fathers*, ed. A. Robertson and J. Donaldson (repr., Grand Rapids: Eerdmans, 1951–57), 5:293.

37. Joseph W. Pokusa, "A Canonical-Historical Study of the Diaconate in the Western Church" (JCD diss., Catholic University of America, 1979), 73 n. 41, citing *Concilia Galliae AD 314–AD 506*, ed. C. Munier, Corpus Christianorum, Series Latina 148 (Turnholt: Brepols, 1963), 225.

38. Ibid., 74 n. 43.

39. Ibid., 75.

40. Augustine, "On the Catechising of the Uninstructed," in *The Nicene and Post-Nicene Fathers of the Christian Church*, ed. Philip Schaff, vol. 3, *St. Augustine On the Trinity, Doctrinal Treatises, Moral Treatises* (Grand Rapids: Eerdmans, 1956), 3:283–314.

41. Ibid., 283.

42. Jerome H. Neyrey, "1 Timothy," in *The Collegeville Bible Commentary*, ed. Dianne Bergant and Robert J. Karris (Collegeville, MN: Liturgical Press, 1989), 1203.

43. "First Council of Arles," in *The Faith of the Early Fathers*, vol. 1, ed. and trans. William A. Jurgens (Collegeville, MN: Liturgical Press, 1970), 273.

44. J. P. Kirsch, "Archdeacon," in *The Catholic Encyclopedia*, vol. 1 (New York: Robert Appleton Company, 1907).

45. For a comprehensive examination of the archdiaconate, see Joseph W. Pokusa, "The Archdeacon's Office and Functions in the Decretals of Gregory IX," (JCL thesis, Catholic University of America, 1977), and the same author's "Canonical-Historical Study of the Diaconate," 210–350.

46. Barnett, *Diaconate*, 104.

47. Ibid.

48. Jurgens, *Faith of the Early Fathers*, 1:255–56. It should be noted that both *presbyter* and *sacerdos* are used in this canon. While Jurgens concludes that the terms are synonymous in this passage, it may also suggest that it is the bishop *[sacerdos]* who must authorize the deacon to give communion to the sinners in question.

49. John J. McCarthy, "The *Diakonia* of Charity in the Permanent Diaconate: Its Application to Certain Clerical Offices as Addressed in the *Directory for the Ministry and Life of Permanent Deacons*," (JCD diss., Pontificia Studiorum Universitas A S. Thoma Aq. In Urbe, 2000), 25.

50. *Council of Nicaea*, can. 18, in Jurgens, *Faith of the Early Fathers*, 1:286.

51. Munier, *Concilia Galliae*, 175, 181.

52. Barnett, *Diaconate*, 66.

53. Norbert Brockman, SM, *Ordained to Service: A Theology of the Permanent Diaconate* (Hicksville, NY: Exposition Press, 1976), 28–29.

4. Preparing for Renewal: The Council of Trent and the 1917 *Code of Canon Law*

1. Philip Hughes, *The Church in Crisis: A History of the General Councils: 325–1870* (Garden City, NY: Hanover House, 1961), 295.

2. Gerard Philips and Herbert Vorgrimler provide a good overview of the discussion and the voting in Herbert Vorgrimler, ed., *Commentary on the Documents of Vatican II*, 5 vols. (New York: Herder & Herder, 1967), vol. 1, esp. 115–19 and 226–30.

3. H. J. Schroeder, ed. and trans., *The Canons and Decrees of the Council of Trent* (Rockford, IL: TAN Books and Publishers, 1978), 174.

4. See, e.g., Norbert Brockman, *Ordained to Service: A Theology of the Permanent Diaconate* (Hicksville, NY: Exposition Press, 1976), 30; William T. Ditewig, *101 Questions & Answers on Deacons* (Mahwah, NJ: Paulist, 2004), 17; Owen F. Cummings, *Saintly Deacons* (Mahwah, NJ: Paulist, 2005), 47–55. For more detailed information on this fascinating churchman, see Thomas F. Mayer, *Reginald Pole: Prince and Prophet* (Cambridge: Cambridge University Press, 2000).

5. Edward P. Echlin, *The Deacon in the Church: Past and Future* (Staten Island, NY: Alba House, 1971), 99.

6. Schroeder, *Canons and Decrees*, 160.

7. At the Council of Trent, the bishops assembled in council were referred to as "major" theologians; other theological experts, such as university professors of theology, were referred to as "minor" theologians. This was because major theologians (the bishops) were entitled to both a consultative and a deliberative vote on the issues and texts; minor theologians had only a consultative vote. The terms *major* and *minor* did not refer to the relative professional competence of the theologians involved. For a comprehensive treatment of this subject, see Nelson H. Minnich, "The Voice of Theologians in General Councils from Pisa to Trent," *Theological Studies* 59 (1998): 420–41, esp. 431–34.

8. *Concilium Tridentinum: Diariorum, actorum, epistularum, tractatuum nova collectio*, ed. Goerresian Society, 13 vols. (Freiburg, 1901–), 9:7.

9. Ibid., 9:11.

10. Ibid., 9:12.

11. Ibid., 9:589.

12. Ibid., 9:41.

13. Ibid., 9:601 (my translation).

14. Ibid., 9:558–59.

15. Echlin, *Deacon in the Church*, 100.

16. *Concilium Tridentinum*, 9:601.

17. James A. Coriden, *An Introduction to Canon Law: Revised Edition* (Mahwah, NJ: Paulist, 2004), 9.

18. Ibid., 27.

19. Edward N. Peters, curator, *The 1917 Pio-Benedictine Code of Canon Law* (San Francisco: Ignatius, 2001), 61.

20. Stanislaus Woywod, *A Practical Commentary on the Code of Canon Law*, vol. 1 (London: Herder, 1926), 49.

21. Peters, *1917 Pio-Benedictine Code*, 64.

5. Vatican II and the Renewal of the Diaconate

1. William T. Ditewig, "The Contemporary Renewal of the Diaconate," in *The Deacon Reader*, ed. James Keating (Mahwah, NJ: Paulist, 2006), 27–55.

2. See, e.g., Karl Rahner and Herbert Vorgrimler, eds., *Diaconia in Christo: Über die Erneuerung des Diakonates*, Quaestiones Disputatae 15/16. Freiburg: Herder, 1962); Otto Pies, "Diakonat, Stufe oder Amt," Theologie und Glaube 50 (1960): 170–93.

3. William T. Ditewig, "The Once and Future Diaconate: Notes from the Past, Possibilities for the Future," *Church* 20, no. 2 (Summer 2004): 52.

4. Josef Hornef, "The Genesis and Growth of the Proposal," in *Foundations for the Renewal of the Diaconate* (Washington, DC: United States Catholic Conference, 1993), 6.

5. See Margret Morche, *Zur Erneuerung des Ständigen Diakonats* (Freiburg: Lambertus-Verlag, 1996), esp. 15–21.

6. G. von Mann, "Der Caritasdiakonat und seine Erneurung," *Caritas* (July/August 1934), cited in Hornef, "Genesis," 7.

7. Hornef, "Genesis," 7–8.

8. Otto Pies, "Block 26: Erfahrungen aus dem Priesterleben in Dachau," *Stimmen der Zeit* 141 (1947–48): 10–28.

9. Wilhelm Schamoni, *Familienväter als geweihte Diakone* (Paderborn: Schöningh, 1953); English translation: *Married Men as Ordained Deacons*, trans. Otto Eisner (London: Burns & Oates, 1955).

10. Ibid., 7.

11. Morche, *Zur Erneuerung*, 36–39.

12. Hornef, "Genesis," 18.

13. Rahner and Vorgrimler, *Diaconia in Christo.*

14. Willem van Bekkum, "The Liturgical Revival in the Service of the Missions," in *The Assisi Papers* (Proceedings of the First International Congress on Pastoral Liturgy, Assisi-Rome, September 18–22, 1956) (Collegeville, MN: Liturgical Press, 1957), 95–112.

15. Johannes Hofinger, "The Case for Permanent Deacons," *Catholic Mind* 57 (1959): 116.

16. Ibid., 119.

17. Michael Warren, ed., *Source Book for Modern Catechetics* (Winona, MN: St. Mary's Press, 1983), 25.

18. Eugene D'Souza, "Permanent Deacons in the Missions," in *Liturgy and the Missions: The Nijmegen Papers*, ed. Johannes Hofinger (New York: P. J. Kenedy & Sons, 1960), 177–90.

19. Ibid., 188.

20. Michel-Dominique Epagneul, "Du role des diacres dans l'Église d'aujourd'hui," *Nouvelle revue théologique* 79 (1957): 153–68.

21. See Paul Winninger, *Vers un renouveau du diaconat* (Paris: Desclée de Brouwer, 1958), 13.

22. See Bruno Kleinheyer, "Le diaconat a la lumière du rituel d'ordination selon le Pontifical Romain," trans. Joseph Breitenstein, in *Le diacre dans L'Église et le Monde d'aujourd'hui*, ed. Paul Winninger and Yves Congar, Unam Sanctam 59 (Paris: Éditions du Cerf, 1966), 109.

23. Pius XII, "Quelques aspects fondamentaux de l'apostolat des laïcs: Hiérarchie et Apostolat," *Acta Apostolicae Sedis* 49 (1957): 925.

24. See Piercarlo Beltrando, *Diaconi per la Chiesa* (Milan: Instituto Propaganda, 1977), for a detailed discussion of the various theological contributions made.

25. *Acta et documenta Concilio oecuminco Vaticano II apparando, Series prima (antepraeparatoria)* (Vatican City: Typis Polyglottis Vaticanis, 1960–61) (hereafter cited as *ADA*).

26. *Acta et documenta Concilio oecuminco Vaticano II apparando, Series secunda (praeparatoria)* (Vatican City: Typis Polyglottis Vaticanis, 1969) (hereafter cited as *ADP*).

27. *Acta Synodalia Sacrasancti Concilii Vaticani II* (Vatican City: Typis Polyglottis Vaticanis, 1970–78) (hereafter cited as *AS*).

28. *ADA*, II/II, 115–21.

29. *ADA*, II/II, 122–28.

30. *ADA*, II/II, 128–31.

31. *ADA*, II/II, 131–32.

32. Only eight U.S. bishops listed the diaconate as a topic for discussion, and none recommended against it. Foery of Syracuse, O'Connor of Madison, and Primeau of Manchester supported a proposal to discuss the diaconate in general. The bishops of Stanford, Dubuque, Dallas-Ft. Worth, Rockford, and Sacramento supported a different proposal which specified that married men should be admitted to the diaconate (*ADA*, II/II, 125).

33. *ADA*, II/II, 115–21.

34. *ADA*, II/II, 128–31.

35. Gerard Philips, "History of the Constitution," in *Commentary on the Documents of Vatican II*, ed. Herbert Vorgrimler, 5 vols. (New York: Herder & Herder, 1967–69), 1:106.

36. *ADP*, II/II, 138–50.

37. *ADP*, II/II, 150–53.

38. *ADP*, II/II, 154-68.

39. *ADP*, II/II, 167.

40. *ADP*, II/II, 154, 159–61.

41. *ADP*, II/VI, 262.

42. Ibid., 265.

43. *ADP*, II/III, 211.

44. Ibid., 212.

45. Ibid.

46. Ibid.

47. Ibid., 213.

48. *AS*, I/IV, 23–24.

49. See Vorgrimler, *Commentary*, 1:111.
50. *AS* II/I, 235.
51. *AS* II/ I, 340.
52. Ibid., 345 and 360.
53. *AS*, II/II, 82–87.
54. In the recently published journal of Yves Congar, the French theologian's entry for October 4, 1963, reads that Spellman did not think the topic of the diaconate belonged in a dogmatic constitution. "Il est contre un diaconat permanent. Il ne comprend rien. Pour lui, ce serait archéologisme condamné par Pie XII" (Yves Congar, *Mon Journal du Concile*, 2 vols. (Paris: Éditions du Cerf, 2002), 1:433. ("He is against a permanent diaconate. He does not understand anything. For him, this would be an archeologism condemned by Pius XII" [my translation].)
55. *AS*, II/II, 120.
56. Ibid., 227–30.
57. Ibid., 229.
58. Ibid., 314–17.
59. Ibid., 317–19.
60. Leo Cardinal Suenens, "The Coresponsibility of Deacons," in *Diaconal Reader: Selected Articles from the "Diaconal Quarterly"* (Washington, DC: National Conference of Catholic Bishops, 1985), 47.
61. *AS*, II/II, 319.
62. Ibid., 346–48.
63. Ibid., 358–60.
64. Ibid.
65. Vorgrimler, *Commentary*, 115.
66. *AS*, II/III, 573–75.
67. Ibid.
68. *AS*, III/I, 227–29.
69. *AS*, III/VIII, 53.
70. See Vorgrimler, *Commentary*, 227.
71. *AS*, III/VIII, 811.
72. Paul VI, *Hodie concilium*, *Acta Apostolicae Sedis* 58 (1966): 57–64.

6. Charting a Theology of Diaconate: An Exercise in Ecclesial Cartography

1. An earlier version of this chapter appeared in *Theology of the Diaconate: The State of the Question* (Mahwah, NJ: Paulist, 2005). It has been

adapted and is offered here as an introduction to the more developed treatment of the following chapters.

2. Augustinus Kerkvoorde, OSB, "Theology of the Diaconate," in *Foundations for the Renewal of the Diaconate* (Washington, DC: United States Catholic Conference, 1993, reissued in 2003), 91.

3. Ibid., 92

4. See, e.g., James M. Barnett, *The Diaconate: A Full and Equal Order*, rev. ed. (Valley Forge, PA: Trinity Press International, 1995); Piercarlo Beltrando, *Diaconi per la Chiesa* (Milan: Instituto Propaganda, 1977); Alphonse Borras and Bernard Pottier, *Le grâce du diaconat: Questions actuelles autour du diaconat latin* (Brussels: Editions Lessius, 1998); Norbert Brockman, *Ordained to Service: A Theology of the Permanent Diaconate* (Hicksville, NY: Exposition Press, 1976); Leo M. Croghan, "The Theology and the Spirit of the Diaconate's Restoration," *American Ecclesiastical Review* 161 (1969): 293–301; Edward P. Echlin, SJ, *The Deacon in the Church: Past and Future* (Staten Island, NY: Alba House, 1971); Josef Hornef, "The Order of Diaconate in the Roman Catholic Church," trans. Patrick Russell, in *The Diaconate Now*, ed. Richard T. Nolan (Washington, DC: Corpus, 1968), 57–79; idem, "The Genesis and Growth of the Proposal," in *Foundations for the Renewal of the Diaconate*, Bishops' Committee on the Permanent Diaconate (Washington, DC: United States Catholic Conference, 1993), 5–27; Joseph A. Komonchak, "The Permanent Diaconate and the Variety of Ministries in the Church," *Diaconal Quarterly* 3, no. 3 (1977): 15–23; 3, no. 4 (1977): 29–40; 4, no. 1 (1978): 13–25; Karl Rahner and Herbert Vorgrimler, eds., *Diaconia in Christo: Über die Erneuerung des Diakonates*, Quaestiones Disputatae 15/16 (Freiburg: Herder, 1962).

5. United States Catholic Conference, *A National Study on the Permanent Diaconate of the Catholic Church in the United States, 1994–1995* (Washington, DC: United States Catholic Conference, 1996).

6. Ibid., 15.

7. Ibid.

8. Ibid., 16.

9. Congregation for Catholic Education, *Basic Norms for the Formation of Permanent Deacons* (Vatican City: Libreria Editrice Vaticana, 1998), #3.

10. Ibid.

11. Ibid.

12. Ibid., with the "authoritative points of reference" being presented in #4–#8.

13. Ibid.

14. James H. Provost, "Canonical Reflection on Selected Issues in Diocesan Governance," in *The Ministry of Governance*, ed. James K. Mallet (Washington, DC: Canon Law Society of America, 1986), 211, citing Paul VI, allocution to Code Commission, November 20, 1965: *Acta Apostolicae Sedis* 57 (1965): 988.

15. Paul VI, *Hodie concilium*, *Acta Apostolicae Sedis* 58 (1966): 57–64.

16. Mary Ann Fatula, OP, "Autonomy and Communion: Paying the Price," *Spirituality Today* 39 (Summer 1987): 164.

17. Cardinal Roger Mahony, "Church of the Eucharist, a Communion for Mission," *Origins* 33:42 (April 1, 2004): 723.

18. John Paul II, *Fides et Ratio* (Vatican City: Vatican Polyglot Press, 1998), #93.

19. Christ's kenotic path to glory as found in Phil 2:6–11 is described by Walter Kasper as a "downwardly mobile career....which prescribes the basic Christian virtue, as the spiritual tradition teaches, namely, the attitude of humility, which is a willingness to serve. This must *a fortiori* be the basic attitude of the deacon" (Walter Kasper, *Leadership in the Church: How Traditional Roles Can Serve the Christian Community Today* [New York: Crossroad, 2003], 39).

20. Jean Corbon, *The Wellspring of Worship* (New York: Paulist, 1988), 106–7, cited in Michael Downey, "Theology as a Way of Life," *New Theology Review* 15, no. 1 (February 2002): 60.

21. John Paul II, Homily at the Mass of the Lord's Supper, 2004. Reported in Vatican Information Service 040414, N. 67, April 14, 2004.

22. Francis J. Moloney, *The Gospel of John* (Collegeville, MN: Liturgical Press, 1998), 375.

23. Ibid., 376.

24. Patrick McCaslin and Michael G. Lawler, *Sacrament of Service: A Vision of the Permanent Deacon Today* (New York: Paulist, 1986), 62–63.

25. Edward J. Kilmartin, SJ, "Lay Participation in the Apostolate of the Hierarchy," in *Official Ministry in a New Age*, ed. James H. Provost (Washington, DC: Canon Law Society of America, 1981), 94.

26. John Paul II, "The Heart of the Diaconate—Servants of the Mysteries of Christ and Servants of Your Brothers and Sisters," Allocution to the Permanent Deacons and Their Wives Given in Detroit, Michigan (September 19, 1987): *Origins* 17 (1987): 327–29.

27. Helmut Hoping, "Diakonie als Aufgabe des kirchlichen Leitungsamtes," *Dokumentation 13—Jahrestagung 1996* (Tübingen: Arbeitsgemeinschaft Ständiger Diakonat, Bundesrepublik Deutschland, 1996), 34.

28. Nathan Mitchell, OSB, *Mission and Ministry: History and Theology*

in the Sacrament of Order (Wilmington, DE: Michael Glazier, 1982), 304 (emphasis in original).

29. Kasper, "Diaconate," 40.

30. Ibid.

31. Ibid., 23.

32. United States Catholic Conference (USCC), *National Study, 1994–1995*, 13.

33. Kasper, "Diaconate," 27.

34. John Paul II, "Deacons Serve the Kingdom of God," Allocution at the General Audience on October 6, 1993, *Insegnamenti* 16, no. 2 (1993), 954, #6; English translation in *L'Osservatore Romano* (English edition), no. 141, October 13, 1993.

7. Foundational Theological Themes and the Diaconate: *Kenōsis* and *Theōsis*

1. John Paul II, *Fides et Ratio* (Vatican City: Vatican Polyglot Press, 1998), #93.

2. Congregation for the Doctrine of the Faith, "Instruction on the Ecclesial Vocation of the Theologian," promulgated May 24, 1990 (*Acta Apostolicae Sedis* 82 [1990]: 1550–70, #2).

3. Lucien Richard, OMI, *Christ: The Self-Emptying of God* (New York/Mahwah, NJ: Paulist, 1997), 84, 94.

4. Ibid., 22.

5. Ibid., citing Hans Urs von Balthasar, *Love Alone* (New York: Herder & Herder, 1969), 15.

6. Johannes Baptist Metz, *Poverty of Spirit* (New York: Paulist, 1968, 1998), 6.

7. Ibid., 10–11.

8. The example of Ephrem of Edessa is illustrative, not exhaustive, of Eastern thought. In addition to the works cited below, see also Vladimir Lossky, *The Mystical Theology of the Eastern Church* (Crestwood, NY: St. Vladimir's Seminary Press, 1976); and John Meyendorff, *Byzantine Theology: Historical Trends and Doctrinal Themes* (New York: Fordham University Press, 1974, 1979). Lossky writes, for example, "As we have said many times, the perfection of the person consists in self-abandonment: the person expresses itself most truly in that it renounces to exist for itself. It is the self-emptying of the Person of the Son, the Divine κένωσις. 'The entire mystery of economy'—said St. Cyril of Alexandria—'consists in the self-emptying and abase-

ment of the Son of God'" (p. 144). Lossky includes a section of his study on "The Way of Union" (pp. 196ff.), focused entirely on the subject of *theōsis*.

9. Seely Beggiani, *Introduction to Eastern Christian Spirituality: The Syriac Tradition* (London: University of Scranton Press, Associated University Presses, 1991), 13.

10. Ibid., 13–14.

11 *Nat.* 21.12; cf. *Nat.* 22.4 and 22.16–18. English translations are taken from *Ephrem the Syrian: Hymns*, trans. Kathleen E. McVey (New York/Mahwah, NJ: Paulist, 1989), 31.

12. Ibid.; cf. *Nat.* 1.99. Simplicity of expression is not limited to Ephrem. Perhaps the simplest comes from St. Athanasius of Alexandria, a deacon and bishop as well as a contemporary of Ephrem: "God became human that we might become God" (*Second Discourse Against the Arians* #70, in *A Select Library of Nicene and Post-Nicene Fathers of the Christian Church*, second series, 14 vols. [Grand Rapids: Eerdmans, 1989], 4:386). The sixth-century bishop Philoxenus of Mabboug echoes Athanasius: "God became human so humans might become God" (cited in Beggiani, *Introduction*, 49).

13. John Paul II, "The Spirit Enables Us to Share in Divine Nature," General Audience, May 27, 1998, #3.

14. Prosper of Aquitaine, *Capitulae Coelestini* 8, provided in Paul de Clerk, "'Lex orandi, lex credendi': The Original Sense and Historical Avatars of an Equivocal Adage," *Studia Liturgica* 24 (1994) (my translation).

15. Seely Beggiani, *Early Syriac Theology: With Special Reference to the Maronite Tradition* (Lanham, MD: University Press of America, 1983), 43.

16. Richard, *Christ*, 94.

17. Canon 1008; see also canon 1009. English citations from the *New Commentary on the Code of Canon Law*, ed. John P. Beal, James A. Coriden, and Thomas J. Green (Washington, DC: Canon Law Society of America, 2000).

18. *Catechism of the Catholic Church*, 2nd ed. [hereafter abbreviated *CCC*] (Washington, DC: United States Catholic Conference, 1997), #1570.

19. John Paul II, "The Deacon's Ordination: Deacons Are Configured to Christ the Servant," an address to the joint *plenarium* of the Congregation for the Clergy and the Congregation for Catholic Education (November 30, 1995), #3.

20. Congregation for Catholic Education, *Basic Norms for the Formation of Permanent Deacons* (Vatican City: Libreria Editrice Vaticana, 1998), #11.

21. Congregation for the Clergy, *Directory for the Ministry and Life of Permanent Deacons* (Vatican City: Libreria Editrice Vaticana, 1998), #23.

22. Ibid.

23. In popular understanding, as well as in some scholarly studies, the deacon is often discussed in almost exclusively functional terms. Parishioners often ask their deacons, "Can you do everything that Father does, except for saying Mass and hearing confession?" In scholarly circles, while many theologians are ready to discuss the distinct sacramental nature of the sacerdotal orders (especially the presbyterate, although relatively few focus on the episcopate), the diaconate is often ignored altogether (since it is not priestly) or dismissed as an order whose functions flow out of sacramental initiation. Such approaches fail to appreciate the distinct sacramental nature of the diaconate. Categorizing the diaconate as neither fish nor fowl, people simply put aside discussions about deacons and the diaconate for another day.

24. Nathan Mitchell, OSB, *Mission and Ministry: History and Theology in the Sacrament of Order* (Wilmington, DE: Michael Glazier, 1982), 304.

25. If this were a text on leadership theory, it would be helpful at this point to discuss the necessary distinctions to be made between notions of "leadership" and "management." While the time for such a discussion is not available in this work, the distinctions are important ones. Leadership is a category that engages the human person in relationships and touches the human at the core of being. Leadership in any context involves vision, inspiration, attractiveness, and a sense of mission and purpose. Management on the other hand, in my opinion, is more focused on the implementation of leadership. Some observers make a distinction between leadership as related to people and management as related to things. Whatever the value of this observation, it is nonetheless true that leadership is distinct from, but related to, management. Some leaders are excellent managers as well; while other exceptional leaders are incompetent managers. The obverse is true: excellent managers may also be excellent leaders, but not necessarily so. This may be seen in the frequent examples of managers who are promoted to leadership positions and fail miserably in that role. For now, it is sufficient to keep the distinction between leadership and management in mind; the conversation here is strictly about *leadership*.

26. Edmund Hill, OP, *Ministry and Authority in the Catholic Church* (London: Geoffrey Chapman, 1988), 11–12.

27. James A. Coriden, *Canon Law as Ministry: Freedom and Good Order for the Church* (New York/Mahwah: Paulist, 2000), 108.

28. Ibid., 112.

29. Patrick McCaslin and Michael G. Lawler, *Sacrament of Service: A Vision of the Permanent Deacon Today* (New York/Mahwah, NJ: Paulist, 1986), 41.

30. Ibid., 62–63.

31. Karl Rahner, "Power," in *Sacramentum Mundi: An Encyclopedia of Theology*, ed. Karl Rahner et al., 6 vols. (New York: Herder & Herder, 1970), 72.

32. Walter Kasper, "The Diaconate," in *Leadership in the Church: How Traditional Roles Can Serve the Christian Community Today* (New York: Crossroad, 2003), 21.

33. Ibid., citing Ignatius, *Trallians* 3:3.

34. It may also be noted that, while matrimony is no more intrinsic to the sacramental nature of the diaconate than celibacy is intrinsic to the sacramental nature of the presbyterate, nonetheless, as has been seen, the vast majority of deacons participate not solely in the sacrament of orders, but in the sacrament of matrimony as well. For those deacons who are also married, they experience a kind of dual sacramentality of keno-theotic service.

35. Max De Pree, "Servant-Leadership: Three Things Necessary," in *Focus on Leadership: Servant-Leadership for the 21st Century*, ed. Larry C. Spears and Michele Lawrence (New York: John Wiley & Sons, 2002), 89–97.

36. Ibid., 91.

37. Ibid.

38. Ibid., 91–92.

39. Ibid., 92.

40. Ibid.

41. Kasper, "Diaconate," 39.

42. De Pree, "Servant-Leadership," 92, citing *Gaudium et Spes* 31.

43. De Pree, "Servant-Leadership," 92.

44. Ibid.

45. Ibid., 93.

46. Ibid., 94.

47. Ibid.

48. Ibid.

49. Ibid.

50. Ibid., 95.

51. Ibid.

52. Ibid.

53. Ibid.

54. Ibid.

55. Paul Philibert, OP, "Issues for a Theology of Priesthood: A Status Report," in *The Theology of Priesthood*, ed. Donald J. Goergen and Ann Garrido (Collegeville, MN: Liturgical Press, 2000), 3–4.

56. Ibid., 4.

57. Kasper, "Diaconate," 23.

58. United States Catholic Conference (USCC), *A National Study on the Permanent Diaconate of the Catholic Church in the United States, 1994–1995* (Washington, DC: United States Catholic Conference, 1996), 13.

59. John Paul II, "Deacons Serve the Kingdom of God," catechesis at the General Audience of October 6, 1993, *Insegnamenti* 16, no. 2 (1993): 954, #6; English translation in *L'Osservatore Romano* (English edition), n. 41, October 13, 1993.

8. The Meaning of Diaconal Ordination: A Conversation with Susan K. Wood

1. See pp. 150–51.

2. David N. Power, OMI, "Appropriate Ordination Rites: A Historical Perspective," in *Alternative Futures for Worship, Volume 6: Leadership Ministry in Community*, ed. Bernard J. Lee, (Collegeville, MN: Liturgical Press, 1987), 131.

3. See, in particular, Susan K. Wood, *Sacramental Orders, Lex Orandi* series (Collegeville, MN: Liturgical Press, 2000); and Susan K. Wood, ed., *Ordering the Baptismal Priesthood: Theologies of Lay and Ordained Ministry* (Collegeville, MN: Liturgical Press, 2003).

4. Bernard Cooke, *Ministry to Word and Sacraments: History and Theology* (Philadelphia: Fortress, 1976), 347.

5. Ibid.

6. Pierre Jounel, "Ordinations," in *The Church at Prayer*, vol. 3, *The Sacraments*, ed. A. G. Martimort (Collegeville, MN: Liturgical Press, 1988), 139.

7. Ibid., 140; and Herman A. J. Wegman, *Christian Worship in East and West: A Study Guide to Liturgical History* (New York: Pueblo, 1985), 138.

8. Jounel, "Ordinations," 140.

9. John D. Zizioulas, *Being as Communion: Studies in Personhood and the Church*, (Crestwood, NY: St. Vladimir's Seminary Press, 1985), 216.

10. Ibid., 141; see also Wegman, *Christian Worship*, 138.

11. Everett Ferguson, "Hippolytus," in *Encyclopedia of Early Christianity*, 2nd ed., ed. Everett Ferguson (New York: Garland, 1998), 531–32; B. R. Suchla, "Hippolytus," in *Dictionary of Early Christian Literature*, ed. Siegmar Döpp and Wilhelm Geerlings (New York: Herder & Herder, 2000), 287–89.

12. Burton Scott Easton, trans. and ed., *The Apostolic Tradition of Hippolytus: Translated into English with Introduction and Notes* (Cambridge:

Cambridge University Press, 1934), 38–39.

13. Ibid.

14. Jounel, "Ordinations," 144.

15. Ibid., 153.

16. Edward P. Echlin, *The Deacon in the Church: Past and Future* (Staten Island, NY: Alba House, 1971), 64.

17. This language is found at the conclusion of the consecratory prayers in each of the texts cited.

18. Wegman, *Christian Worship*, 204.

19. Jounel, "Ordinations," 164.

20. Wood, *Sacramental Orders*, xi–xii.

21. Pius XII, Apostolic Constitution *Sacramentum Ordinis* (1947): *Acta Apostolicae Sedis* 40 (1948): 5.

22. Jan Michael Joncas, "The Public Language of Ministry Revisited: *De Ordinatione Episcopi, Presbyterorum et Diaconorum* 1990," *Worship* 68, no. 5 (September 1994): 386.

23. Wood, *Sacramental Orders*, xii–xiv.

24. Joncas enumerates these changes in "Public Language of Ministry Revisited," 397–98.

25. For a critique of the language of ordination rites with respect to status elevation, see Mary Collins, "The Public Language of Ministry," in *Official Ministry in a New Age*, ed. James H. Provost, Permanent Seminar Studies 3 (Washington, DC: Canon Law Society of America, 1981); Joncas, "Public Language of Ministry Revisited," 386–403. Joncas argues that the elevation language has been much mitigated in the 1990 rite.

26. Joncas, "Public Language of Ministry Revisited," 386, citing Annibale Bugnini, *The Reform of the Liturgy 1948–1975*, trans. Matthew J. O'Connell (Collegeville, MN: Liturgical Press, 1990), 721–23.

27. A better translation of *ministerium* is "service" rather than "charity." As noted in chapter 3, the original form of this text referred to the deacon being ordained to the service "of the bishop" *(ministerium episcopi)* and although *episcopi* would be dropped later in the tradition, the meaning is consistent that we are not speaking of "charity" being extended to the bishop; rather, we are speaking of the service offered by the deacon to and on behalf of the bishop.

28. *Rites*, 46.

29. Nathan Mitchell, OSB, *Mission and Ministry: History and Theology in the Sacrament of Order* (Wilmington, DE: Michael Glazier, 1982), 202.

30. See Pius XII, above.

31. Wood, *Sacramental Orders*, 150.

32. Joncas, "Public Language of Ministry Revisited," 392.

33. Ibid.

34. See n. 25 above; Collins, "Public Language of Ministry"; and Joncas, "Public Language of Ministry Revisited."

35. Wood, *Sacramental Orders*, 151.

36. "Like the men the apostles chose for works of charity, you should be a man of good reputation, filled with wisdom and the Holy Spirit. Show before God and mankind that you are above every suspicion of blame, a true minister of Christ and of God's mysteries, a man firmly rooted in faith. Never turn away from the hope which the Gospel offers; now you must not only listen to God's word but also preach it. Hold the mystery of faith with a clear conscience. Express in action what you proclaim by word of mouth. Then the people of Christ, brought to life by the Spirit, will be an offering God accepts. Finally, on the last day, when you go to meet the Lord, you will hear him say: 'Well done, good and faithful servant, enter into the joy of your Lord.'"

37. One may only surmise, since the majority of deacons are married, why the phrasing could not more appropriately be, "Whether or not you have been called to holy matrimony," when introducing the section on celibacy in the homily. This observation is made with tongue planted firmly in cheek.

38. Wood, *Sacramental Orders*, 161.

39. Ibid., 151.

40. Joncas, "Public Language of Ministry Revisited," 395.

41. Jounel, "Ordinations," 178.

42. Wood, *Sacramental Orders*, 96.

43. Ibid., 108–9.

44. Helmut Hoping, "Diakonie als Aufgabe des kirchlichen Leitungsamtes," *Dokumentation 13—Jahrestagung 1996* (Tübingen: Arbeitsgemeinschaft Ständiger Diakonat, Bundesrepublik Deutschland, 1996), 34.

45. Wood, *Sacramental Orders*, 154–58.

46. Ibid., 157.

47. Joncas, "Public Language of Ministry Revisited," 398.

48. Wood, *Sacramental Orders*, 160.

49. Ibid., citing James M. Barnett, *The Diaconate: A Full and Equal Order*, rev. ed. (Valley Forge, PA: Trinity Press International, 1995), 80–83, 211–12.

50. See, e.g., Joseph W. Pokusa, "A Canonical-Historical Study of the Diaconate in the Western Church" (JCD diss., Catholic University of America, 1979).

51. Joncas, "Public Language of Ministry Revisited," 401.

52. Ibid., 402, citing BCL *Newsletter*, 34.

53. Wood, *Sacramental Orders*, 160.

54. Power, "Appropriate Ordination Rites," 134–35.

9. The Emerging Challenges: Issues for Reflection and Action

1. Owen F. Cummings, "Response to Bishop Campbell: The Impact of the New *National Directory*," *in Today's Deacon: Contemporary Issues and Cross-Currents* (Mahwah, NJ: Paulist, 2006), 75.

2. I have translated this passage in a manner slightly different from others. A common English translation has been, "In language intelligible to every generation…." However, the official Latin text reads, *modo unicuique generationi accommodato*. I believe that it is more accurate to reflect that what the council seems to be saying here goes beyond the category of language, but refers rather to a much broader set of categories: through intelligible language, certainly, but in other ways *(modi)* as well, the church must translate its vision for each and every *(unicuique)* generation.

3. John P. McIntyre, "*In persona Christi Capitis:* A Commentary on Canon 1008," *Studia Canonica* 30 (1996): 371–401, esp. 373. See also Thomas Lane, "In the Person of Christ—by Baptism," in *A Priesthood in Tune: Theological Reflections in Ministry* (Dublin: Columbia, 1993), 91–98.

4. See also *AA* 1: "this Sacred Council now earnestly turns to the lay Christian faithful, whose roles in the church's mission have already been mentioned in other places as proper to them and indispensable. For the apostolate of the laity, deriving from the very vocation of being a Christian, can never be lacking in the Church."

5. Joseph A. Komonchak, "The New Diaconate Guidelines," in *Proceedings of the 1986 Convention of the National Association of Permanent Diaconate Directors in Baltimore, Maryland, April 28–1 May, 1986* (Chicago: National Association of Permanent Diaconate Directors, 1986), 7.

6. David N. Power, "Order," in *Systematic Theology: Roman Catholic Perspectives*, vol. 2, ed. Francis Schüssler Fiorenza and John P. Galvin (Minneapolis: Fortress, 1991), 302.

7. Susan K. Wood, *Sacramental Orders*, *Lex Orandi* Series (Collegeville, MN: Liturgical Press, 2000), 166.

8. Ibid., 182.

9. James M. Barnett, *The Diaconate: A Full and Equal Order*, rev. ed. (Valley Forge, PA: Trinity Press International, 1995), 104.

10. Patrick McCaslin and Michael G. Lawler, *Sacrament of Service: A Vision of the Permanent Deacon Today* (New York/Mahwah, NJ: Paulist, 1986), 62–63.

11. Wood, *Sacramental Orders*, 180.

12. Phyllis Zagano, *Holy Saturday: An Argument for the Restoration of the Female Diaconate in the Catholic Church* (New York: Crossroad, 2000); Canon Law Society of America, *The Canonical Implications of Ordaining Women to the Permanent Diaconate* (Washington, DC: Canon Law Society of America, 1995); International Theological Commission, *From the Diakonia of Christ to the Diakonia of the Apostles* (Mundelein, IL: Hillenbrand Books, 2004).

13. See John J. McCarthy, "The *Diakonia* of Charity in the Permanent Diaconate: Its Application to Certain Clerical Offices as Addressed in the *Directory for the Ministry and Life of Permanent Deacons* (JCD diss., Pontifical University of St. Thomas, 2000), 107–20.

14. *Communicationes: Pontificium Consilium De Legum Textibus Interpretandis* 24 (1992) (Vatican City: Typografia Vaticana, 1969 et seq.) (hereafter cited as *Communicationes*), 137.

15. Ibid., 138–39.

16. Ibid., 205.

17. Ibid., 231.

18. *Communicationes* 25 (1993): 201.

19. *Communicationes* 13 (1981): 306.

20. McCarthy, "*Diakonia* of Charity," 114.

21. Pontifical Commission for the Revision of the Code of Canon Law, *Relatio complectens synthesim animadversionum ab Em.mis atque Exc.mis Patribus Commissionis ad Novissimum Schema Codicis Iuris Canonici Exhibitarum, cum responsibus a Secretaria et Consultoribus datis* (Vatican City: Typis Polyglottis Vaticanis, 1981).

22. Ibid., 123.

23. Ibid.

24. Ibid.

25. McCarthy, "*Diakonia* of Charity," 118.

26. Congregation for the Clergy et al., instruction *Ecclesiae de mysterio*, August 15, 1997: *Acta Apostolicae Sedis* 89 (1997): 852–76, here art. 4; English translation in *Origins* 27 (November 27, 1997): 397–409.

27. Edward N. Peters, *The 1917 Pio-Benedictine Code of Canon Law* (San Francisco: Ignatius, 2001), 174: "In order that one validly assume a parish, he must be constituted in the sacred presbyteral order."

28. Ibid., 74.

29. Stanislaus Woywod, *A Practical Commentary on the Code of Canon Law*, vol. 1 (London: Herder, 1926), 62.

30. National Conference of Catholic Bishops, *Permanent Deacons in the United States: Guidelines for Their Formation and Ministry, 1984 Revision* (Washington, DC: National Conference of Catholic Bishops, 1984), 21.

SELECTED BIBLIOGRAPHY

Primary Sources

Abbott, Walter M., ed. *The Documents of Vatican II, All Sixteen Texts Promulgated by the Ecumenical Council 1963–65*. New York: Guild, 1966.

Acta et documenta Concilio oecumenico Vaticano II apparando, Series prima (antepraeparatoria). Vatican City: Typis Polyglottis Vaticanis, 1960–61.

Acta et documenta Concilio oecumenico Vaticano II apparando, Series secunda (praeparatoria). Vatican City: Typis Polyglottis Vaticanis, 1969.

Acta Synodalia Sacrosancti Concilii Vaticani II. Vatican City: Typis Polyglottis Vaticanis, 1970–78.

Bishops' Committee on the Permanent Diaconate. *Diaconal Reader: Selected Articles from the Diaconal Quarterly*. Washington, DC: United States Catholic Conference, 1985.

_______. *Foundations for the Renewal of the Diaconate*. Washington, DC: United States Catholic Conference, 1993.

_______. *A National Study of the Permanent Diaconate in the United States*. Washington, DC: United States Catholic Conference, 1981.

_______. *Permanent Deacons in the United States: Guidelines on Their Formation and Ministry*. Washington, DC: United States Catholic Conference, 1971; rev. 1984.

Catechism of the Catholic Church. 2nd ed. Washington, DC: United States Catholic Conference, 1997.

Catéchisme de l'Église Catholique. Ottawa: Conférence des Évêques catholiques du Canada, 1993.

Catechismus Catholicae Ecclesiae. Vatican: Libreria Editrice Vaticana, 1997.

Center for Applied Research in the Apostolate. "Catholic Ministry Formation Directory Statistical Summary: 2005–2006." Washington, DC: CARA, April 2006.

_______. "Diaconate Post-Ordination Survey." Washington, DC: CARA, May 2006.

———. "The Permanent Diaconate Today." Washington, DC: CARA, June 2000.

———. "Profile of the Diaconate in the United States: A Report of Findings from CARA's Deacon Poll." CARA Working Paper Series 6. Washington, DC: CARA, April 2004.

Clement. "The Letter of the Church of Rome to the Church of Corinth, Commonly called Clement's First Letter." In *Early Christian Fathers*. Translated and edited by Cyril C. Richardson. Library of Christian Classics. Philadelphia: Westminster, 1953.

Code of Canon Law: Latin-English Edition. Washington, DC: Canon Law Society of America, 1999.

Code of Canons of the Eastern Churches. Washington, DC: Canon Law Society of America, 1990.

Codex Iuris Canonici Pii X Pontificis Maximi iussu digestus Benedicti Papae XVAuctoritate Promulgatus. *Acta Apostolicae Sedis* 9 (1917): (II).

Concilium Tridentinum: Diariorum, actorum, epistularum, tractatuum nova collectio. Edited by Goerresian Society. 13 vols. Freiburg, 1901–.

Congregation for Catholic Education. *Basic Norms for the Formation of Permanent Deacons*. Vatican City: Libreria Editrice Vaticana, 1998.

Congregation for the Clergy. *Directory for the Ministry and Life of Permanent Deacons*. Vatican City: Libreria Editrice Vaticana, 1998.

———. *General Directory for Catechesis*. Vatican City: Libreria Editrice Vaticana, 1997.

———. *et al. Instruction on Certain Questions Regarding the Collaboration of the Non-Ordained Faithful in the Ministry of Priest*. Vatican City: Libreria Editrice Vaticana, 1997.

"De Ordinatione Episcopi, Presbyterorum et Diaconorum." *Pontificale Romanum ex Decreto Sacrosancti Oecumenici Concilii Vaticani II Renovatum Auctoritate Pauli PP. VI Editum Ioannis Pauli PP. II Cura Recognitum*. Vatican City: Typis Polyglottis Vaticanis, 1990.

Easton, Burton Scott, trans. and ed. *The Apostolic Tradition of Hippolytus: Translated into English with Introduction and Notes*. Cambridge/New York: Cambridge University Press, 1934.

John Paul II. "The Deacon Has Many Pastoral Functions." Allocution on the Permanent Diaconate given at the General Audience on October 13, 1993. English translation in *L'Osservatore Romano* (English edition), n. 42 (October 20, 1993): 11.

———. "Deacons Are Called to a Life of Holiness." Allocution on the Permanent Diaconate given at the General Audience on October 20, 1993. English translation in *L'Osservatore Romano* (English edition), n. 43 (October 27, 1993): 11.

_______. "Deacons as Apostles of the New Evangelization." Address to Permanent Deacons and Their Families during the Jubilee Day for Deacons on February 19, 2000. *L'Osservatore Romano* (English edition), February 23, 2000.

_______. "The Deacon's Ordination: Deacons Are Configured to Christ the Servant." Allocution to a Joint Plenary Session of the Congregation for the Clergy and the Congregation for Catholic Education. Given on November 30, 1995. English translation in *L'Osservatore Romano* (English edition), n. 51/51 (December 20/27, 1995): 5.

_______. "Deacons Serve the Kingdom of God." Allocution on the Permanent Diaconate given at the General Audience on October 6, 1993. English translation in *L'Osservatore Romano* (English edition), n. 41 (October 13, 1993): 11.

_______. *Fides et Ratio*. Vatican City: Vatican Polyglot Press, 1998.

_______. "The Heart of the Diaconate—Servants of the Mysteries of Christ and Servants of Your Brothers and Sisters." Allocution to the Permanent Deacons and Their Wives. Given in Detroit, Michigan, on September 19, 1987. *Origins* 17 (1987): 327–29.

Munier, C., ed. *Concilia Galliae AD 314–AD 506*. Corpus Christianorum, Series Latina 148. Turnholt: Brepols, 1963.

National Conference of Catholic Bishops. "Minutes of the Second General Meeting of the National Conference of Catholic Bishops," 32–34. April 11–13, 1967.

_______. "Minutes of the Fourth General Meeting of the National Conference of Catholic Bishops," 37–45. April 23–24, 1968.

Paul VI. *Hodie concilium*. *Acta Apostolicae Sedis* 58 (1966).

_______. *Motu proprio, Ad pascendum*. August 15, 1972. *Acta Apostolicae Sedis* 64 (1972): 534–40.

_______. *Motu proprio, Ministeria quaedam*. August 15, 1972. *Acta Apostolicae Sedis* 64 (1972): 529–34.

_______. *Motu proprio, Sacrum Diaconatus Ordinem*. June 18, 1967. *Acta Apostolicae Sedis* 59 (1967): 697–704.

Pius XII. "Quelques aspects fondamentaux de l'apostolat des laïcs: Hiérarchie et Apostolat." *Acta Apostolicae Sedis* 49 (1957): 925.

Pontifical Commission for the Revision of the Code of Canon Law. *Relatio complectens synthesim animadversionum ab Em.mis atque Exc.mis Patribus Commissionis ad Novissimum Schema Codicis Iuris Canonici Exhibitarum, cum responsibus a Secretaria et Consultoribus datis*. Vatican City: Typis Polyglottis Vaticanis, 1981.

Richardson, Cyril C., ed. *Early Christian Fathers*. New York: Collier Books, Macmillan, 1970.

Roberts, Alexander, and James Donaldson, eds. *The Ante-Nicene Fathers: Translations of the Writings of the Fathers Down to A.D. 325*. American reprint, ed. A. Cleveland Coxe. Grand Rapids: Eerdmans, 1951–57. Vol. 1, *The Apostolic Fathers with Justin Martyr and Irenaeus* (1956). Vol. 2, *Fathers of the Second Century: Hermas, Tatian, Athenagoras, Theophisbus, and Clement of Alexandria* (1956). Vol. 3, *Latin Christianity: Its Founder, Tertullian* (1957). Vol. 4, *Tertullian, Part Fourth; Minucius Felix; Commodian; Origen, Parts First and Second* (1956). Vol. 5, *Fathers of the Third Century: Hippolytus, Cyprian, Caius, Novatian, Appendix* (1951). Vol. 7, *Lactantius, Venantius, Asterius, Victorinus, Dionysius, Apostolic Teaching and Constitutions, Homily, and Liturgies* (1951). Vol. 8, *Fathers of the Third and Fourth Centuries: The Twelve Patriarchs, Excerpts and Epistles, the Clementina, Apocrypha, Decretals, Memoirs of Edessa and Syriac* (1951). Vol. 9, *Documents, Remains of the First Ages; Biographical Synopsis; Index* (1951).

Schaff, Philip, ed. *Nicene and Post-Nicene Fathers of the Christian Church*. First Series. Vol. 3, *St. Augustin: On the Trinity, Doctrinal Treatises, Moral Treatises*. Grand Rapids: Eerdmans, 1956.

Schaff, Philip, and Henry Wace, ed. *Nicene and Post-Nicene Fathers of the Christian Church*. Second Series. Vol. 6, *St. Jerome: Letters and Select Works*. Grand Rapids: Eerdmans, 1954.

United States Catholic Conference. *A National Study on the Permanent Diaconate of the Catholic Church in the United States, 1994–1995*. Washington, DC: United States Catholic Conference, 1996.

United States Conference of Catholic Bishops. *National Directory for the Formation, Ministry and Life of Permanent Deacons in the United States*. Washington, DC: United States Conference of Catholic Bishops, 2004.

———. *The Roman Pontifical as Renewed by Decree of the Second Vatican Council, Published by Authority of Pope Paul VI and Further Revised at the Direction of Pope John Paul II. Rites of Ordination of a Bishop, of Priests, and of Deacons, Second Typical Edition*. Washington, DC: United States Conference of Catholic Bishops, 2003.

Secondary Sources

Alberigo, Guiseppe, and Joseph A. Komonchak, eds. *History of Vatican II*. 5 vols. Maryknoll, NY: Orbis; Leuven: Peeters, 1995–.

Aquinas, Thomas. *Summa Theologiae*. 5 vols. Madrid: Biblioteca de Autores Cristianos, 1952.

Audet, Jean-Paul. *Structures of Christian Priesthood: A Study of Home, Marriage, and Celibacy in the Pastoral Service of the Church*. Translated by Rosemary Sheed. New York: Macmillan, 1967.

Barnett, James M. *The Diaconate: A Full and Equal Order.* Rev. ed. Valley Forge, PA: Trinity Press International, 1995.

Beal, John P. "The Exercise of the Power of Governance by Lay People: State of the Question." *The Jurist* 55 (1995): 1–92.

Beal, John P., James A. Coriden, and Thomas J. Green, eds. *New Commentary on the Code of Canon Law.* Commissioned by the Canon Law Society of America. Washington, DC: Canon Law Society of America, 2000.

Bekkum, Willem van. "The Liturgical Revival in the Service of the Missions." In *The Assisi Papers,* 95–112. Proceedings of the First International Congress on Pastoral Liturgy, Assisi-Rome, September 18–22, 1956. Collegeville, MN: Liturgical Press, 1957.

Beltrando, Piercarlo. *Diaconi per la Chiesa.* Milan: Instituto Propaganda, 1977.

Bernardin, Joseph. "The Call to Service: Pastoral Statement on the Permanent Diaconate." Chicago: Archdiocese of Chicago, 1993.

Bernier, Paul. *Ministry in the Church: A Historical and Pastoral Approach.* Mystic, CT: Twenty-Third Publications, 1992.

Blancy, Alain. "Diaconie et diaconat: Place, rôle, charge des diacres et d'un diaconat dans l'Église." *Etudies théologiques et religieuses* 42 (1967): 129–42.

Borras, Alphonse. "Les effets canoniques de l'ordination diaconal." *Revue théologique de Louvain* 28 (1997): 469–80.

Borras, Alphonse, and Bernard Pottier. *Le grâce du diaconat: Questions actuelles autour du diaconat latin.* Brussels: Editions Lessius, 1998.

Bouscaren, T. "Canon 453." *Canon Law Digest* 1 (1934): 246.

Brockman, Norbert, SM. *Ordained to Service: A Theology of the Permanent Diaconate*. Hicksville, NY: Exposition Press, 1976.

Brown, Raymond E. *The Gospel According to John: Introduction, Translation, and Notes.* 2 vols. Anchor Bible 29, 29A. New York: Doubleday, 1966, 1970.

_______. *Priest and Bishop: Biblical Reflections*. New York: Paulist, 1970.

Buckley, Joseph C. "The Permanent Diaconate." *The Furrow* 23 (1972): 476–82.

Buechlein, Daniel M. "The Sacramental Identity of the Ministerial Priesthood: '*In Persona Christi.*'" In *Priests for a New Millennium: A Series of Essays on the Ministerial Priesthood*, by Bishops' Committee on Priestly Life and Ministry, 37–52. Washington, DC: United States Conference of Catholic Bishops, 2000.

Catholic Theological Society of America. "Report on Permanent Diaconate." *American Ecclesiastical Review* 164 (1971): 190–204.

Coffee, David. "The Common and the Ordained Priesthood." *Theological Studies* 58, no. 2 (June 1997): 209–36.

Collins, John N. *Diakonia: Re-interpreting the Ancient Sources.* New York/Oxford: Oxford University Press, 1990.

Colson, Jean. "Le diaconat aux premiers siècles de l'Église." *Vocation* 234 (1966): 294–315.

———. Les diacres à la lumière de l'histoire." *La vie spirituelle* 116 (1967): 442–67.

———. *La fonction diaconale aux origines de l'Église*. Paris: Descleé de Brouwer, 1960.

———. *Les fonctions ecclésiales aux deux premiers siècles*. Paris: Descleé de Brouwer, 1956.

Congar, Yves. "Le diaconat dans le théologie des ministères." In *Le Diacre dans l'Eglise et le monde d'aujourd'hui*, edited by Paul Winninger and Yves Congar, 121–41. Unam Sanctam 59. Paris: Éditions de Cerf, 1966.

———. "Le diacre dans la théologie des ministères." *Vocation* 234 (1966): 273–93.

———. *Lay People in the Church*. Translated by Donald Attwater. Westminster, MD: Newman, 1965.

Cooke, Bernard. *Ministry to Word and Sacraments: History and Theology.* Philadelphia: Fortress, 1976.

Corbon, Jean. *The Wellspring of Worship*. New York: Paulist, 1988.

Coriden, James A. *Canon Law as Ministry: Freedom and Good Order for the Church*. New York/Mahwah, NJ: Paulist, 2000.

———. "The Permanent Diaconate: Meaning of Ministry." *Origins* 7/41 (March 30, 1978): 653–56.

Coriden, James A., Thomas J. Green, and Donald E. Hentschel, eds. *The Code of Canon Law: A Text and Commentary.* Commissioned by the Canon Law Society of America. New York/Mahwah, NJ: Paulist, 1985.

Cranfield, C. E. B. "*Diakonia* in the New Testament." In *Service in Christ*, edited by James I. McCord and T. H. L. Parker, 37–48. Grand Rapids: Eerdmans, 1966.

Croghan, Leo M. "The Theology and the Spirit of the Diaconate's Restoration." *American Ecclesiastical Review* 161 (1969): 293–301.

Cummings, Owen F. *Deacons and the Church.* Mahwah, NJ: Paulist, 2004.

Cummings, Owen F., William T. Ditewig, and Richard R. Gaillardetz. *Theology of the Diaconate: The State of the Question*. Mahwah, NJ: Paulist, 2005.

Cuneo, J. James. "The Power of Jurisdiction: Empowerment for Church Functioning and Mission Distinct from the Power of Orders." *The Jurist* 39 (1979): 200.

Cunningham, Agnes, SSCM. "Power and Authority in the Church." In *The Ministry of Governance*, edited by James K. Mallett, 80–97. Washington, DC: Canon Law Society of America, 1986.

Davis, Kortright. *Serving with Power: Reviving the Spirit of Christian Ministry*. New York/Mahwah, NJ: Paulist, 1999.

Denzler, George A. "The Pastoral Letters." In *The Jerome Biblical Commentary*, edited by Raymond E. Brown, Joseph A. Fitzmyer, and Roland E. Murphy, 350–61. Englewood Cliffs, NJ: Prentice-Hall, 1968.

Deutsch Bischofskonferenz. "Le prêtre, le diacre et le laïc dans la pastorale." *Documentation Catholique* 74/no. 1721 (June 5, 1971): 517–22.

Ditewig, William T. "Charting a Theology of the Diaconate: An Exercise in Ecclesial Cartography." In Owen F. Cummings, William T. Ditewig, and Richard R. Gaillardetz, *Theology of the Diaconate: The State of the Question*, 31–65. Mahwah, NJ: Paulist, 2005.

———. "The Contemporary Renewal of the Diaconate." In *The Deacon Reader*, edited by James Keating, 27–55. Mahwah, NJ: Paulist, 2006.

———. "The Deacon as Voice of Lament and Link to Thanksgiving and Justice." *Liturgical Ministry* 13 (Winter 2004): 24–28.

———. "The Exercise of Governance by Deacons: A Theological and Canonical Study." Ph.D. diss. Catholic University of America, 2002.

———. "The Kenotic Leadership of Deacons." In *The Deacon Reader*, edited by James Keating, 248–77. Mahwah, NJ: Paulist, 2006.

———. "The Once and Future Diaconate: Notes from the Past, Possibilities for the Future." *Church* 20, no. 2 (Summer 2004): 51–54.

———. *101 Questions & Answers on Deacons*. Mahwah, NJ: Paulist, 2004.

Dix, Gregory. *The Treatise on the Apostolic Tradition of St. Hippolytus of Rome*. London: SPCK, 1968.

Donovan, Daniel. *What Are They Saying about the Ministerial Priesthood?* New York: Paulist, 1992.

Döpp, Siegmar, and Wilhelm Geerlings, eds. *Dictionary of Early Christian Literature*. Translated by Matthew O'Connell. New York: Crossroad, 2000.

Duquoc, Christian. "Ministère et pouvoir." *Spiritus* 70, no. 19 (January 1978): 8–18.

Echlin, Edward P., SJ. *The Deacon in the Church: Past and Future*. Staten Island, NY: Alba House, 1971.

———. "The Origins of the Permanent Diaconate." *American Ecclesiastical Review* 162 (1970): 92–105.

———. "Theological Frontiers of the Deacon's Ministry." *American Ecclesiastical Review* 166 (1972): 479–91.

Ellis. Peter F. *The Genius of John: A Composition-Critical Commentary on the Fourth Gospel.* Collegeville, MN: Liturgical Press, 1984.

Epagneul, Michel-Dominique. "Du role des diacres dans l'Église d'aujourd'hui." *Nouvelle revue théologique* 79 (1957): 153–68.

Ferguson, Everett, ed. *Encyclopedia of Early Christianity.* 2nd ed. New York: Garland, 1998.

Florovsky, George. "The Problem of Diaconate in the Orthodox Church." In *The Diaconate Now,* edited by Richard T. Nolan, 81–98. Washington, DC: Corpus Books, 1968.

Galligan, Timothy, and Bruce Harbert. "*Diaconus alter Christus.*" *Clergy Review* 66 (1981): 355–60.

Galot, Jean, SJ. *Theology of the Priesthood.* Washington, DC: National Conference of Catholic Bishops, 1984.

Goergen, Donald J., and Ann Garrido, eds. *The Theology of Priesthood.* Collegeville, MN: Liturgical Press, 2000.

Greenleaf, Robert K. *Servant Leadership: A Journey into the Nature of Legitimate Power and Greatness.* New York: Paulist, 1977.

Greshake, Gisbert. *The Meaning of Christian Priesthood.* Westminster, MD: Christian Classics, 1989.

Griffin, Bertram F. "The Three-Fold *Munera* of Christ and the Church." In *Code, Community, Ministry: Selected Studies for the Parish Minister Introducing the Revised Code of Canon Law,* edited by James H. Provost, 19–20. Washington, DC: Canon Law Society of America, 1982, 1983.

Gula, Richard. "A Theology of Diaconate." *American Ecclesiastical Review* 169 (1975): 621–35, 669–80.

Haquin, André, and Philippe Weber, eds. *Diaconat, XXIe siècle: Actes du Colloque de Louvain-la-Neuve (13–15 septembre 1994).* Brussels: Lumen Vitae, 1997.

Hardy, Edward R. "Deacons in History and Practice." In *The Diaconate Now,* edited by Richard T. Nolan, 11–36. Washington, DC: Corpus Books, 1968.

Harnack, Adolf. *Sources of the Apostolic Canons.* Translated by John Owen. London: F. Norgate, 1895.

Hennessey, Lawrence R., ST. "*Diakonia* and *Diakonoi* in the Pre-Nicene Church." In *Diakonia: Studies in Honor of Robert T. Meyer,* edited by Thomas Halton and Joseph P. Williman, 60–86. Washington, DC: Catholic University of America Press, 1986.

Hilberath, Bernd Jochen. *Zwischen Vision und Wirklichkeit: Fragen nach dem Weg der Kirche*. Würzburg: Echter, 1999.

Hill, Edmund, OP. *Ministry and Authority in the Catholic Church*. London: Geoffrey Chapman, 1988.

Hite, Jordan, and Daniel J. Ward. *Readings, Cases, Materials in Canon Law: A Textbook for Ministerial Students*. Rev. ed. Collegeville, MN: Liturgical Press, 1990.

Hofinger, Johannes. "The Case for Permanent Deacons." *Catholic Mind* 57 (1959): 116.

———. "Ist in der Mission ein eigener Stand der Diakone anzustreben?" *Zeitschrift fur Missionswissenschaft und Religionswissenschaft* 41 (1957): 201–13.

Hoping, Helmut. "Diakonie als Aufgabe des kirchlichen Leitungsamtes." In *Dokumentation 13–Jahrestagung 1996*, 24–40. Tübingen: Arbeitsgemeinschaft Ständiger Diakonat, Bundesrepublik Deutschland, 1996.

Hornef, Josef. "The Genesis and Growth of the Proposal." In *Foundations for the Renewal of the Diaconate*, by Bishops' Committee on the Permanent Diaconate, 5–27. Washington, DC: United States Catholic Conference, 1993.

———. "The Order of Diaconate in the Roman Catholic Church." Translated by Patrick Russell. In *The Diaconate Now*, edited by Richard T. Nolan, 57–79. Washington, DC: Corpus, 1968.

Horvath, Tibor. "Theology of a New Diaconate." *Revue de l'Université d'Ottawa* 38 (1968): 248–76, 495–523.

Huels, John M. *The Pastoral Companion: A Canon Law Handbook for Catholic Ministry*. Rev. ed. Quincy, IL: Franciscan, 1995.

———. "The Power of Governance and Its Exercise by Lay Persons: A Juridical Approach." *Studia Canonica* 35, no. 1 (2001): 59–96.

International Theological Commission. *From the Diakonia of Christ to the Diakonia of the Apostles*. Historico-Theological Research Document. Mundelein, IL: Hillenbrand Books, 2003.

Johnson, Luke Timothy. "The Eucharist and the Identity of Jesus." *Priest and People* 15, no. 6 (June 2001): 230–35.

Jurgens, William A., ed. and trans. *The Faith of the Early Fathers: A Sourcebook of Theological and Historical Passages from the Christian Writings of the Pre-Nicene and Nicene Eras*. 3 vols. Collegeville, MN: Liturgical Press, 1970–79.

Kasper, Walter. "The Diaconate." In *Leadership in the Church: How Traditional Roles Can Serve the Christian Community Today*. New York: Crossroad, 2003.

Keating, James, ed. *The Deacon Reader*. Mahwah, NJ: Paulist, 2006.

Kilmartin, Edward J. "Apostolic Office: Sacrament of Christ." *Theological Studies* 36 (1975): 243–64.

———. *Christian Liturgy: Theology and Practice*. Kansas City: Sheed & Ward, 1988.

———. "Lay Participation in the Apostolate of the Hierarchy." In *Official Ministry in a New Age*, edited by James H. Provost, 89–116. Washington, DC: Canon Law Society of America, 1981.

King, John J. "Vatican II: De Ecclesia Chapter II: Collegiality and the Diaconate," *Homiletic and Pastoral Review* 64 (1964): 571–80.

Komonchak, Joseph A. "Authority and Conversion or: the Limits of Authority." *Cristianesimo nella Storia* 21 (2000): 207–29.

———. "The New Diaconate Guidelines." In *Proceedings of the 1986 Convention of the National Association of Permanent Diaconate Directors in Baltimore, Maryland, April 28–1 May, 1986*, 5–9. Chicago: National Association of Permanent Diaconate Directors, 1986.

———. "The Permanent Diaconate and the Variety of Ministries in the Church." *Diaconal Quarterly* 3, no. 3 (1977): 15–23; 3, no. 4 (1977): 29–40; 4, no. 1 (1978): 13–25.

Kramer, Hannes. "Der Diakonat der Liebe." *Caritas* 31 (1953): 289–94.

———. "Twenty-five Years: The Diaconate Circle and Diaconate Movement: A Historical Review." Translated by John Fullenbach. *Diaconal Quarterly* 3, no. 3 (1977): 7–12.

Lane, Thomas. "In the Person of Christ—by Baptism." In *A Priesthood in Tune: Theological Reflections in Ministry*, 91–98. Dublin: Columbia, 1993.

LeClair, Douglas M. *The Deacon as Icon of Christ: An Assessment and Reflection of the Functional Approach Versus the Mission Approach Following the Golden Age, the Decline and the Restoration*. Phoenix, AZ: Catholic Sun Publishing, 2001.

Lobinger, Fritz. *Like His Brothers and Sisters: Ordaining Community Leaders*. New York: Crossroad, 1999. Originally published in the Philippines by Claretian Publications, 1998.

Mallett, James K., ed. *The Ministry of Governance*. Washington, DC: Canon Law Society of America, 1986.

Marliangeas, Bernard Dominique. *Clés pour une théologie du ministère: In persona Christi, in persona Ecclesiae*. Paris: Beauchesne, 1978.

McCarthy, John J. "The *Diakonia* of Charity in the Permanent Diaconate: Its Application to Certain Clerical Offices as Addressed in the *Directory for the Ministry and Life of Permanent Deacons*." JCD diss. Pontificia Studiorum Universitas A S. Thoma Aq. in Urbe, 2000.

McCaslin, Patrick, and Michael G. Lawler. *Sacrament of Service: A Vision of the Permanent Diaconate Today*. New York: Paulist, 1986.

McIntyre, John P. "*In persona Christi Capitis*: A Commentary on Canon 1008." *Studia Canonica* 30 (1996): 371–401.

McKenzie, John L. *Authority in the Church*. New York: Sheed & Ward, 1966.

Medina, José Casanas. "The Law for the Restoration of the Permanent Diaconate: A Canonical Commentary." JCD diss. Catholic University of America, 1968.

Michalski, Melvin. *The Relationship between the Universal Priesthood of the Baptized and the Ministerial Priesthood of the Ordained in Vatican II and Subsequent Theology: Understanding "Essentia et non Gradu Tantum" in Lumen Gentium No. 10*. Lewiston: Edwin Mellen, 1996.

Miguens, Manuel, OFM. *Church Ministries in New Testament Times*. Arlington: Christian Culture Press, 1976.

Mitchell, Nathan, OSB. *Mission and Ministry: History and Theology in the Sacrament of Order*. Wilmington, DE: Michael Glazier, 1982.

Moloney, Francis J., SDB. *The Gospel of John*. Collegeville, MN: Liturgical Press, 1998.

Morche, Margret. *Zur Erneuerung des Ständigen Diakonats*. Freiburg: Lambertus-Verlag, 1996.

Munley, Anne, Rosemary Smith, Helen Maher Garvey, Lois MacGillivray, and Mary Milligan, eds. *Women and Jurisdiction: An Unfolding Reality*. Silver Spring, MD: Leadership Conference of Women Religious, 2001.

Neyrey, Jerome H., SJ. "1 Timothy." In *The Collegeville Bible Commentary*, edited by Dianne Bergant and Robert J. Karris, 1200–1207. Collegeville, MN: Liturgical Press, 1989.

Nolan, Richard, ed. *The Diaconate Now*. Washington, DC: Corpus Books, 1968.

Noll, Ray Robert. *Christian Ministerial Priesthood: A Search for Its Beginnings in the Primary Documents of the Apostolic Fathers*. San Francisco/London: Catholic Scholars, 1993.

Nowell, Robert. *The Ministry of Service: Deacons in the Contemporary Church*. New York: Herder & Herder, 1968.

O'Meara, Thomas F., OP. "Karl Rahner on Parish, Priest and Deacon." *Worship* 40 (1966): 103–10.

———. *Theology of Ministry*. Rev. ed. New York/Mahwah, NJ: Paulist, 1999.

Osborne, Kenan B., OFM. *The Diaconate in the Christian Church: Its History and Theology*. Chicago: National Association of Diaconate Directors, 1996.

———. *Ministry: Lay Ministry in the Roman Catholic Church*. New York/Mahwah, NJ: Paulist, 1993.

———. *Priesthood: A History of the Ordained Ministry in the Roman Catholic Church*. New York/Mahwah, NJ: Paulist, 1988.

Pagé, Roch. *Diaconat permanent et diversité des ministères: Perspective du droit canonique*. Montreal: Les Éditions Paulines, 1988.

Perkin, David R. "A Comparative Analysis of the 1971 and 1984 Editions of *Permanent Deacons in the US: Guidelines of Their Formation and Ministry*." JCL thesis. Catholic University of America, 1987.

Perrin, Norman, and Dennis C. Duling. *The New Testament: An Introduction*. 2nd ed. San Diego: Harcourt, Brace, Jovanovich, 1982.

Peters, Edward N., curator. *The 1917 Pio-Benedictine Code of Canon Law*. San Francisco: Ignatius, 2001.

Petrolino, Enzo. *I Diaconi: Annunziatori della Parola ministri dell'altare e della carità*. Milan: San Paulo, 1998.

Pfeffer, J. *Power in Organizations*. Marshfield, MA: Pitman, 1981.

Philibert, Paul, OP. "Issues for a Theology of Priesthood: A Status Report." In *The Theology of Priesthood*, edited by Donald J. Goergen and Ann Garrido, 1–42. Collegeville, MN: Liturgical Press, 2000.

Pies, Otto. "Block 26: Erfahrungen aus dem Priesterleben in Dachau." *Stimmen der Zeit* 141 (1947–48): 10–28.

———. "Diakonat, Stufe oder Amt." *Theologie und Glaube* 50 (1960): 170–93.

Pokusa, Joseph W. "The Archdeacon's Office and Functions in the Decretals of Gregory IX." JCL thesis. Catholic University of America, 1977.

———. "A Canonical-Historical Study of the Diaconate in the Western Church." JCD diss. Catholic University of America, 1979.

———. "The Diaconate: A History of Law Following Practice." *The Jurist* 45 (1985): 95–135.

Power, David N. "The Basis for Official Ministry in the Church." In *Official Ministry*, edited by James H. Provost, 60–88. Washington, DC: Canon Law Society of America, 1981.

———. "Order." In *Systematic Theology: Roman Catholic Perspectives*, vol. 2, ed. Francis Schüssler Fiorenza and John P. Galvin, 291–304. Minneapolis: Fortress, 1991.

Provost, James H. "Canonical Reflections on Selected Issues in Diocesan Governance." In *The Ministry of Governance*, edited by James K. Mallett, 209–51. Washington, DC: Canon Law Society of America, 1986.

———. "Permanent Deacons in the 1983 Code." *Canon Law Society of America Proceedings* 46 (1984): 175–91.

Provost, James H., ed. *Code, Community, Ministry: Selected Studies for the Parish Minister Introducing the Revised Code of Canon Law.* Washington, DC: Canon Law Society of America, 1982.

———, ed. *Official Ministry in a New Age.* Permanent Seminar Studies 3. Washington, DC: Canon Law Society of America, 1981.

Quasten, Johannes. *Patrology.* 4 vols. Westminster, MD: Newman, 1950.

Rahner, Karl. "On the Diaconate." In *Foundations for the Renewal of the Diaconate,* 192–212. Translated by David Bourke. Washington, DC: United States Catholic Conference, 1993.

———. "The Teaching of the Second Vatican Council on the Diaconate." In *Theological Investigations,* 10:222–32. Translated by David Bourke. New York: Seabury, 1977.

———. "The Theology of the Restoration of the Diaconate." In *Theological Investigations,* 5: 268–314. Translated by Karl-H. Kruger. New York: Crossroad, 1983.

Rahner, Karl, and Herbert Vorgrimler, eds. *Diaconia in Christo: Über die Erneuerung des Diakonates.* Quaestiones Disputatae 15/16. Freiburg: Herder, 1962.

Rahner, Karl, et al., eds. *Sacramentum Mundi: An Encyclopedia of Theology.* 6 vols. New York: Herder & Herder, 1968–70.

Rashke, Richard L. *The Deacon in Search of Identity.* New York: Paulist, 1975.

Rausch, Thomas P. *Priesthood Today: An Appraisal.* New York/Mahwah, NJ: Paulist, 1992.

Richard, Lucien. *Christ: The Self-Emptying of God.* New York/Mahwah, NJ: Paulist, 1997.

Schamoni, Wilhelm. *Familienväter als geweihte Diakone.* Paderborn: Schöningh, 1953. English translation: *Married Men as Ordained Deacons.* Translated by Otto Eisner. London: Burns & Oates, 1955.

Scheffczyk, Leo. "Laypersons, Deacons, and Priests: A Difference of Ministries." *Communio* 23 (1996): 639–55.

Schillebeeckx, Edward. "The Catholic Understanding of Office in the Church." *Theological Studies* 30 (December 1969): 567–87.

———. *The Layman in the Church.* Staten Island, NY: Alba House, 1963.

———. *Ministry: Leadership in the Community of Jesus Christ.* New York: Crossroad, 1986.

Schroeder, H. J., ed. *Canons and Decrees of the Council of Trent.* St. Louis: Herder, 1950. Reprint, Rockford, IL: TAN Books and Publishers, 1978.

Sennett, Richard. *Authority*. New York/London: W. W. Norton, 1980.

Shugrue, Timothy J. *Service Ministry of the Deacon*. Washington, DC: Bishops' Committee on the Permanent Diaconate, National Conference of Catholic Bishops, 1988.

Tanner, Norman P., ed. *Decrees of the Ecumenical Councils*. 2 vols. Washington, DC: Georgetown University Press, 1990.

Timms, Noel, and Kenneth Wilson, eds. *Governance and Authority in the Roman Catholic Church: Beginning a Conversation*. London: SPCK, 2000.

Varvaro, William A. "Proposed Legislation for Permanent Deacons: Developments and Difficulties." *Canon Law Society of America Proceedings* 44 (1981): 238–53.

Vorgrimler, Herbert, ed. *Commentary on the Documents of Vatican II*. 5 vols. New York: Herder & Herder, 1967–69.

Winninger, Paul. *Les diacres: histoire et avenir du diaconat*. Paris: Centurion, 1967.

———. *Vers un renouveau du diaconat*. Paris: Desclée de Brouwer, 1958.

Winninger, Paul, and Yves Congar, eds. *Le diacre dans l'Eglise et le monde d'aujourd'hui*. Unam Sanctam 59. Paris: Éditions du Cerf, 1966.

Woestman, William H.. *The Sacrament of Orders and the Clerical State: A Commentary on the Code of Canon Law*. Ottawa: St. Paul Université, 1999.

Wood, Susan K. *Sacramental Orders. Lex Orandi* Series. Collegeville, MN: Liturgical Press, 2000.

———, ed. *Ordering the Baptismal Priesthood: Theologies of Lay and Ordained Ministry*. Collegeville, MN: Liturgical Press, 2003.

Woywod, Stanislaus, OFM. *A Practical Commentary on the Code of Canon Law*. London: Herder, 1926.

Zagano, Phyllis. *Holy Saturday: An Argument for the Restoration of the Female Diaconate in the Catholic Church*. New York: Crossroad, 2000.

Ziegler, John. *Let Them Anoint the Sick*. Collegeville, MN: Liturgical Press, 1987.

———. "Toward a Theology of the Diaconate." *Diaconal Quarterly* 3, no. 1 (1977): 12–20; 3, no. 2 (1977): 8–14.

John D. Zizioulas. *Being as Communion: Studies in Personhood and the Church*. Crestwood, NY: St. Vladimir's Seminary Press, 1985.

Paulist Press is committed to preserving ancient forests and natural resources. We elected to print *The Emerging Diaconate* on 50% post consumer recycled paper, processed chlorine free. As a result, for this printing, we have saved:

18 Trees (40' tall and 6-8" diameter)
7,536 Gallons of Wastewater
3,031 Kilowatt Hours of Electricity
831 Pounds of Solid Waste
1,632 Pounds of Greenhouse Gases

Paulist Press made this paper choice because our printer, Thomson-Shore, Inc., is a member of Green Press Initiative, a nonprofit program dedicated to supporting authors, publishers, and suppliers in their efforts to reduce their use of fiber obtained from endangered forests.

For more information, visit www.greenpressinitiative.org